International Tax Planning for Inward Investment

International Tax Planning for Inward Investment

by Allan Cinnamon
International tax consultant, BDO Stoy Hayward, London

Richard Citron
International tax partner, BDO Stoy Hayward, London

LexisNexis™ UK

Members of the LexisNexis Group worldwide

United Kingdom	LexisNexis UK, a Division of Reed Elsevier (UK) Ltd, Halsbury House, 35 Chancery Lane, LONDON, WC2A 1EL, and 4 Hill Street, EDINBURGH EH2 3JZ
Argentina	LexisNexis Argentina, BUENOS AIRES
Australia	LexisNexis Butterworths, CHATSWOOD, New South Wales
Austria	LexisNexis Verlag ARD Orac GmbH & Co KG, VIENNA
Canada	LexisNexis Butterworths, MARKHAM, Ontario
Chile	LexisNexis Chile Ltda, SANTIAGO DE CHILE
Czech Republic	Nakladatelství Orac sro, PRAGUE
France	Editions du Juris-Classeur SA, PARIS
Germany	LexisNexis Deutschland GmbH, FRANKFURT and MUNSTER
Hong Kong	LexisNexis Butterworths, HONG KONG
Hungary	HVG-Orac, BUDAPEST
India	LexisNexis Butterworths, NEW DELHI
Ireland	LexisNexis, DUBLIN
Italy	Giuffrè Editore, MILAN
Malaysia	Malayan Law Journal Sdn Bhd, KUALA LUMPUR
New Zealand	LexisNexis Butterworths, WELLINGTON
Poland	Wydawnictwo Prawnicze LexisNexis, WARSAW
Singapore	LexisNexis Butterworths, SINGAPORE
South Africa	LexisNexis Butterworths, Durban
Switzerland	Stämpfli Verlag AG, BERNE
USA	LexisNexis, DAYTON, Ohio

First published in 2003

A CIP Catalogue record for this book is available from the British Library.

ISBN 0 406 96290 1

Typeset by Kerry Press, Luton, Beds

Printed and bound in Great Britain by Hobbs the Printers Ltd, Totton, Hampshire
Visit LexisNexis UK at www.lexisnexis.co.uk

Preface

The main objective of this book is to serve as a reference guide to the UK and foreign tax aspects of doing business, or investing, in the UK.

The book describes in detail the relevant UK tax legislation and case law relevant to each aspect of the foreign investor's UK activity. At the same time, the foreign tax consequences are considered from the viewpoint of the foreign investor's home jurisdiction. A balance is then struck between the two in terms of international tax planning techniques so as to minimise the overall tax burden.

This book will therefore be of interest to the UK tax adviser, who needs to appreciate the nuances of the tax rules in the foreign investor's home country in order to sensibly advise an incoming client. It will be of equal interest to the foreign investor and tax adviser who must similarly appreciate the nuances of the UK tax system.

As a result of its transaction-based approach the book should also serve as a useful checklist and planning tool to be referred to whenever an inward UK investment or activity is being considered.

Allan Cinnamon
BDO Stoy Hayward
Allan.Cinnamon@bdo.co.uk

Richard Citron
BDO Stoy Hayward
Richard.Citron@bdo.co.uk

August 2003

Acknowledgements

The authors would like thank their respective families; and to acknowledge the invaluable assistance of Paul Ayres, Martin Dane, Janine Elliott, Zigurds Kronbergs and Debbie Thorne of the BDO Stoy Hayward international tax team.

List of contributors – BDO offices

Warwick James	Australia	wjames@bdosyd.com.au
Margit Widinski	Austria	widinski@bdoauxilia.at
Marc Verbeek	Belgium	marc.verbeek@bdo.be
John Wonfor	Canada	jwonfor@bdo.ca
Hans-Henrik Nilausen	Denmark	hhn@bdo.dk
Heikki Muikku	Finland	heikki.muikku@bdo.fi
Jacques Dubarry	France	jdubarry@bdo-gendrot.fr
Gerhard Engler	Germany	gerhard.engler@bdo.de
John Tentes	Greece	Hac@internet.gr
Katherine Yeung	Hong Kong	katherine_yeung@bdo.com.hk
Frank Sheedy	Ireland	Fsheedy@bdosx.ie
Giorgio Farina	Italy	giorgio.farina@bdo.it
Paul Houston	Japan	Paul.houston@bdo.or.jp
Claude Zimmer	Luxembourg	Claude.zimmer@bdo-cf.lu
Leo Wesenhagen	Netherlands	Leo.wesenhagen@bdo.nl
Paulo Alves	Portugal	paulo.alves@bdo.pt
Simon Poh	Singapore	simonpoh@bdo.com.sg
Carlos Lopez	Spain	carlos.lopez@bdo.es
Pether Rombo	Sweden	pether.rombo@bdo.se
Roland Etienne	Switzerland	roland.etienne@visura.ch
John Santamaria	USA	Jsantamaria@bdo.com

List of abbreviations

ACT	=	Advance corporation tax
APA	=	Advanced pricing agreement
art	=	Article
CAA	=	Capital Allowances Act
CFC	=	Controlled foreign company
CNR	=	Inland Revenue's Centre for Non-Residents
EAC	=	European Arbitration Convention
EC	=	European Communities
EEA	=	European Economic Area
EEC	=	European Economic Community
EHC	=	European holding company
EU	=	European Union
FA	=	Finance Act
FEU	=	Foreign Entertainers' Unit
FOREX	=	Foreign exchange
HL	=	House of Lords
ICTA	=	Income and Corporation Taxes Act
IHTA	=	Inheritance Tax Act
IM	=	Inland Revenue's Inspector's Manual
IP	=	Intellectual property
ISP	=	Internet service provider
ITEPA	=	Income Tax (Earnings and Pensions) Act
LLP	=	Limited liability partnership
MAP	=	Mutual agreement procedure
OECD	=	Organisation for Economic Co-operation and Development
PE	=	Permanent establishment
R&D	=	Research and development
RSA	=	Regional Selective Assistance
SA	=	Stamp Act
s	=	section
Sch	=	Schedule
SME	=	Small and medium-sized enterprise
SP	=	Inland Revenue Statement of Practice
Sp C	=	Special Commissioners
SI	=	Statutory Instrument
TCGA	=	Taxation of Chargeable Gains Act
TMA	=	Taxes Management Act
UK	=	United Kingdom
VAT, VATA	=	Value added tax, Value Added Tax Act
WHT	=	Withholding tax

Contents

Table of Cases

References to the Appendices are in Italic.

W

Table of Statutes

1 Introduction

> **Overview**
>
> - UK—a popular inward investment destination for doing business in Europe.
> - Grants, financial assistance and tax incentives available to foreign investors.
> - Consideration of the home country/UK crossborder tax position of 21 of the most popular foreign investor jurisdictions.

The business background to inward investment

1.1 The UK economy is characterised by the importance of international trade and of foreign investment. In return, UK businesses are major investors abroad. Confidence in the UK's business and economic environment remains strong despite difficult market conditions caused by the slowdown in the economies of most developed nations, fierce competition and the continuing uncertainty over eventual membership of the Euro. The economy is enjoying historically low inflation and interest rates.

The UK continues to receive a large volume of foreign direct investment. It is marked by economic, political and social stability, and has benefited from a sustained period of freedom from major industrial unrest. The importance of London as a global financial centre and the use of English as the language of worldwide communication cannot be overestimated. Other factors in the UK's favour are:

(a) membership of the European Union, giving access to a single market of 380 million consumers (soon to be expanded from 15 to 25 Member States giving an estimated 454 million consumers);

(b) the size of its own domestic economy, the fourth largest in the world by some measures;

(c) a generally open and deregulated economy;

(d) a track record of technological and scientific innovation;

(e) a large stock of commercial property;

(f) a relatively flexible labour market; and

(g) some of the lowest corporate and personal tax rates in the EU.

Grants and financial assistance

1.2 A wide variety of financial assistance from both the UK government and the EU is available to investors.

Regional Selective Assistance (RSA) is the main form of government support for new investment. It is offered on a discretionary basis to companies opening a new plant or expanding or modernising an existing plant in an 'assisted area'.

RSA is intended to provide assistance with projects involving fixed capital expenditure of over £500,000. Its aims are to:

(a) help to attract and retain investment that would otherwise not come to the UK;

(b) increase prosperity by improving the productivity and competitiveness of the national and regional economy; and

(c) create and/or safeguard jobs, preferably skilled jobs, in the assisted areas.

Assistance is usually offered in the form of a grant, which is taxable, although loans may be available in particular cases.

Companies wishing to obtain RSA must make a grant application. In England, the minimum grant that may be applied for is £75,000. In Wales, grants from upwards of £50,000 are available, whereas in Scotland there is no minimum. In Northern Ireland, there are special arrangements for financial assistance.

Broadly speaking, grant offers of between 5% to 15% of the projected capital expenditure are offered. Grants are normally paid in instalments, linked to the creation of jobs, capital expenditure and the progress of the project. The investment and jobs have to be maintained for at least five years after the first instalment has been paid or at least 18 months after payment of the last instalment.

In 1999/00, by way of example, 1,226 awards were made, at an average of £249,200, comprising an average of 13.8% of the total project cost.

The assisted areas map of the UK is divided into three 'tiers', plus Northern Ireland. Tier one consists of much of Wales, Cornwall, Merseyside and South Yorkshire. This tier qualifies for the highest levels of assistance. Tier two includes parts of the West Midlands conurbation, the Highlands and Islands of Scotland and the North East of England. In tier three areas, RSA is not available but there is assistance in the form of enterprise grants, aimed largely at small and medium-sized businesses (SMEs). Enterprise grants are also available in tier one and tier two areas.

Enterprise grants are one-off grants of up to 15% of fixed capital investment on projects of up to £500,000, subject to a maximum of £75,000, made available to 'high quality' businesses employing no more than 250 people. There is a bias towards manufacturing and specialist service industries with a national or international customer base. The linkage to job creation, while still important, is not crucial.

Enterprise grants and the RSA are the two chief grant-aid programmes, but there are several other, more specialised programmes. Assistance may also be obtainable from local authorities.

European funding comes via the European Union Structural Funds. Between 2000/06, approximately £10,000 million has been allocated to the UK, in respect of three 'Objective' areas. Objective 1 is intended to promote the development of regions lagging behind in development terms. In the UK, Objective 1 areas are coextensive with the tier one RSA area, ie Cornwall and the Scilly Isles, West Wales and the Welsh Valleys, Merseyside and South Yorkshire. Northern Ireland and the Highlands and Islands of Scotland are entitled to transitional funding as their Objective 1 status was withdrawn in the revision of EU Structural Funds in 1999.

Objective 2 is aimed at regions seriously affected by industrial decline or crisis. Whereas Objective 1 and 2 funding is limited to designated areas, Objective 3 funding is available throughout England and selectively in Wales and Scotland. Objective 3 is designed to help people to adapt and prepare for change through education, training and employment.

Other forms of European funding may be available for investors locating in areas benefiting from 'Community Initiatives'. This may be in designated rural areas (the LEADER+ scheme), urban areas (URBAN), border regions (INTEREG) or for transnational cooperation to promote equal opportunities in the labour market (EQUAL).

Low-interest loans may also be available from the European Investment Bank, for up to 50% of eligible projects. Minimum loan amounts are €40,000 (£28,000) based on capital expenditure of €80,000 (£56,000).

Research and development in the UK is encouraged by special tax benefits. These are detailed in **Appendix 6**.

Foreign companies and individuals

1.3 The UK is host to foreign investors from almost every jurisdiction. The jurisdictions selected in this book comprise the 21 most popular; namely all the present EU countries outside the UK together with Australia, Canada, Hong Kong, Japan, Singapore, Switzerland and the USA.

The bulk of foreign business investors into the UK comprise companies, whether publicly or privately owned. However, foreign individuals carry on business in the UK from time to time and will often derive business-related income such as dividends, interest, royalties, and salary received from the business. Furthermore, foreign entertainers and sportsmen can derive substantial income from performances in the UK, foreign individuals purchase homes in the UK, and property investment is often undertaken by foreign individuals.

There may also be cases when it is more beneficial from a tax viewpoint for a privately owned UK company to be owned, financed or licensed by its foreign individual owners rather than by the foreign company itself.

For all these reasons, the UK and foreign tax position of the individual as well as that of the foreign company is considered in most Chapters.

Organisation

1.4 This book considers each stage of the typical business cycle of transactions undertaken by a foreign investor. It begins with the export of goods, services and intangibles to the UK without the foreign business establishing a UK base; and progresses by stages to the realisation of a mature UK business. It similarly deals with UK property investment, including the purchase of a home in the UK, together with the special UK tax regime for foreign entertainers and athletes.

In most Chapters there is a basic assumption that the foreign investor is a company. There then follows a separate section assuming instead that the foreign investor is an individual.

Each Chapter considers the specific aspect of the business cycle from both the UK and the foreign tax viewpoints, and suggests planning structures which combine facets of the two tax systems designed to provide the most efficient overall result.

Examples, which include planning techniques, are also provided throughout the text.

For ease of reference, most Chapters begin with an overview of their contents.

Double tax treaties

1.5 Apart from Hong Kong, the UK has entered into double tax treaties with all of the foreign-investor countries surveyed in the text.

All these treaties are based on the Model Tax Convention on Income and Capital published by the Organisation for Economic Co-operation and Development (OECD). Rather than giving examples of articles from treaties with selected countries, reference is generally made to the relevant article of the OECD Model Convention, which is reproduced in full in **Appendix 1**.

Appendix 2 contains a table of withholding tax rates applicable to payments of UK source interest (**Chapter 19**) and royalties (**Chapter 6**) paid to non-UK residents in each of the countries with which the UK has concluded a tax treaty.

Controlled foreign companies

1.6 In considering the optimum corporate structure for investing into the UK, the foreign investor will wish to take account of the legitimate use of third country low-tax jurisdictions to function, for example, as holding trading, financing, licensing or management companies.

In more than half the 21 countries considered, controlled foreign company ('CFC') rules or their equivalents operate to curtail the use of foreign low-tax companies by immediately taxing their income and gains in the home country jurisdiction. Consideration must always be given to CFC rules when utilising third country companies between the home country and the UK.

Appendix 3 provides an overview that summarises the broad principles applying in those of the 21 selected countries where CFC legislation or its equivalent is in force. It discusses the wide scope of the rules but also pinpoints situations in which they do not apply and where income and gains may be properly accumulated in a low-tax jurisdiction, reflecting business reality and reducing potential UK and home country taxes.

Transfer pricing

1.7 Another limiting factor to the use of third country low-tax jurisdictions is the existence of transfer pricing rules in both the UK and the home country jurisdiction. These are discussed in **Chapter 17**.

2 UK residence

Overview

- UK corporate residence determined by incorporation or central management and control.
- Dually resident companies—residence determined under 'tie-breaker' article of tax treaty.
- Foreign investors must ensure third country companies resident in neither UK nor their home jurisdiction.
- Assumed foreign individuals are not UK resident.

2.1 Non-resident individuals and companies doing business, or making investments, in the UK often do so through UK or foreign companies.

Companies incorporated in the UK are thereby UK resident [FA 1988, s 66]. However, it is perfectly possible for a company to be resident in the UK under UK law and at the same time to be resident in another jurisdiction under that jurisdiction's law. This condition is known as dual residence (see paragraph **2.9** et seq).

Setting aside dual residence for the moment, this Chapter considers the circumstances in which a company incorporated outside the UK may nevertheless be classified as resident in the UK for UK tax purposes.

It will be seen in **Chapters 13** and **14** below that, whether a foreign investor carries on a UK trade through a UK company or the UK permanent establishment of a foreign company, there is little or no difference in the UK tax consequences so far as the taxation of the ongoing profits, gains and dividend distributions are concerned. Briefly, this is because there are no UK withholding taxes on outbound dividends of a UK company, and the inter-group transfer provisions of ICTA 1988, s 171 and group relief provisions of ICTA 1988, s 402 et seq now apply as equally to a UK permanent establishment as they do to a UK company. (There may well be differences in the foreign tax consequences, which are considered in **Chapter 25**.)

However in the case of an investment activity in the UK, such as property investment, there is a crucial difference between UK and non-UK residence in that capital gains accruing to a non-UK resident company will generally be free of UK tax. Additionally, a non-resident company's rental income will be taxed at a lower rate (see paragraphs **32.1** and **32.2**).

Determining residence

2.2 For companies not incorporated in the UK the basic rule, developed by the courts over the last 100 years or more, is that such a company is resident in the

UK if its 'central management and control'—meaning essentially the place where the strategic decisions concerning the company are taken—is situated here.

There are a number of landmark decisions of the courts that have established this principle.

2.3 In *Calcutta Jute Mills Co Ltd v Nicholson* (1876) 1 TC 83, it was held that a company's residence could be regarded as the place where its business is carried on, and that the real business is carried on where the central management and control abides. This test was reiterated in *De Beers Consolidated Mines Ltd v Howe* (1905) 5 TC 198.

2.4 In *Unit Construction Co Ltd v Bullock* [1960] AC 351, although the Articles of Association of East African subsidiaries of a UK company specified that the boards had to meet locally and manage the companies, the facts were that the directors' meetings simply rubber-stamped decisions already taken in London and thereby the subsidiaries were held to be centrally managed and controlled in the UK and therefore UK resident.

2.5 In contrast, in the comparatively recent case of *Untelrab Ltd v McGregor* [1996] STC (SCD) 1, a foreign finance subsidiary of a UK company made loans to group companies which resulted from telexed requests from the group head office in the UK. However, it was established that, had any of the requests not been in the interests of the local subsidiary, they would have been refused. The Commissioners found that the board met in Bermuda, the proposals from head office were discussed, and the board would have refused to carry out unreasonable proposals. Accordingly, it was held that the subsidiary was not resident in the UK.

2.6 Statement of Practice SP 1/90 (reproduced in **Appendix 4**) sets out the Revenue's views on central management and control.

General disciplines

2.7 Reference should be made to paragraph **32.10** for practical steps to be taken to ensure as far as possible that corporate residence is located outside the UK in relation to UK property investment.

In general terms the following disciplines should be adhered to:

(a) A majority (preferably all) of the company directors should be non-UK residents.

(b) At least one director from the country of incorporation should hold an executive position with the company and if possible be given the position and power equivalent to those of an English managing director.

(c) The directors must be, or must include, persons with sufficient knowledge and competence to mange the company's business independently, and must receive remuneration commensurate with their duties and the scale of the business. If not, they should seek (preferably independent), expert help.

(d) Overseas directors must have sufficient information to enable them to make decisions.

(e) In particular, no UK resident director should be able to exert a dominant influence over the non-UK resident directors. In addition, UK resident directors must not inadvertently exercise central management and control actively or tacitly through oversight.

(f) All major decisions should be made, negotiations carried out, and contracts signed by the directors at board meetings. Concise but accurate Minutes should be kept of such meetings and full documentation supporting the Minutes should be kept on file, to put it beyond dispute that the meetings are the sole forum for arriving at relevant decisions, and are demonstrably not held merely to ratify decisions already taken elsewhere.

(g) Any decisions not made at board meetings should be supported by documentary evidence that the directors were fully and properly involved outside the UK in the more important aspects of the decision making process.

(h) Board meetings should be held regularly and at frequent intervals, to establish that the board is operating effectively to manage and control the business.

(i) Board meetings should be held outside the UK and preferably not at airports or hotels, but if possible at permanent premises of the company.

(j) The board should be provided with such accounts and other information as are reasonably necessary for it to control the company's activities, and such accounts and information should be discussed in board meetings and the discussions minuted.

(k) If functions of central management and control are delegated by the board, eg to a committee of directors, the same guidelines must be adopted by the committee as would be adopted in relation to the full board (eg all meetings of the committee should be held outside the UK).

(l) Books and records of the company should be kept outside the UK, preferably in the country of incorporation.

(m) In relation to its parent company, it is important that all communications should be in terms of giving information about, rather than asking approval for, decisions of the non-resident company. Conversely, all communications from the parent and its personnel to the board of the subsidiary should be in terms of general advice or guidance, rather than of specific instructions or orders, on the conduct of the company.

(n) Decisions not made at board meetings should be supported by documentary evidence that the directors were fully and properly involved outside the UK in the more important aspects of the decision making process.

(o) The company must not use a UK address or telephone number in any aspect of its business.

(p) Any parent company staff utilised by the non-resident company should be formally seconded. Such employees should refrain from acting in connection with the foreign company's business while in the UK and should at all times act under instructions from its board of directors.

Residence in foreign jurisdictions

2.8 Broadly similar concepts to UK corporate residence apply in the foreign jurisdictions surveyed (apart from the USA). In most European countries the concept of the 'seat of management' is the broad equivalent of the UK's central management and control.

Throughout the text reference is sometimes made to the foreign investor utilising companies in third country jurisdictions such as the Netherlands, to function as holding, finance companies etc. In such cases the foreign investor must ensure that the seat of management of such companies is not in the home jurisdiction, nor indeed, in the UK.

Dual residence

2.9 As we have seen, it is possible for a company to be resident in the UK for UK tax purposes because its central management and control is in the UK, but for the company to be resident outside the UK under the tax laws of a foreign jurisdiction applying a different test of residence. In cases where there is a double tax treaty between the UK and the foreign jurisdiction, the OECD Model Tax Convention article 4.3 (see **Appendix 1**) specifies that a person other than an individual is deemed for tax treaty purposes to be a resident only of the State in which its effective management is situated. (This definition is currently under discussion.)

The Revenue's view that in most cases (but not always) effective management is equivalent to central management and control (see the Inland Revenue's International Tax Handbook, and Tax Bulletin Issue 14 (December 1994).

2.10 In considering whether the 'effective management' of a trust was located in Ireland for the purposes of the UK/Ireland double tax treaty, a Special Commissioner, giving a decision in principle, considered that on the facts effective management of the trust was not located in Ireland. It was not sufficient that some sort of management was carried on in Ireland, such as operating a bank account in the name of the trustees. 'Effective' implied realistic, positive management. The place of effective management was 'where the shots were called' [*Wensleydale's Settlement Trustees v IRC* [1996] STC (SCD) 241].

2.11 In these 'tie breaker' situations in which a company is incorporated in one jurisdiction but is effectively managed in another, FA 1994, s 249 provides that, if the company is classified as resident outside the UK under the terms of a double tax treaty, it is to be treated as non-UK resident for all purposes of the Taxes Acts.

2.12 This provision is primarily aimed at UK incorporated companies effectively managed and controlled outside the UK and is therefore of little relevance to foreign companies operating inside the UK.

VAT and 'business establishment'

2.13 A business investing or trading in the UK will need to consider whether or not it has a business establishment in the UK for VAT purposes. The concept of 'business establishment' differs from the concept of residence or permanent establishment for tax purposes. European case law has found that the business establishment must have a certain minimum size and both the human and technical resources available on a permanent basis necessary for the provision of the particular activity undertaken (see *Berkholz v Finanzamt Hamburg–Mitte–Altstadt* [1985] ECR 2251, ECJ). It is important to note that the 'business establishment' test does not depend on the existence of corporate residence or a permanent establishment in the UK.

2.14 It should also be noted that having a business establishment in one EU Member State does not preclude a multinational business from also having business establishments in other EU Member States, provided that the business establishment test is met or the VAT provisions prevailing in the countries in question deem the activities to take place in that country for VAT purposes.

2.15 It is also the case that certain types of business activity can give rise to VAT issues and liabilities in the UK even though the business has no business establishment in the UK. These activities are considered in more detail in paragraphs **3.14** et seq, **4.3** et seq and in **Chapter 8**.

Tax implications in the foreign jurisdiction

2.16 There may be cases in which a company incorporated in the foreign investor's home jurisdiction is resident in the UK because of central management and control in the UK. Assuming that the company was to be treated as UK resident under a 'tie-breaker' article in the UK's tax treaty with the home country, this could restrict the home country's taxing rights.

Example 1

Solal SA is a company incorporated in France (and thereby resident in France). It is managed and controlled in the UK (and thereby resident in the UK).

By virtue of articles 3(1) and (2) of the France/UK tax treaty, the company is to be treated as UK resident only, because effective management is in the UK (see paragraph **2.9** et seq):

> '3(1) For the purposes of this Convention, the term "resident of Contracting State" means any person who, under the laws of that State, is liable to tax therein by reason of his domicile, residence, place of management or any other criterion of a similar nature. But this term does not include any person who is liable to tax in that State in respect only of income from sources in that State.
>
> 3(3) Where by reason of the provisions of paragraph (1) a person other than an individual is resident of both Contracting States, then it shall be deemed to be a resident of the Contracting State in which its place of effective management is situated.'

Solal SA receives interest from a French bank. Article 11(1) of the treaty specifies that interest arising in a Contracting State and paid to a resident of the other Contracting State shall be taxable only in that other State.

Therefore, French source interest received by the French company is exempt from French tax.

Foreign individuals

2.17 It is assumed that the individual foreign investor is resident for tax purposes in his home jurisdiction but is not resident in the UK. This will be the case for the vast majority of inward investors. Therefore, this book does not consider in any detail the cases where a foreign investor becomes UK resident and it is assumed in the rest of the book that the foreign individual retains his or her non-resident status.

This will be the case unless the foreign individual spends substantial periods of time in the UK; namely 183 days in any tax year to 5 April, or an average of 91 days per tax year for at least 4 consecutive tax years [Revenue Booklet IR20 paras 1.2 and 3.3].

As with companies, it is perfectly possible for an individual to be resident both in the UK under UK domestic law as well as in another jurisdiction, according to the law of that jurisdiction. If the UK has a tax treaty with the foreign jurisdiction, it will invariably include a 'tie-breaker' article specific to individuals that will settle the question one way or the other, for the purposes of applying the treaty (see article 4.2 in **Appendix 1** in relation to the OECD Model Convention). The article applies criteria such as the location of the person's permanent home, personal and economic relations, habitual abode, centre of vital interests, nationality etc. If none of these tests is conclusive, article 4.2(d) leaves it to the two tax authorities to determine the question by mutual agreement.

The typical foreign investor who may become tax resident in the UK will only do so because of the length of his or her stay in the UK (see above). However the foreign individual will normally have his or her sole home or main personal and economic interests in the home country. As a result, article 4.2(a) will have the effect of treating the foreign individual as a non-resident of the UK for the purposes of the tax treaty.

3 Exporting product to the UK: trading with the UK or in the UK?

Overview

- Foreign companies exporting product to the UK without a fixed place of business or dependent or habitual agent unlikely to be liable to UK tax.
- Particularly where there is tax treaty between UK and foreign exporter's jurisdiction of residence.
- Consequently, in most cases profits arising from exports fully taxable in foreign exporter's home jurisdiction.
- However where UK taxes are lower than home country, consider setting up UK branch or subsidiary to handle exports. Could reduce taxes on export profits.
- UK VAT and customs duties could be payable even though export profits not liable to UK tax.

3.1 It is quite possible for a foreign company or individual to generate profits from the UK by simply exporting products from outside the UK without maintaining any physical presence or representative capacity in the UK. In other words the foreign company or individual will be trading with, rather than in, the UK.

This Chapter discusses whether or not a foreign company or individual is trading with or in the UK.

3.2 *However even if trading takes place in the UK, it will be seen from paragraphs* **11.2** *and* **12.2** *et seq that in practice a UK tax liability will only arise if the foreign company or individual actually maintains a permanent establishment or habitual agency in the UK through which the product is sold.*

The tax consequences of doing so are discussed in **Chapter 13** 'UK permanent establishment'.

Trading in the UK

3.3 ICTA 1988, s 18(1)(a)(iii) charges a non-resident to income tax in respect of annual profits or gains arising or accruing from any trade, profession or vocation exercised within the UK. For corporation tax purposes, a non-resident company is liable to tax if it carries on a trade (a company cannot carry on a profession or vocation) in the UK through a permanent establishment [ICTA 1988, s 11(1)] (see paragraph **11.2**).

3.4 The basic principle of what constitutes 'trading in the UK' has been the subject of a number of cases beginning in the late 19th Century.

3.5 Before discussing these cases it should be stated that the mere purchase of goods in the UK does not constitute trading in the UK. This was decided in *Sulley v A-G* (1860) 2 TC 149. A US firm had a UK office that purchased goods and shipped them to the USA for sale there. It was held that the firm's profits did not accrue in the UK, but rather in the USA, where the main business was conducted. Basically trading profits from the purchase and sale of goods arise only when the sale is made. Without the sale, no profit is realised. Consequently where the trade consists of the mere purchase and sale of goods, a trade will not be carried on in the UK if no sales are made here.

3.6 On the question of trading in the UK, in *Erichsen v Last* (1881) 4 TC 422, a Danish telegraph company had an agency and offices in the UK dealing with calls received in this country on the company's wires. Contracts for the company's services were concluded in the UK. The courts found the company to be trading in the UK and upheld assessments on its net UK profits. In *Pommery & Greno v Apthorpe* (1886) 2 TC 182, French wine merchants sold their French-produced wine in the UK through their UK agent, who concluded contracts on their behalf. They were held to be exercising their trade in the UK. The same result was reached in two similar cases also involving French wine exporters (*Tischler & Co v Apthorpe* (1885) 2 TC 89 and *Werle & Co v Colquhoun* (1888) 2 TC 402).

3.7 The French firms also produced the wine but it is reasonably clear from these cases and from *Grainger v Gough* (see paragraph **3.9**) that the Revenue did not seek to tax the element of the overall profit attributable to the production activities as these took place in France.

3.8 On the same lines, a Norwegian ship owner whose vessel was chartered by a Glasgow agent who also collected all the receipts and made all the disbursements, was held to be trading in the UK (*James Wingate & Co v Webber* (1897) 3 TC 569).

3.9 These cases should be contrasted with that of *FL Smidth & Co v Greenwood* (1922) 8 TC 193, in which a Danish firm maintained an office in London staffed by an employee. The employee discussed prospective customers' requirements with them and reported back to Denmark but all the contracts were negotiated from, and made in, Denmark. The House of Lords held that the Danish company was not exercising a trade in the UK. In another French wine case, the French merchant's English agent transmitted all orders back to the merchant in France for execution. It was held that the merchant was not trading in the UK (*Grainger & Son v Gough* (1896) 3 TC 462).

3.10 Briefly, the principle illustrated by these cases is that, in the case of a sale of goods to the UK, the non-resident will be trading in the UK if contracts of sale are concluded in the UK. Therefore, in the case of merchanting goods, there is a possibility of avoiding UK tax if contracts of sale are concluded outside the UK. However concluding contracts outside the UK is not by itself a guarantee that the activities will escape UK tax. The real test, formulated as long ago as 1922 by Lord Justice Atkin in *Smidth* (see paragraph **3.9**), is 'where do the operations take place from which the profits in substance arise?' This is as true of a simple sale of goods as it is in situations where some other activity (performance of services, manufacturing etc) takes place in the UK. As Mr Justice Peter Gibson put it in *Hafton Properties Ltd v McHugh* [1987] STC 16, '. . . it is not correct to say that because a contract is concluded in the UK in the course of a business, the business is necessarily carried on in the UK.'

3.11 In *Firestone Tyre and Rubber Co Ltd v Lewellin* (1957) 37 TC 111, Firestone, the US tyre manufacturer, had a manufacturing subsidiary in the UK. Under an agreement between the two, the UK company fulfilled orders obtained by European agents of the US parent. The purchasers paid the UK company which remitted the sale proceeds to the US parent after deducting its costs and a 50% mark-up. The House of Lords held that the US parent was trading in the UK and that the UK subsidiary was correctly assessed as its UK agent.

UK agents

3.12 Acts performed by a UK agent on behalf of his non-resident principal constitute acts performed by the non-resident principal. In this way the agent's acts could cause the non-resident to be carrying on a trade in the UK.

However it will be seen from what follows that the actions of an independent agent carrying out functions in the ordinary course of his business will not lead to his non-resident principal carrying on a trade in the UK. There is a logic in this as an agent performing services on behalf of many principals does not have the characteristic of constituting any sort of permanent UK base for his principal.

In contrast, a UK dependent agent, or one habitually exercising authority to do business on behalf of his non-resident principal, normally constitutes the necessary permanence (see paragraph **11.11** for the status and position of dependent agents). Under this heading would normally be included a so-called commissionaire agent.

Conclusion of contracts

3.13 The cases discussed above place an emphasis on where contracts are concluded as a factor in determining whether a trade is carried on in the UK.

It is a matter of law as to where a contract is concluded. Although this can occur orally, contracts are normally concluded in writing. Contracts accepted by mail are considered concluded at the place where the letter or other notification of acceptance is posted as once posted the letter is held by the postal authorities as agent for the addressor on behalf of the addressee. On the other hand contracts concluded by instantaneous communication, such as telephone, fax or e-mail, are concluded at the place where the acceptance is received. The various processes by which the contract is negotiated and concluded are crucial.

Example 2

Peterson Inc, a Canadian company, distributes a price list to UKco as purchaser, with a standard acceptance form attached:

(a) UKco posts the acceptance form to Peterson Inc.

The contract is made in the UK where the acceptance form is posted.

(b) UKco faxes the acceptance form to Peterson Inc.

The contract is made abroad where the fax is received.

(c) UKco faxes Peterson Inc a counter-offer, proposing a reduced price for a larger quantity of goods. Peterson Inc faxes acceptance to UKco.

The contract is made in the UK where the fax is received.

In cases where the contract is made in the UK, Peterson Inc will not be taxable in the UK unless the contract is made by its UK permanent establishment or its regular agent (see paragraphs **11.2** and **12.3**).

A contract can also be made by performance (ie where the offeror performs the transaction that is the subject of the contract without having received a formal acceptance).

Example 3

Hong Kongco ships goods to an independent warehouse. With a view to avoiding UK tax, Hong Kongco ensures that all contractual communications with its UK customers are conducted from Hong Kong. Customers fax their requests to Hong Kongco which, if it accepts the offer, instructs the UK warehouse to deliver the goods. This is followed by a confirmation posted by Hong Kongco.

The contract is made by delivery of the goods from the UK warehouse. The postal confirmation is of a contract already made by the delivery. So the contract is made in the UK.

However, if Hong Kongco has no UK permanent establishment or regular agency, an assessment to UK tax is unlikely in practice (see paragraphs **11.2** and **12.3**).

VAT and customs duties

3.14 See **Chapters 8** and **9** for the basic rules.

The VAT treatment of physical goods being moved to the UK from outside the UK will depend on the source of the goods, the ownership of the goods and the contract under which they are supplied. This section can only give a brief summary of the basic principles relating to the movement of physical goods into the UK. Individual transactions will need to be considered on their own facts and the VAT and customs duty position determined accordingly.

3.15 Goods which are not of EU source or origin are deemed not to be in 'free circulation' in the UK/EU until import VAT and any customs duties have been paid, usually at the point of importation or removal from a UK/EU located Customs Warehouse. VAT and duty-unpaid goods cannot be lawfully moved or traded in the UK/EU, although there are a range of reliefs available for goods which are: temporarily imported; located in the EU solely as a point in a trans-shipment destined for a non-EU location; or are temporarily in the EU for process or repair.

3.16 If a business without a business establishment in the UK exports goods to a specific UK customer and the customer is responsible for the importation of the goods, then the VAT and customs duties consequences rest with the customer. However, if a non-resident business imports its own goods into the UK with the intention of establishing and holding a stock of goods for subsequent resale, it will be its responsibility to bring the goods into free circulation within the UK/EU by accounting for any VAT and customs duties at the time of importation.

3.17 This would normally mean the non-established business has to register itself for UK VAT on the basis that it wishes to recover any VAT incurred on importation and on the basis that it will at some future point supply those goods to customers within the UK/EU and need to account either for UK VAT on their sale, or be in a position to meet the requirements for the intra-EU movement of goods.

3.18 For goods which are already in free circulation within the EU, the procedures are slightly different. The initial point to note is that there will be no customs duty payable on intra-EU movements of goods. If goods are being moved from another EU source where the supplier is already locally VAT registered and the movement is to a UK VAT registered customer, then no VAT is accounted for in the place of dispatch but the UK VAT registered customer is required to account for VAT in the UK on the acquisition of the goods by adjusting its periodic VAT return. For UK acquiring businesses which make only taxable supplies in the UK, any VAT on the acquisition should be recoverable in full and thus not lead to a VAT cost.

3.19 An EU VAT registered business moving its own goods from an EU place of despatch to the UK would need to register for UK VAT itself in order to account for the VAT on the acquisition. It would also need to account for UK VAT on any sales made to UK customers from its own stocks located in the UK.

Tax implications in the foreign jurisdiction

3.20 In this section, it is assumed that a foreign company is exporting product to the UK. Contracts may or may not be concluded in the UK and the company may or may not be trading in the UK. In any event there is no physical presence or representative capacity in the UK; in other words, there is no UK branch, permanent establishment or regular agency and so, as will be seen in paragraphs **11.2** and **12.3**, no exposure to UK tax.

In these circumstances, the profits arising will continue to be exclusively taxed in the foreign jurisdiction. However, of the jurisdictions surveyed, it is possible that Hong Kong might consider the export profits to be foreign source income, particularly if sales contracts and all of the business functions relating to the sales were performed outside the UK. If this was the case, Hong Kong would exempt the profits from tax as it only taxes Hong Kong source income.

Example 4

While this Chapter assumes that there is no liability to UK tax, the overall tax position may be improved if a liability to UK tax actually arises.

As will be seen from Table 2 at paragraph **13.3(f)**, many countries exempt foreign profits from tax, especially if they are generated by a permanent establishment taxed abroad. As UK tax rates are often comparatively low, an overall tax saving then arises. For example:

Grappelli SA is a French company that currently exports its product to the UK. All of its profits, including those arising from the UK exports, are taxable in France at the current rate of approximately 35%.

If Grappelli SA sets up a UK permanent establishment to effect the UK sales, the profits arising will be liable to UK corporation tax of up to 30%. France will normally exempt the profits of the permanent establishment from tax, and therefore a minimum saving of 5% arises.

The same result could be achieved if Grappelli SA were to set up a UK subsidiary to handle the UK export sales.

Foreign individuals

3.21 The comments in this Chapter apply as much to foreign individuals as to foreign companies.

4 Exporting services to the UK

Overview

- Where the foreign business provides services in the UK, profits are taxable in principle.
- However in absence of a UK fixed place of business or dependent or habitual agent, UK tax liability unlikely to arise.
- Particularly so where there is a tax treaty between foreign country and the UK.
- Assuming no liability to UK tax, profits arising to foreign business likely to be taxed in home jurisdiction.
- Despite absence of tax on profits, VAT liabilities could arise.

4.1 In situations that do not involve a simple sale of goods, such as where a non-resident company or individual renders services in the UK (or where manufacturing takes place in the UK), the place of conclusion of the contract for services is less relevant. Furthermore, Lord Atkin's test in *F L Smidth & Co v Greenwood* (where do the operations take place from which the profits in substance arise?) will, in the great majority of cases, lead to the conclusion that there is trading in the UK if the services are rendered in the UK(see paragraph **3.10**).

Example 5

Foreignco sends computer experts to service UK customers in return for service fees.

Foreignco is taxable in the UK on the service fees earned.

(However, if Foreignco has no UK fixed place of business or dependent or habitual agency, an assessment to UK tax is unlikely in practice (see paragraphs **11.2** and **12.3**.)

4.2 A relatively recent case illustrating this point is *Brackett v Chater* [1986] STC 521. A Jersey company had as its sole employee a chartered surveyor who was resident in the UK. The company's main activity was the exploitation of the surveyor's services, which he carried out from his base in the UK. The Jersey company was held to be trading in the UK through its UK permanent establishment.

Increasingly, services are delivered by e-commerce (see **Chapter 7**).

Again, a UK tax liability will only arise if the foreign company or individual actually maintains a UK fixed place of business or dependent or habitual agency through which the services are rendered (see paragraphs **11.2** and **12.3**).

VAT: place of supply of services

4.3 As with supplies of goods it is necessary to consider the UK VAT impact of importing services into the UK. The basic rule for supplies of services is that they are deemed to be made where the supplier of the service has his business establishment. Therefore, in most cases a foreign business with no UK establishment that is supplying services to the UK should be able to do so without itself suffering any VAT consequences (but see paragraphs **7.11** et seq and **8.4**). The recipient will need to consider the effect that receiving such services would have on its UK VAT position. The receipt by a UK VAT registered business of services that are supplied by a supplier established outside the UK will normally give rise to a 'reverse charge' in the UK [VATA 1994, s 8].

4.4 Broadly, this requires the recipient to account for output VAT on the deemed value of the supply. Normally, the business would be able to recover the same amount as input VAT under the usual VAT provisions, unless it makes partly exempt supplies.

4.5 There are a broad range of services that are deemed to be supplied where the recipient belongs, in cases where the recipient of those services is in business in another EU Member State or belongs outside the EU. In the UK, these are set out in VATA 1994, Sch 5.

The services listed in Sch 5 are as follows:

(a) Transfers and assignments of copyright, patents, licences, trademarks and similar rights.

(b) Advertising services.

(c) Services of consultants, engineers, consultancy bureaux, lawyers, accountants and other similar services; data processing and provision of information (excluding services relating to land).

(d) Acceptance of any obligation to refrain from pursuing or exercising in whole or in part any business activity or any of the rights in para 1.

(e) Banking, financial and insurance services (including reinsurance but not including the provision of safe-deposit facilities).

(f) The supply of staff.

(g) The letting on hire of goods other than means of transport.

(h) Telecommunications services.

(i) Services rendered by one person to another in procuring any of the above services for the latter.

(j) Any services not specified above (excluding telecommunications services) when supplied to a VAT-registered person in the UK.

4.6 Conversely to paragraph **4.3**, supplies of such services by UK businesses are outside the scope of UK VAT when supplied to an EU business or non-EU located recipient, but they do attract the right of the supplier to deduct associated input tax.

4.7 A UK established recipient of services which is not required to be VAT registered under the normal rules, can find itself liable to be registered for UK VAT if it receives supplies set out VATA 1994, Sch 5. In these circumstances a VAT cost can arise if there is any restriction on that business's ability to recover the reverse charge VAT as input tax.

It should be noted that the supply of most intellectual property and associated rights is covered by these provisions (see **Chapter 6**).

Tax implications in the foreign jurisdiction

4.8 At this stage it is assumed that there is in fact no UK permanent establishment or regular agency and so, as will be seen from paragraphs **11.2** and **12.3**, no exposure to UK tax.

In these circumstances the profits arising from the services performed in the UK will generally continue to be exclusively taxed in the foreign jurisdiction. However, of the jurisdictions surveyed, it is possible that Hong Kong would consider the fees from the services to constitute foreign source income even though there was no UK permanent establishment. If this was the case, Hong Kong would exempt the fee income from tax as it only taxes Hong Kong source income.

Foreign individuals

4.9 The comments in this Chapter apply as much to foreign individuals as to foreign companies.

Example 6

See Example 4 at paragraph **3.20**.

In specific circumstances an overall saving could be achieved if the foreign company or individual had the UK services performed by a UK branch, permanent establishment or subsidiary.

5 Manufacturing in the UK

Overview

- Profits arising from UK manufacturing activities liable to UK tax even if no sales are made in the UK.
- Additional taxable profits arise if sales made in the UK.
- UK tax exposure may exempt profits from tax in home country.

5.1 Unlike a mere seller of products or services, a foreign business carrying on a manufacturing trade in the UK will necessarily do so through a UK permanent establishment, namely the manufacturing premises. In these circumstances liability to UK tax will invariably arise (see paragraphs **11.2** and **12.2**). The actual tax consequences are discussed in **Chapter 13** 'UK permanent establishment'.

5.2 ICTA 1988 s 832(1) defines 'trade' to include manufacture. Thus manufacturing in the UK constitutes the carrying on of a trade even if there are no sales of the manufactured product in the UK (because it is shipped abroad for sale outside the UK).

5.3 In such a case, liability to UK tax will be limited to the manufacturing profit. Clearly, the profit attributable to selling the product arises outside the UK. This conclusion is supported by a Privy Council case, *Taxation Comrs v Kirk* [1900] AC 588.

5.4 However it is important to ascertain in these circumstances what is the trade, and what is the profit generated from that trade. Where manufacturing is carried on in the UK but sale contracts, negotiations etc are concluded elsewhere, it is only the manufacturing profit (the profit of the trade carried on in the UK) that is assessable to UK tax (see paragraph **3.10**). Any mark-up on sales remains outside the scope of UK tax, subject to any transfer pricing considerations (see **Chapter 17**).

5.5 An exercise will need to be carried out to establish the value of the manufactured product constituting the gross notional proceeds, from which manufacturing costs and overhead expenses will be deductible.

Example 7

Instead of manufacturing itself, it may be preferable for the foreign company or individual to form a UK company to specifically carry out the manufacturing activity. The UK company could then sell the manufactured product to a related company outside the UK at a sustainable arm's length price.

5.6 *Manufacturing in the UK*

In addition to manufacturing the product the UK company would then be carrying out selling activities that would attract additional taxable UK profits. In view of the UK's comparatively low tax rates, this could be advantageous.

However, if it was instead preferable to minimise taxable UK profits, this could be done by having the UK company manufacture the product to order rather than organise sales to its foreign affiliate.

In fact, this organisation of the functions of the UK company to determine the profits attributable to it on an arm's length basis anticipates the functional analysis relevant to transfer pricing discussed in paragraph **17.18**.

Tax implications in the foreign jurisdiction

5.6 As mentioned at paragraph **5.1**, the foreign business's UK manufacturing activity will necessarily constitute a UK permanent establishment. The foreign tax consequences relevant to a UK permanent establishment are discussed in **Chapter 13**. In a number of jurisdictions the manufacturing profits generated in the UK will be exempt from tax in the home country. See Table 2 at paragraph **13.3(f)**.

Instead of manufacturing in the UK, it may be possible for the foreign investor to have all or part of the manufacturing function performed by a subsidiary located in a low-tax jurisdiction. Apart from low tax rates a number of these jurisdictions offer additional incentives including grants, cheap loans and low labour costs.

While the home country jurisdiction may impose controlled foreign company rules designed to frustrate the accumulation of profits in low-tax jurisdictions, these are primarily aimed at passive income and are generally inapplicable to real trading activities carried out by a local workforce, especially when there are no dealings with related parties (see **Appendix 3**).

Transfer pricing rules will also require consideration if the offshore manufacturing company trades with its home jurisdiction and when it sells its product to the UK branch or subsidiary (see **Chapter 17**).

Foreign individuals

5.7 The comments in this Chapter apply as much to foreign individuals as to foreign companies.

6 Licensing to the UK

> **Overview**
>
> - UK source patent, copyright and design royalties subject to UK withholding tax, reducible under a tax treaty.
> - Licensors resident in non-treaty jurisdictions could sublicense rights to intermediary company, for example the Netherlands. However UK Revenue tending to challenge such 'treaty shopping'.
> - As alternative to royalty, foreign licensor could sell UK rights for capital sum. With exception of UK patent rights, sale proceeds could be free of UK tax.
> - In most cases, royalty received in foreign jurisdiction fully taxable with credit for UK withholding taxes suffered.

6.1 Increasingly, foreign entrepreneurs are able to do business in the UK without an actual presence, by licensing intellectual property such as computer software, patents, trademarks, know-how or other intangibles, to a UK licensee in return for a royalty payable to the foreign company or individual.

Chapter 21 discusses the tax position of the UK licensee. This Chapter is concerned with the tax position of the foreign licensor. See paragraph **7.9** et seq for the e-commerce implications.

UK source royalties

6.2 Royalties payable by a UK person for the right to use intangible property in the UK are sourced, and so taxable, in the UK. ICTA 1988, s 18(1)(a)(iii) charges non-residents to UK income tax under Schedule D Case VI on income from property in the UK. However in most cases the royalty will simply be part of the gross revenue of the foreign company's or individual's business and thus merely a component in the calculation of its overall profits, much like export sales. On that basis the source of the income would be the foreign resident's non-UK business which, in the absence of a UK permanent establishment, would not be exposed to UK tax.

6.3 But it is arguable that, if a non-resident can enforce his rights in the UK, the royalty income does arise from property in the UK taxable under s 18(1)(a)(iii). For example under the Berne and Universal Copyrights Conventions, to which the UK and most other OECD countries are signatories, a foreign person acquires rights to enforce copyright in a state that is a signatory to the agreement.

6.4 In principle all types of royalty sourced in the UK are liable to income tax at rates of up to 40% to foreign individuals, and 22% to foreign companies. In practice it is only UK patent, copyright and registered design royalties that are actually taxed as a result of the requirement for the payer to withhold tax at source (see paragraph **6.5** et seq). Other royalties could be taxable by direct assessment under Schedule D Case VI (see above) if sourced in the UK. In practice such assessments are rare. Apart from the difficulty of collecting the tax, the position is probably taken that such royalties are not sourced in the UK because they are part of the profits of the foreign licensor's business and the business is located outside the UK (see paragraph **6.2**).

Withholding tax and double tax treaties

6.5 As a tax collection mechanism, ICTA 1988 ss 349(1)(b), 536 and 537B basically require a UK payer to deduct tax at the basic rate (currently 22%) from payments of UK patent, copyright and registered design royalties, to non-residents. Film and video copyright royalties are excluded together with royalties in respect of exported products that have attracted copyright and design royalties [ICTA 1988, s 536(2)].

6.6 The deduction of tax at source is also inapplicable to royalty payments made to authors on the basis that the source of income is not the copyright but rather the author's profession. This is reinforced by a response to a Parliamentary question (HC Vol 791, Col 31, 10 November 1969). In practice, the UK Revenue accepts that this same treatment applies to royalties payable in respect of literary, dramatic, musical or artistic work written or executed in the ordinary course of the creative artist's profession [Inspector's Manual para IM4001].

6.7 Where withholding tax applies, and assuming that the foreign licensor is resident in a jurisdiction that has entered into a double tax treaty with the UK and that the royalties are not derived through the foreign licensor's UK permanent establishment, the rate of UK withholding tax will invariably be reduced to (typically) 0%, 5% or 10% under the relevant tax treaty (see **Appendix 2**), based on article 12.1 of the OECD Model Tax Treaty (see **Appendix 1**).

6.8 Before deducting tax at the appropriate treaty rate, it was previously the case that the UK licensee was required to obtain prior permission from the Inland Revenue's Centre for Non-Residents ('CNR'). From 1 October 2002, that requirement has been relaxed for all royalties if the payer is a company. Companies may now deduct the appropriate treaty rate (including zero) without prior permission, provided that they have reasonable grounds for believing that the payee is entitled to relief under the treaty [ICTA 1988, s 349E]. However as this places the responsibility on the payer, it is likely that permission to apply the treaty rate will continue to be sought from the CNR.

6.9 There is no legislative authority for the deduction of tax at source from royalties other than for patents, copyright and designs. As discussed at paragraph **6.4**, royalties for example, for trademarks, franchises and know-how are not normally liable to UK tax in the hands of a non-resident unless they:

(a) are derived through the foreign licensor's UK permanent establishment and so constitute part of UK trading profits directly taxable under ICTA 1988, s 11 for companies or s 18 for individuals (see paragraphs **11.2** and **12.1**); or

(b) constitute 'pure income profit' to the licensor and thus an annual payment from which tax is deductible at the basic rate (currently 22%), under ICTA 1988, s 349(1)(a) (see paragraph **6.10** et seq).

Annual payments

6.10 The 'pure income profit' concept is an abstruse and somewhat archaic product of case law, being the defining characteristic of an 'annual payment', which is itself a concept arguably ripe for reform if not abolition. It has been held in a series of cases, beginning with *Re Hanbury* (1939) 38 TC 588, that an annual payment is a recurrent payment that is 'pure income profit' in the hands of the recipient and not, by contrast, one the proper treatment of which is as 'an element to be taken into account in discovering what the profits of the recipient are'. In other words, a payment that is 'pure income profit' is one such that the whole of it can be properly regarded as an addition to the total income of the recipient. Where, under generally accepted accounting principles, the profit of the recipient in this respect can be ascertained only after a deduction of all the associated items of expenditure, the payment cannot be pure income profit.

Example 8

Foreignco's only asset is the rights to a brand name which it licenses to a UK company in return for a royalty.

The royalty it receives constitutes 'pure income profit'. It is not a mere element in the calculation of Foreignco's profits. It constitutes the true measure of its total profits (re *Hanbury* 38 TC 588).

The royalty is therefore an annual payment, subject to deduction of 22% income tax, reducible under a double tax treaty (see paragraph **6.11**).

6.11 However assuming, as is normal, that there is an 'Other Income' article in the UK's tax treaty with the jurisdiction in which the foreign licensor is resident, the annual payment will fall within this article. It will invariably specify that the income is to be taxed only in the foreign licensor's jurisdiction of residence and so exempt from the 22% withholding tax (see article 21.1 of the OECD Model Convention, **Appendix 1**).

The 'Other Income' article is a sweeping-up process by which items of income not specified in other articles of the treaty fall within its scope.

Impending changes

6.12 It should be added that, arising from recent consultations on the modernisation of the taxation of intangible property (which culminated in legislation contained in FA 2002 (see **Chapter 21**), the UK Government suggested widening the ambit of withholding tax on OECD lines so as to extend it to all royalties including, for example, trademarks, franchises and know-how [Inland Revenue Technical Note of 22 June 2000 'Reform of the taxation of intellectual property goodwill and other intangible assets']. But to date no legislative action has been taken on this proposal.

6.13 The European Council adopted the Interest and Royalties Directive (2003/49/EC) on 3 June 2003. It will eliminate withholding taxes on payments of interest and royalties between affiliated companies (25% shareholding relationships) in Member States. The Inland Revenue will be consulting on the legislative and practical changes needed to implement the Directive in the autumn of 2003, with the legislation promised for inclusion in the Finance Bill 2004. The Directive is due to be implemented by 1 January 2004, but this date may yet be set back unless disputes in the EC concerning the tax package of which the Directive is a part are settled quickly.

Chapter 21 deals in more detail with the licensing or acquisition of intellectual property from the licensee's point of view.

Offshore licensing company

6.14 Licensors whose country of residence has no tax treaty with the UK, for example Hong Kong, have tended to use intermediate companies in order to avoid the imposition of the 22% withholding tax on their UK source royalty income from patents, copyrights and registered designs, and in those cases where the royalty constitutes an annual payment.

6.15 Typically, the Netherlands has been used as a sub-licensee jurisdiction.

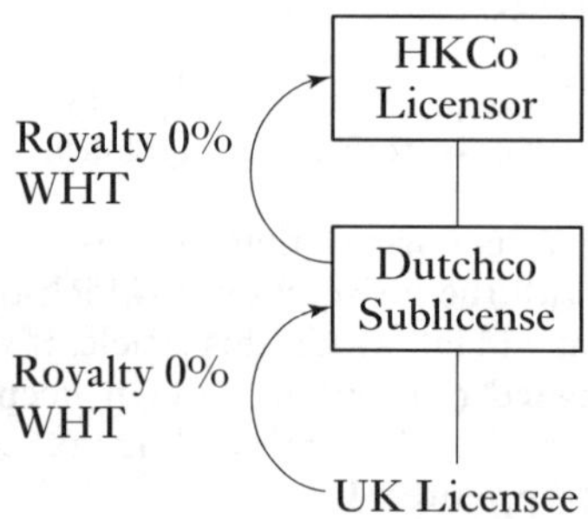

The Dutch company derives a margin of profit between the royalty it receives, and the royalty it pays to the Hong Kong company. Until recently an advance ruling was obtainable in the Netherlands that the margin be in the region of 7%. This process has now been abolished to be replaced by a requirement for the Dutch company to demonstrate what would be an arm's-length margin of profit.

Article 12(1) of the UK/Netherlands tax treaty provides for a 0% withholding tax on the royalty paid by the UK licensee. The Netherlands domestically imposes no withholding tax on outgoing royalties. The Dutch company is liable to a 34.5% corporate income tax on its 7% margin of profit, so the effective tax rate is approximately 2.5% rather than 22%.

Treaty shopping

6.16 However, article 12(5) (which is not based on the OECD Model Convention) contains an anti-treaty shopping provision which renders the 0% rate inapplicable if the rights giving rise to the royalties were created or assigned mainly to take advantage of the treaty and not for bona fide commercial reasons. It reads as follows:

> '12(5) The provisions of this Article shall not apply if the right or property giving rise to the royalties was created or assigned mainly for the purpose of taking advantage of this Article and not for *bona fide* commercial reasons.'

6.17 The UK Revenue is tending to use article 12(5) to a greater extent than previously in asserting that the full 22% withholding tax applies. For example, it has been argued that the decision in *Wood Preservation Ltd v Prior* (1968) 45 TC 112, (relating to transfer of losses to a company under the same 75% beneficial ownership) is in point in that 93% of the royalties received are destined to leave the company and so are not in its beneficial ownership.

6.18 It is also interesting to note that the Netherlands Underminister of Finance has stated that a person cannot be considered the beneficial owner of income if, for example, he is contractually obliged to pay the largest part of the income to third parties.

6.19 Subject to the anti-treaty shopping comments above, an offshore licensing company (say, Gibraltar) might also be used by a foreign licensor in a high tax country wishing to defer home country tax on the royalty income, for example using this structure:

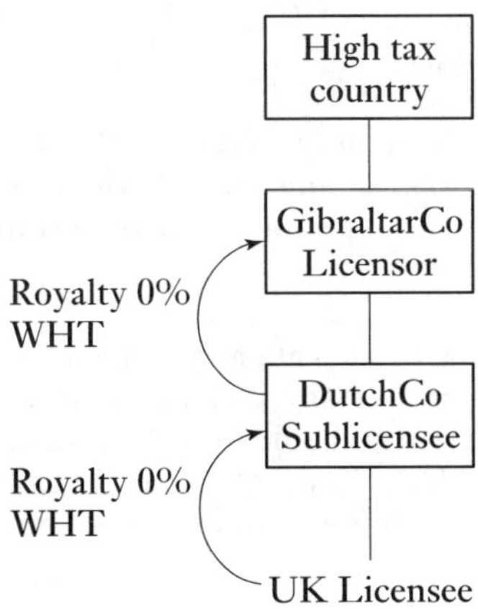

6.20 *Licensing to the UK*

The problem that needs considering in this situation will be controlled foreign company rules that could immediately tax the royalty income of the Gibraltar company in the high tax country (see **Appendix 3**).

Sale of intellectual property

6.20 An interesting alternative to the grant of a UK licence in return for a recurring royalty would be for the foreign company or individual to dispose of the UK rights to the intellectual property by way of a grant, in return for a lump sum payment by the UK grantee.

6.21 The grant of the rights for a lump sum would normally constitute a capital gain to the non-resident company or individual. In the absence of a UK permanent establishment, the gain would be outside the ambit of capital gains tax [TCGA, 1992, s 2(1)], and the lump sum would not be subject to withholding tax as a royalty.

6.22 However, the mere fact that a payment is made in one lump sum rather than on a recurring basis does not by itself guarantee that it is a capital sum and not a revenue receipt. Whether a payment is of an income nature or a capital nature depends on the facts in each case. For instance, a lump-sum payment in respect of past use or future use, where there is no acquisition by the purchaser of a defined portion of the rights concerned would be regarded by the Inland Revenue as an income payment, and hence equivalent to a royalty, from which withholding tax may be due, depending on the nature of the right and the place of abode of the recipient. See, for example, the Revenue's Inspector's Manual para IM3922 (in respect of patent royalties).

6.23 Be that as it may, gains on the sale of UK patent rights wholly or partly for a capital sum are in any case taxable as income under Schedule D Case VI [ICTA 1988, s 524]. Where the seller is a non-resident, the UK purchaser must withhold 22% basic rate tax at source [ICTA 1988, s 524(3)] but this is subject to potential relief under a tax treaty.

It is doubtful that the sale of the rights would fall within the royalty article of the treaty. For example, article 12.2 of the OECD Model Convention defines a royalty as payment for the use of (rather than the acquisition of) intangible property (see **Appendix 1**).

However, although the UK taxes the gain as income, it is in fact a capital gain. Provided the patent is not part of any UK permanent establishment of the licensor, all of the UK's tax treaties should exempt the gain from UK tax, based on article 13.5 of the OECD Model Convention (see **Appendix 1**). Taxing rights would be reserved to the licensor's country of residence (see also paragraph **21.13**).

The tax position of the UK purchaser of the rights is discussed in **Chapter 21**.

Example 9

In situations where the owner of the rights is unable to take advantage of a tax treaty with the UK, the sale of rights (other than patent rights) for a lump sum could avoid a 22% withholding tax that would be suffered on royalty income. This is particularly appropriate to group situations where the terms of the sale can be more flexible than with third parties.

For example, a Hong Kong company allows its UK subsidiary to use copyrights. Hong Kong has no tax treaty with the UK. The UK rights can be sold in return for a lump sum.

For UK tax purposes the subsidiary will be able to amortise the lump sum paid over the term of the licence provided the rights were acquired or created by the Hong Kong company after 31 March 2003 (see paragraphs **21(5)(b)** and **(c)**). The Hong Kong company will not be liable to UK tax on the lump sum proceeds. For Hong Kong tax purposes the lump sum will probably be regarded as a capital gain. Hong Kong does not tax capital gains.

VAT

6.24 See paragraph **4.3** et seq. Supplies by a foreign business of the services specified there are outside the scope of UK VAT and subject to the 'reverse charge' procedure.

Tax implications in the foreign jurisdiction

6.25 As with the export of products and services to the UK, the derivation of UK royalties in the absence of a UK permanent establishment or regular representative will normally result in the royalties remaining taxable in the foreign jurisdiction.

Generally this will be so in all of the jurisdictions surveyed even though UK withholding tax may be deductible from the royalties received (see **Appendix 2**). The withholding tax will normally be allowed as a deduction or credit when calculating tax on the royalty income in the foreign jurisdiction.

However, this general rule may not apply in Hong Kong which only taxes Hong Kong source profits. Depending on the facts it could be arguable that the royalties were sourced in the UK.

In cases of inter-group etc licensing, transfer pricing rules in the foreign jurisdiction will generally require that the foreign affiliate charge the UK entity an arm's length rate of royalty. However, of the jurisdictions surveyed, Hong Kong and Ireland do not provide for transfer pricing adjustments.

A foreign licensor may license intellectual property through an offshore company. Licensors resident in countries with controlled foreign company legislation may be constrained from doing so (see **Appendix 3**). Other considerations in the foreign jurisdiction may be the tax arising on the transfer of the intellectual property to the offshore company as governed by transfer pricing rules (see **Chapter 17**).

Foreign individuals

6.26 The comments made in this Chapter apply equally to foreign individuals as they do to foreign companies.

7 E-commerce

Overview

- Existence of UK website or server is insufficient in itself to constitute taxable permanent establishment.
- Digital information for customer's own use is business profits, not royalty.
- Non-EU providers required to register for VAT when providing services to EU non-business customers.

7.1 With the emergence of electronic commerce as an increasingly common method of doing business, governments and the business community have deliberated on how and where the profits derived should be taxed. One of the most important tax considerations has been whether the existence of a server or website constitutes a taxable permanent establishment (see paragraph **11.3**).

7.2 The UK's position was clearly stated at a conference in Lisbon on 11 April 2000. The Director of the Inland Revenue's International Division, Mr Gabs Makhlouf said:

> 'The OECD has been reviewing with the business community the long term future of the 'permanent establishment' concept – the threshold in the OECD's model tax treaty below which a country will not tax non-residents carrying on a business in that country. This is crucial work. And it is important that it is carried out with due consideration, and in partnership between representatives of Government and business.
>
> "Permanent establishment" is a long standing concept. It is tried and tested. And it is widely supported. As yet, we do not know enough about how e-commerce will develop for anyone to make reasoned decisions on whether or not to move away from it. But now is clearly the time for the debate to begin.
>
> In the meantime, early decisions are needed on the status of web sites and servers under the existing rules of permanent establishment. Businesses need to know where they stand in order to make investment decisions and calculate their tax liabilities.
>
> A particularly important policy objective is that the outcome is a practical one. One that works in the real world as well in the heads of lawyers. Governments and businesses need an outcome that allows e-commerce to flourish, that keeps down compliance costs, and that is enforceable.
>
> In the UK, we take the view that a web site of itself is not a permanent establishment. And we take the view that a server is insufficient of itself to constitute a permanent establishment of a business that is conducting e-commerce through a web site on the server. We take that view regardless of whether the server is owned, rented or otherwise at the disposal of the business.'

7.3 However international thinking continues to develop in this area and it is unlikely that the UK would wish to deviate significantly from a collective view, such as the OECD's. The latest thinking of the OECD is reflected in the January 2003 version of the commentary on the OECD Model Convention.

7.4 With respect to article 5 (the permanent establishment article, see **Appendix 1**), the commentary now states, in paragraph 42.2:

> 'Whilst a location where automated equipment is operated by an enterprise may constitute a permanent establishment in the country where it is situated . . . a distinction needs to be made between computer equipment, which may be set up at a location so as to constitute a permanent establishment under certain circumstances, and the data and software which is used by, or stored on, that equipment. For instance, an internet website, which is a combination of software and electronic data, does not in itself constitute tangible property. It therefore does not have a location that can constitute a "place of business" as there is no "facility such as premises or, in certain instances, machinery or equipment" . . . as far as the software and data constituting that website is concerned. On the other hand, the server on which the website is stored and through which it is accessible is a piece of equipment having a physical location and such location may thus constitute a "fixed place of business" of the enterprise that operates the server.'

(See paragraph **11.9** et seq.)

7.5 The commentary goes on to distinguish between a website hosted and maintained by a separate ISP (internet service provider) and one at the disposal of the enterprise concerned itself (where, for example, the enterprise owns or leases and operates the server on which the website is stored and used). In the former case, there is no permanent establishment of the enterprise; in the latter case, there may be.

7.6 Such a server may constitute a permanent establishment if it satisfies the criteria of article 5. It must be fixed, which in the case of a server, means that it needs to be located at a certain place for a sufficient period of time. The business of the enterprise must be wholly or partly carried on at the location at which it has the server at its disposal. The presence of personnel would not be essential. If the functions performed by the server were preparatory or auxiliary, it could not constitute a permanent establishment. Examples of activities generally regarded as preparatory or auxiliary, unless forming in themselves an essential and significant part of the business activity of the enterprise as a whole are, according to paragraph 42.7 of the commentary:

(a) providing a communications link (much like a telephone line) between suppliers and customers;

(b) advertising goods or services;

(c) relaying information through a mirror server for the purposes of security and efficiency;

(d) gathering marketing data; and

(e) supplying information.

(See paragraph **10.3**.)

7.7 In the case of a business (an 'e-tailer') selling products through the internet, the mere fact that it operates a server at a given location is not enough, in the opinion of the commentary, to conclude that activities performed at that location are more than preparatory and auxiliary. If, however, the typical functions related to a sale—for example, the conclusion of a contract with the customer, the processing of the payment and the delivery of the products—are performed automatically through the equipment, these activities could not be considered merely preparatory or auxiliary, and a permanent establishment could exist.

7.8 Based on its position discussed at paragraph **7.2**, the UK has indicated its reservations on paragraphs 42.1 to 42.10 of the OECD commentary, reiterating the view that a server used by an e-tailer, either alone or together with websites, could not as such constitute a permanent establishment. Spain, Portugal and Greece also reserve their position. See paragraph **11.10**, which discusses a case in the German tax courts in Schleswig Holstein (*Finanzgericht Schleswig)* relating to a computer server.

7.9 A significant part of the debate organised by the OECD on the taxation of e-commerce has been the question of whether the revenue produced constitutes a royalty or consideration for a service. Put briefly the general consensus is that information supplied for the exclusive use of the customer constitutes a service to the customer and business profits to the provider. However if the customer is permitted to transmit the information to third parties, the customer's payment constitutes a royalty (see paragraph **6.2** et seq).

7.10 An extract from the revised OECD commentary on Model article 12 (royalties) illustrates the point:

> '17 Software payments may be made under mixed contracts. Examples of such contracts include sales of computer hardware with built-in software and concessions of the right to use software combined with the provision of services. The methods set out in paragraph 11 above for dealing with similar problems in relation to patent royalties and know-how are equally applicable to computer software. Where necessary the total amount of the consideration payable under a contract should be broken down on the basis of the information contained in the contract or by means of a reasonable apportionment with the appropriate tax treatment being applied to each apportioned part.
>
> 17.1 The principles expressed above as regards software payments are also applicable as regards transactions concerning other types of digital products such as images, sounds or text. The development of electronic commerce has multiplied the number of such transactions. In deciding whether or not payments arising in these transactions constitute royalties, the main question to be addressed is the identification of that for which the payment is essentially made.
>
> 17.2 Under the relevant legislation of some countries, transactions which permit the customer to electronically download digital products may give rise to use of copyright by the customer, eg because a right to make one or more copies of the digital content is granted under the contract. Where the consideration is essentially for something other than for use of, or right to use, rights in the copyright (such as to acquire other types of contractual rights, data or services), and the use of copyright is limited to such rights as are required to enable downloading, storage and operation

on the customer's computer, network or other storage, performance or display device, such as use of copyright should not affect the analysis of the character of the payment for purposes of applying the definition of "royalties".

17.3 This is the case for transactions that permit the customer (which may be an enterprise) to electronically download digital products (such as software, images, sounds or text) for that customer's own use or enjoyment. In these transactions, the payment is essentially for the acquisition of data transmitted in the form of a digital signal and therefore does not constitute royalties but falls within Article 7 or Article 13, as the case may be. To the extent that the act of copying the digital signal onto the customer's hard disk or other non-temporary media involves the use of a copyright by the customer under the relevant law and contractual arrangements, such copying is merely the means by which the digital signal is captured and stored. This use of copyright is not important for classification purposes because it does not correspond to what the payment is essentially in consideration for (ie to acquire data transmitted in the form of a digital signal), which is the determining factor for the purposes of the definition of royalties. There also would be no basis to classify such transactions as "royalties" if, under the relevant law and contractual arrangements, the creation of a copy is regarded as use of copyright by the provider rather than by the customer.

17.4 By contrast, transactions where the essential consideration for the payment is the granting of the right to use a copyright in a digital product that is electronically downloaded for that purpose will give rise to royalties. This would be the case, for example, of a book publisher who would pay to acquire the right to reproduce a copyrighted picture that it would electronically download for the purposes of including it on the cover of a book that it is producing. In this transaction, the essential consideration for the payment is the acquisition of rights to use the copyright in the digital product, ie the right to reproduce and distribute the picture, and not merely for the acquisition of digital content.'

VAT

7.11 In May 2002 the European Commission issued a Directive requiring Member States to introduce provisions with effect from 1 July 2003 requiring non-EU established providers of electronic services to non-business customers within the EU to register for VAT.

7.12 The definition of electronic services is widely drawn and includes:

(a) most web based services supplied on-line, including web hosting;

(b) the supply of services over the web, such as internet gaming and the provision of games and for software; and

(c) broadcasting services.

7.13 Providers of such services are required to register in a minimum of one EU Member State and account for VAT at the rate prevailing in each EU country in which they supply services. Although there is no associated right to deduct input VAT with a VAT registration of this type, a non-EU established business is able to make claims for VAT incurred using the EC 13th Directive refund system.

As an alternative, a provider may wish to create a business establishment within the EU and register for VAT under the usual provisions. This would require it to add VAT at the rate prevailing in the country in which it has registered, but it would be entitled to VAT recovery in the usual way.

8 VAT

Overview

- Foreign businesses must establish whether they are required to register for VAT in the UK. They may need to do so even though the profits generated by their supplies are not liable to UK tax.

8.1 Unlike forms of direct taxation, VAT is chargeable on supplies of goods or services made in the course of business. In practice, VAT is charged at each stage in a transaction chain and borne by either the final consumer or further up the chain by a business or organisation that is unable to recover the VAT which it incurs.

See also the comments at paragraphs **3.14** et seq, **4.3** et seq, **6.24** and **7.11** et seq.

Business activities

8.2 It is important to establish whether the activity a business undertakes amounts to a 'business having economic activities' for VAT purposes. For most companies looking to undertake normal trading activities, this should not be a significant problem. But, for example, a company which is a pure holding company receiving only dividend income from its investments is not deemed to be undertaking 'economic activities' (*Polysar Investments Netherlands BV v Inspecteur der Invoerrechten en Accijnzen* Case C60/90, [1993] STC 222, ECJ).

Place of supply

8.3 For a supply of goods to be subject to UK VAT the supply must take place within the territory of the UK [VATA 1994, s 7]. This includes the Isle of Man and Northern Ireland but excludes the Channel Islands.

8.4 For supplies of services the basic rule is that in order for a supply to be subject to VAT, the supplier must have a business establishment in the UK from which the supply is made. However, there are certain overriding provisions which deem the supply to take place:

(a) in the case of supplies relating to land/real property, where the land is physically located [VAT (Place of Supply of Services) Order, SI 1992/3121 art 5];

(b) for

(i) cultural, artistic, sporting, scientific, educational or entertainment services;

(ii) services relating to exhibitions, conferences or meetings;

(iii) work carried out on goods; and,

(iv) ancillary transport services,

the place of supply is where the services are physically carried out.

8.5 It is important to note that, where a foreign business supplies the services detailed at paragraph **8.4(a)** and **(b)**, it will be deemed to have a business establishment in the UK with the attendant requirement to register for VAT.

Exempt activities

8.6 Certain supplies are exempted from VAT. These include a number of the following:

(a) financial and insurance services—including certain share/rights issues and similar transactions;

(b) land transactions;

(c) gaming-related activities;

(d) educational services;

(e) state-run postal services; and

(f) health and welfare services.

Exemption from VAT means that no VAT is chargeable but that the supplier is not making taxable supplies. A business that makes only exempt supplies is unable to register for VAT as it is not a 'taxable person'.

Zero-rated activities

8.7 The UK also applies a zero rate of VAT to certain supplies of goods and services [VATA 1994, Sch 8]. Whilst the supplier of such goods or services does not charge VAT on them, the supply *is* a taxable supply. Accordingly, there is a requirement to notify a liability to register for VAT, although the business can apply for exemption from registration if it expects to be in a regular net repayment position. In practice, most businesses making zero-rated supplies will wish to register in order to recover the VAT which they incur.

Zero-rated supplies include:

(a) books, newspapers, periodicals and similar printed matter;

(b) most young children's clothing and footwear;

(c) certain foodstuffs for human or animal consumption;

(d) certain domestic construction services and the sale or long lease of new dwellings;

(e) imports/exports;

(f) drugs, medicines and aids for the handicapped;

(g) international services;

(h) certain trades in gold;

(i) certain transportation services.

Deduction of VAT incurred

8.8 A business which undertakes or intends to undertake taxable activities or activities which are outside the scope of UK VAT, but with the right of input tax deduction, is able to recover the VAT that it incurs in relation to these activities.

There is no right of VAT recovery in relation to exempt or non-business activities. This is an important point as any non-recoverable VAT represents an additional cost which will need to be taken into account when setting budgets and financial forecasts.

VAT recovery is restricted in relation to certain costs. These include business entertaining, the purchase of a car by a business for both business and private use and certain costs relating to directors' living accommodation.

Compliance

8.9 A business that has activities which are undertaken or are deemed to be undertaken in the UK must register for VAT if the value of its taxable supplies in any 12 month period exceeds the registration threshold then in force (currently £56,000). A business which is making taxable supplies but is not required to be registered can voluntarily register. It may wish to do so if, for example, it expects to incur significant costs on which it will be entitled to recover VAT.

8.10 In addition, a company which *intends* to make taxable supplies is able to register in advance of making such supplies at the discretion of Customs and Excise. Again, this is a significant cashflow advantage if it expects to incur significant costs on which it would be entitled to recover VAT. This can be of particular use for start-ups.

8.11 It is possible for a number of corporate bodies to register for VAT as a single taxable person, known as a group registration. For VAT purposes, a group consists of a company and all the other companies that it controls, or a number of companies under the common control of another person (who can be an individual), or of two or more persons carrying on a business in partnership (VATA 1994, s 43A). Each of the companies must be established, or have a fixed establishment, in the UK.

8.12 Transactions between VAT group members are disregarded for VAT purposes—no VAT is added—which can be an advantage with inter-company trading. VAT grouping can also be of benefit where there is a UK holding company which is not 'in business' (see paragraph **8.2**). The inclusion of the holding company within a VAT group with its trading subsidiaries would enable it to recover some, if not all, of the VAT it incurred.

8.13 The taxable person is the legal entity undertaking the activity. This could be an individual acting as a sole proprietor, a partnership (of either individuals or corporate bodies), a corporate body, a joint venture, a body of trustees, a limited liability partnership or other organisation.

VAT is a self-assessed tax and VAT registered persons must submit and pay the VAT due on periodic (quarterly or monthly) VAT returns.

9 Customs duties

Overview

- Customs duty may be payable whenever a UK-based business imports goods from outside the EU.
- Rates of duty vary from 0% to 14%.
- Customs duty implications need reviewing before goods are exported to UK.

(a) Customs duty legislation is uniform throughout the EU—there are no legislative differences in any of the Member States.

(b) All goods moving into the EU, including capital equipment, are chargeable with customs duty. The rate at which duty is charged is determined by the tariff classification of the goods and ranges from zero to 14% for most goods.

(c) Capital equipment being moved to the UK as a result of the transfer of business activities from another country may be imported free of customs duty.

(d) Preferential rates of import duty apply to goods which qualify as originating in certain countries, i.e. those that have preferential trade agreements with the EU.

(e) The customs value of imported goods is the value used to calculate the duty payable. In general terms, the customs value is the price paid or payable for the goods, plus the cost of shipping to the EU, providing the price paid is on an 'arm's length' basis. Planning techniques can strip out non-dutiable elements which are typically included in the invoice price, thus reducing the customs value and, therefore, the duty payable.

(f) Customs duty need not be paid immediately at the point of import. Subject to approval from the Customs authorities, goods may be stored in a duty-free environment until they are removed for a manufacturing process or for onward sale in the EU.

(g) There are many duty relief schemes in the EU, whereby customs duty can be suspended at import or reclaimed once the conditions of a particular duty relief scheme have been fulfilled. Eligibility for duty reliefs depends on the use to which imported goods are put and the way in which they are disposed of. To benefit from a duty relief scheme, prior authorisation is required from Customs.

(h) Once customs duty has been paid in an EU Member State, goods can then move freely within all EU Member States.

(i) The ideal time to consider the customs duty implications of a transaction is before goods leave the exporting country, sometimes even before they are manufactured. It is rarely possible to influence the tariff classification, origin and customs valuation once goods have been shipped. It is strongly recommended that foreign exporters consider the customs duty position at the decision making stage in order that the customs duty costs of moving goods to the EU can be properly addressed.

10 Non-revenue producing activities in the UK

Overview

- Auxiliary activities will not attract UK tax.
- Typical examples are premises used to perform research, to purchase goods, or to display products. But it may be beneficial to register for VAT to obtain refunds of VAT incurred on inputs.

10.1 A company that is not resident in the UK is outside the charge to corporation tax unless it carries on a trade in the UK through a permanent establishment [ICTA 1988, s 11(1)]. Briefly, this is defined as a fixed place of business or habitual agency (see paragraph **11.3**).

10.2 Non-resident individuals are chargeable to income tax under Schedule D Case I on the annual profits or gains arising or accruing from a trade, and under Schedule D Case II from any profession or vocation exercised in the UK [ICTA 1988, s 18(1)(a)(iii), (3)] (see paragraph **12.1**).

10.3 If profits or gains do not arise from the activities conducted in the UK there is no liability to UK tax. This is the case whether or not a double tax treaty is in place between the foreign company or individual's country of residence and the UK. For example, UK premises may be used in order to perform research, or to purchase goods. Similarly, premises may be used to market a product without any sales being effected from the UK. Such auxiliary activities do not by themselves generate profits. They are merely ancillary to the earning of profits.

This concept is also reflected in the UK's double tax agreements with other countries, which are generally based on article 5.4 of the OECD Model Convention (see **Appendix 1**).

Example 10

Beiderbecke GmbH, a German company, opens a UK display showroom targeted at foreign tourists who are able to view and sample its products. Customers order and purchase the goods from a Beiderbecke office when they return to their home country.

The UK permanent establishment is reimbursed its costs by Beiderbecke's German head office.

There is no taxable profit in the UK following article II(l)(aa) of the UK/Germany double tax treaty.

However, note that if Beiderbecke GmbH had set up a UK subsidiary instead of a permanent establishment, the zero profit would have been uplifted on an arm's length basis under transfer pricing rules to reflect the services provided to Beiderbecke GmbH [ICTA 1988, Sch 28AA] (see **Chapter 17**).

But as tax rates in Germany are higher than in the UK, incorporating a UK subsidiary to derive taxable profits in the UK would actually reduce taxes overall, although consideration would need to be given to the German tax consequences of Beiderbecke GmbH passing on the dividends of its UK subsidiary to its German shareholders in due course (see paragraph **25.8** and Example 40).

VAT

10.4 The fact that the foreign company actually has a UK 'establishment' in VAT terms permits it to register for VAT even though it will not generate any outputs. This would enable it to recover VAT on input incurred [VATA 1994, Sch 1 para 10(1)(a)].

Tax implications in the foreign jurisdiction

10.5 The existence of a non-taxable UK branch or permanent establishment will have no radical impact on the foreign business's tax liability in its home country.

Profits arising as a result of the existence of the UK office, such as sales resulting from enquiries made at a UK showroom, will be taxable in the home country, although the cost of maintaining the showroom should be a tax-deductible expense.

Foreign individuals

10.6 The comments made in this Chapter apply as much to foreign individuals as to foreign companies.

11 Trading in the UK: foreign companies with a permanent establishment

Overview

- UK domestic definition of permanent establishment similar to tax treaty definitions.
- Trading profits attributable to permanent establishment liable to UK corporation tax.
- Permanent establishment is either fixed place of business, construction project, dependent agent with power to include contracts or, (where no tax treaty in force), UK agent habitually exercising authority to do business on behalf of foreign company.
- In foreign company's home jurisdiction, profits of the UK permanent establishment will be either exempt, or taxable with credit for UK corporation tax paid.

This Chapter deals with a foreign company's liability to tax once it is trading in the UK through a permanent establishment. **Chapter 12** deals primarily with the position of foreign individuals, and foreign companies without a permanent establishment in the UK.

Accounting periods beginning before 1 January 2003

11.1 For any accounting period beginning before 1 January 2003, a company that was not resident in the UK was within the charge to corporation tax if it carried on a trade in the UK through a 'branch or agency'. A branch or agency includes any factorship, agency, receivership, branch or management [ICTA 1988, s 834].

Corporation tax liability: accounting periods from 1 January 2003

11.2 The effect of the changes introduced in FA 2003, s 149(1) and (6) is that from 1 January 2003 a company that is not resident in the UK is liable to corporation tax if, and only if, it carries on a trade in the UK through a permanent establishment in the UK [ICTA 1988, s 11(1)]. This legislation replaces the long-established rule that a non-resident company is within the charge to corporation tax only if it carries on a trade in the UK through a branch or agency and brings UK law very much into line with the terms of most double tax treaties (see article 7 of the OECD Model Convention, **Appendix 1**).

It should be noted that this legislation has no impact on non-resident individuals doing business in the UK. They remain liable to income tax under existing legislation; as do companies with no UK permanent establishment (see paragraphs **12.1** and **12.3**).

Permanent establishment

11.3 The revised provisions in FA 2003 have largely aligned the UK's domestic provisions and definitions in ICTA 1988, s 11 with article 7 of the OECD Model Convention (see paragraph **11.8**). However there are a few subtle differences, which are mentioned below.

Under FA 2003, s 148(1) a company has a permanent establishment ('PE') in a territory (including the UK) if, and only if:

(a) it has a fixed place of business in the UK (see paragraph **11.9** et seq) through which the business of the company is wholly or partly carried on [per article 5.1 of the OECD Model Convention]; or

(b) an agent acting on behalf of the company has and habitually exercises (in the UK) authority to do business on behalf of the company [partly based on articles 5.5 and 5.6 of the OECD Model Convention].

This is limited by FA 2003, s 148(3), which excludes an agent of independent status acting in the ordinary course of his business [again, based on articles 5.5 and 5.6 of the OECD Model Convention].

FA 2003, s 148(1)(b) differs from the OECD Model Convention where it will be seen from **Appendix 1** that article 5.5 envisages the dependent agent having power to conclude contracts in the name of the enterprise.

The UK Revenue presumably has in mind that a dependent agent could habitually exercise an authority to carry on his foreign principal's business without being given contractual powers. According to the strict OECD definition, such an agent would not constitute a UK permanent establishment. However it is understood that the UK Revenue consider s 148(1)(b) to reflect the substance of the OECD Model Convention and commentary and that the wording should not cause any confusion as the terminology is well understood.

These general definitions are subject to various provisions which broadly speaking reiterate the terms of the PE article (article 5) in the OECD Model Convention. For example a 'fixed place of business' includes a place of management, branch, office etc [FA 2003, s 148(2)].

A building site or construction or installation project is included in the PE definition but without the normal 6, 9 or 12 month minimum period found in treaties, based on the 12 month suggestion contained in article 5.3 of the OECD Model Convention [FA 2003, s 148(2)(h)]. This is of no consequence where a tax treaty exists with the foreign company's jurisdiction of residence as the treaty definition (which invariably stipulates a minimum period of existence for the construction etc site before it comes to be regarded as a PE) will have precedence (see paragraph **33.17** et seq). However where there is no treaty the possibility exists under the new legislation that a site of very short duration will nevertheless constitute a PE.

Premises or agents used for activities of a preparatory or auxiliary character, in other words non-profit generating activities, are excluded from being a PE [FA 2003, s 148(4)] based on article 5.4 of the OECD Model Convention (see **Appendix 1** and paragraph **10.3**).

Attributable profits

11.4 Where a PE exists in the UK the foreign company is chargeable to corporation tax on all its profits wherever arising that are attributable to that PE, subject to any exceptions provided in the Corporation Tax Acts [ICTA 1988, s 11(2) as amended by FA 2003, s 149(1)]. Such profits consist of:

(a) trading income directly or indirectly arising through or from the PE;

(b) income from property or rights used by, or held by or for, the PE; and

(c) chargeable gains derived from assets used in or for the purposes of the trade carried on through the PE, or assets used or held for the purposes of the PE or acquired for use by or for the purposes of the PE.

[ICTA 1988, s 11(2A) and TCGA 1992, s 10B(1) as amended by FA 2003, s 149(2A) and (4).]

11.5 The profits that are attributable to the PE are those it would have derived if it were a distinct and separate enterprise, dealing wholly independently with the foreign company (the 'head office'), and engaged in the same or similar activities under the same or similar conditions [ICTA 1988, s 11AA(2) as amended by FA 2003, s 149(2)].

11.6 Transactions undertaken with related parties will be subject to adjustment under the transfer pricing rules contained in ICTA 1988, Sch 28AA (see **Chapter 17**). These include the financing arrangements discussed in **Chapters 19** and **20**. Specifically, ICTA 1988, s 11AA(3) as amended by FA 2003, 149(2), provides that:

> '(a) it shall be assumed that the PE has the same credit rating as the non-resident company; and
>
> (b) it shall also be assumed that the PE has such equity and loan capital as it could reasonably be expected in the circumstances specified [in subsection (2)]'.

Namely, that it is a distinct and separate enterprise etc.

No deduction may be made in respect of costs in excess of those that would have been incurred on those assumptions. Nor may deductions be made for interest etc (with exceptions for financial businesses), or royalties paid to the PE's foreign head office [Sch A1 paras 4 and 5 inserted by FA 2003, Sch 25].

See also **Chapter 18** 'Calculating profits and losses of the UK permanent establishment'.

Assessments

11.7 The PE, as the UK representative of the non-resident company, is held responsible for the obligations and liabilities of the company with respect to the assessment, collection and recovery of corporation tax [FA 2003, s 150(1)]. It will be recalled from paragraph **11.3** that a PE is defined as including an agent habitually exercising an authority to do business on behalf of the non-resident company [FA 2003, s 148(1)(b)].

In certain circumstances, brokers, investment managers and Lloyd's agents are not to be considered the PE of a non-resident company, and as a result cannot be the UK representative of that company for these purposes [FA 2003, s 152 and Sch 26].

Double tax treaties

11.8 Until now this Chapter has discussed the UK's domestic rules relating to PE's. As mentioned above these have been broadly based on the OECD Model Convention. However subtle differences will often exist in the specific tax treaty between the UK and the country of residence of the foreign company. Some of the differences from the OECD Model Convention have already been pointed out.

As noted earlier in this Chapter, the UK definition of PE now contained in ICTA 1988, s 11 has mostly been brought into line with the OECD Model Convention.

Example 11

Foreignco sells goods in the UK through a UK agent who negotiates deals and signs contracts with UK customers. The UK agent has many other principals and so does not constitute a taxable permanent establishment of Foreignco.

If a double tax treaty applies, Foreignco has no UK permanent establishment as the agent is not a dependent agent (see article 5.5 of the OECD Model Convention).

The same result applies if there is no double tax treaty with the UK as FA 2003, s 148(3) excludes from the PE definition an agent of independent status acting in the ordinary course of his business.

Example 12

Foreignco provides hotel management services to a UK hotel group. Foreignco's management staff are located at the UK hotel where they have the regular use of an office.

The office constitutes a UK permanent establishment of Foreignco even though Foreignco has no lease or ownership of the office premises.

The office is a permanent establishment within both the tax treaty and domestic definitions (see article 5.2(c) of the OECD Model Convention and FA 2003, s 148(2)(c)).

Example 13

Foreignco constructs an office tower block in the City of London. The duration of the project is 18 months. It has no premises in the UK:

(a) Foreignco carries out the construction work for a fee.

The building site is its permanent establishment (see article 5.3 of the OECD Model Convention and FA 2003, s 148(2)(h)). The services have been rendered in the UK and so Foreignco is taxable by reference to the fee received.

Note that if a tax treaty did not apply the construction site would be a permanent establishment however short its duration [FA 2003, s 148(2)(h)].

(b) The same circumstances as above but Foreignco owns the land and buildings which it constructs to hold as an investment.

Foreignco is not trading in the UK. The existence of a permanent establishment is therefore irrelevant.

Fixed place of business

11.9 As discussed at paragraph **11.3**, this is a PE under both domestic and tax treaty definitions.

It will be noted that article 5 of the OECD Model Convention includes a fixed place of business as constituting a permanent establishment.

Paragraph 10 of the commentary on article 5 of the OECD Model Convention confirms that automatic machines may constitute a permanent establishment if the enterprise setting up the machines also operates and maintains them for its own account. In these circumstances profits from UK-located automatic vending and gaming machines owned by a foreign company will therefore be liable to UK tax.

11.10 Two recent cases in the German courts provide some useful pointers and examples.

In the local tax court (*Finanzgericht Schleswig Holstein*, 6 September 2001) it was held that a German company's computer server constituted a permanent establishment in Switzerland, to which income should be attributed (see paragraph **7.4**). The server operated without personnel, distributing information to Swiss users. (However, in its decision of 5 June 2002, the Federal Tax Court left the issue open.)

In 1996 a federal tax court case held that an underground pipeline which operated without personnel was held to be a permanent establishment (BFH, 30 October 1996).

Dependent agent

11.11 As mentioned at paragraph **11.3**, an agent of independent status is excluded from constituting a UK PE under both domestic and tax treaty definitions.

The case of *Fleming v London Produce Co Ltd* (1968) 44 TC 582 serves as a useful pointer to the determination of a dependent—as opposed to independent—agency. The case was concerned with whether the taxpayer, a London company, was acting as a dependent agent of a South African company under the same control, and could thus be assessed to tax on behalf of the South African principal. The London company maintained it was acting in the course of its business as a broker or general commission agent in the UK. In fact, it did 95% of its business on behalf of its South African principal and also did many activities on its behalf that would not have been performed by a general broker or agent acting for a wide public. The assessment was upheld.

Non-trading income

11.12 With effect for income arising after 31 December 2002 with respect to the tax year 2002/03, and for all subsequent tax years, the income tax liability of a non-resident company is limited by FA 2003, s 151 to the following:

(a) the tax deducted or treated as deducted at source or in respect of which there is a tax credit on:

  (i) interest etc assessable under Schedule D Case III;

  (ii) UK and other dividends assessable under Schedule F;

(b) transactions in deposits taxable under Schedule D Case VI by virtue of ICTA 1988, s 56;

(c) income arising from a transaction carried out through a broker or investment manager in the UK acting as an independent agent in the ordinary course of his business; and

(d) income of any other description as designated by the Treasury in regulations; and

(e) the tax that would be chargeable on the company's total income if it were reduced by the income listed in paragraph (a).

This is the equivalent for non-resident companies of FA 1995, s 128, which imposes a similar limitation on the liability of non-resident individuals. Section 128 no longer applies to companies.

Tax implications in the foreign jurisdiction

11.13 In cases where the foreign company is liable to UK tax from trading in the UK through a PE, article 23 of the OECD Model Convention provides for the avoidance of double taxation by either the exemption method or the credit method (see **Appendix 1**)

A Exemption method

The state of residence is to exempt the profits of the UK PE from tax (see article 23A(1)).

B Credit method

The state of residence of the business which has a PE in the other state (in this case the UK) is to allow the UK tax payable on the profits of the PE as a credit against tax payable in the state of residence (see article 23B(1)).

11.14 Whether the credit or exemption method is adopted by the state of residence depends upon its own domestic rules and the negotiations between the two countries that are parties to the double tax treaty (see Table 2 at paragraph **13.3(f)** for the position in each of the selected countries).

11.15 In the case of Hong Kong and Singapore, trading profits of a UK PE are exempt from tax under domestic legislation as opposed to a tax treaty.

There will be cases where the trading profits generated in the UK are not attributable to a UK PE and so are exempt from UK tax. For example contracts of sale are concluded in the UK but the foreign company has no UK premises, dependent agent or agent habitually exercising an authority to do business in the UK (see paragraph **11.3**).

As a general rule the UK trading profits will then be liable to tax in the foreign jurisdiction. However in relation to the selected jurisdictions, this general rule may not apply in Hong Kong, which only taxes Hong Kong-source profits. Depending on the facts it could be arguable that the profits were sourced in the UK.

12 Trading in the UK: foreign individuals, and foreign companies with no permanent establishment

Overview

- Foreign individuals trading through UK permanent establishment or regular agency taxable on profits generated.
- UK profits either tax-exempt in foreign company's home jurisdiction, or taxable with credit for UK tax paid.

Non-resident individuals

12.1 The revisions in FA 2003 discussed in **Chapter 11** do not apply to non-resident individuals trading, or carrying on a profession, in the UK. Subject to exemption under a tax treaty, they remain taxable under existing legislation on profits arising from a trade, profession or vocation exercised within the UK [ICTA 1988, s 18(1)(a)(iii) and (3)].

Assessments

12.2 The income tax liability will be assessable on the non-resident individual's UK permanent establishment or UK representative [FA 1995, s 126, Sch 23].

FA 1995, s 127 broadly excludes from being a UK representative a person who does not carry on a regular agency for the non-resident and brokers acting in the ordinary course of their business at a customary rate of remuneration.

In practice an assessment is unlikely to arise on the non-resident individual in the absence of a UK permanent establishment or representative. A UK representative is typically a regular agent of the non-resident because a broker, or a person who is not a regular agent, is excluded from being a UK representative [FA 1995, s 127(1)(a) and (b)]

Non-resident companies with no UK permanent establishment

12.3 Such companies are outside the ambit of liability to corporation tax under ICTA 1988, s 11 in the absence of a UK permanent establishment (see paragraph **11.2**).

12.4 *Trading in the UK: foreign individuals and companies with no PE*

An income tax liability would arise in principle [ICTA 1988, s 18(1)(a)(iii), (3)]. But in the absence of a permanent establishment or UK representative, an assessment is unlikely to arise in practice (see paragraph **12.2**).

Tax implications in the foreign jurisdiction

12.4 In cases where the foreign company is liable to UK tax from trading in the UK through a PE, article 23 of the OECD Model Convention (see **Appendix 1**) provides for the avoidance of double taxation by either the exemption method or the credit method (see paragraphs **11.13** and **11.14**).

In the case of an individual, the treaty invariably provides that the profits of the UK permanent establishment are to be taken into account in determining the individual's rate of tax in his or her country of residence (the so-called 'exemption with progression'), see article 23A(3), **Appendix 1**.

Example 14

Individuals resident in Denmark and the Netherlands carry on a UK business through a permanent establishment in the UK. The position of each of them is as follows, assuming they are taxable at the maximum rate of tax in all three countries:

		Danish individual	*Netherlands individual*
UK profits	100		
Danish tax (marginal rate)		59(1)	
Netherlands tax			–(2)
Credit for UK tax		40(1)	–
Danish tax payable		19	–
UK tax		40	40
Danish tax		19	
Total taxes payable		59	40

Notes

(1) Article 22(2)(a), UK/Denmark Treaty.

(2) Article 22(2)(b), UK/Netherlands Treaty.

13 UK permanent establishment ('PE'): tax consequences

Overview

- Operating as UK PE may allow losses to be offset against home country profits.
- Drawback is that gains on disposal of PE liable to UK tax, whereas gains on disposal of UK company shares are free of UK tax.
- PE losses group-relievable against profits of UK subsidiary (and vice versa).
- When UK PE incorporated into UK subsidiary, PE's accumulated losses carried over into subsidiary. Result may be double loss deduction.
- In certain countries, assets may be transferred to UK PE without incurring home country tax.

13.1 This Chapter discusses the tax consequences arising when a foreign company or individual carries on a UK business through a PE. It also compares the tax position with that of a UK company discussed in **Chapter 14**.

13.2 It is assumed that the foreign company or individual is resident outside the UK. However, there may be circumstances in which a foreign company operating a UK PE is in fact resident in the UK because its management and control is situated in the UK (see paragraph **2.2** et seq). This may be the case when the UK PE is a 'standalone' operation comprising the only activity of the foreign company.

Nevertheless, it will be seen from this and the next Chapter that there is little or no difference in the UK tax consequences so far as the taxation of the ongoing profits and gains are concerned as between a UK PE on the one hand and a UK subsidiary on the other. However there are a considerable number of other differences as discussed below.

13.3 The UK and foreign tax consequences arising from the operation of a UK PE may be summarised at paragraphs (a) to (o) below.

(a) The PE's profits will be liable to corporation tax [ICTA 1988, s 11]. Profits of a foreign individual will bc liable to income tax [ICTA 1988, s 18(1)(a)(iii), (3)].

(b) Losses incurred by the UK PE may be available for offsetting against profits in the home country. As many new businesses incur losses during their start-up period an initial PE structure is often selected for that reason. Losses could also be generated in the home country because of large amortisation deductions arising from significant asset acquisitions (see paragraph **27.2**).

Table 1 below provides an overview of the deductibility of UK losses incurred by a UK PE in each of the selected jurisdictions. Some of the conditions required for loss deductibility are noted but the list is not exhaustive.

TABLE 1 Offsetting losses of UK PEs: foreign tax position

Company or individual resident in:	*Offset of losses*	*Recapture*[(7)]
Australia	No[(1)]	–
Austria	Yes[(2)]	Yes
Belgium	Yes	Yes
Canada	Yes	Yes
Denmark	Yes	Yes
Finland	Yes[(2)]	Yes
France	No[(3)]	–
Germany	No[(4)]	–
Greece	No[(5)]	–
Hong Kong	No	–
Ireland	Yes	Yes
Italy	Yes	Yes
Japan	Yes	Yes
Luxembourg	No[(6)]	–
Netherlands	Yes	Yes
Portugal	Yes	Yes
Singapore	No	–
Spain	Yes[(2)]	Yes
Sweden	Yes[(2)]	Yes
Switzerland	Yes	Yes
USA	Yes	Yes

Notes (not exhaustive)

(1) Losses of a UK PE may only offset profits of other foreign branches that are taxable in Australia.

(2) No loss offset when the foreign branch is situated in a country whose tax treaty exempts foreign branch profits. However, the UK's treaties with Austria, Finland, Spain and Sweden allow the profits of a UK PE to be taxed in those countries (see Table 2 at paragraph **13.3(f)**).

(3) But French individuals may offset losses.

(4) No loss offset when the foreign branch is situated in a country whose tax treaty with Germany exempts foreign branch profits. The UK treaty does exempt the UK branch profits from German tax: OECD Model Tax Treaty article 23A.1, see **Appendix 1** and article 18(2)(a) of the UK/Germany tax treaty.

(5) UK PE losses may only offset profits of other foreign PEs.

(6) No loss offset when the foreign PE is situated in a country with which Luxembourg has concluded a tax treaty. However, loss may be deducted if it exceeds Luxembourg company's profits.

(7) Losses recaptured in home country to the extent that profits are earned by the UK PE (see (c) below).

(c) The loss relief in the foreign country will normally be of temporary value as it will be 'recaptured' as and when the UK permanent establishment earns profits. This is clearly the case in foreign countries that tax the profits of the UK permanent establishment rather than exempting them (see Table 2 at paragraph **13.3(f)** below).

In such cases there will normally be no UK tax to offset the foreign tax as the losses carried forward in the UK will offset the profits liable to UK tax and so reduce or eliminate the UK tax liability.

Example 15

UK PE			*UK tax*	*US tax*
Year 1	Loss	(100)		
	Carried forward		(100)	
	Offset profits			(100)
Year 2	Profit	80		
	Loss carried forward		(20)	
	Taxable profit			80
	Relief for UK tax			–

Table 1 above indicates that, of the countries selected, all of those that allow the offset of UK PE losses, recapture them as and when the PE earns profits.

(d) Losses of a foreign company's PE may be surrendered in a UK group relief claim, which can include profits and losses of UK PE's of non-resident companies. However, a PE's loss cannot be surrendered to the extent it is offset for foreign tax purposes in any period, against the profits of the non-resident company or of any other person [ICTA 1988, s 403D(1)].

So to the extent that the PE's losses are offset in the home country against current profits (see Table 1 in (b) above) or are carried forward against future profits of the home country company, they cannot be surrendered for group relief. However, for UK tax purposes they can be carried forward for offset against future profits of the PE [ICTA 1988, s 393(1)].

Example 16

Swedco AB has a UK PE and a UK subsidiary. The UK PE incurs losses which are offset against Swedco's profits for Swedish tax purposes (see Table 1 at paragraph **13.3(b)**).

Therefore, the losses cannot be group relieved against the UK subsidiary's profits.

The losses can be carried forward under ICTA 1988, s 393(1) against future profits of the UK PE. While this will reduce UK tax, it will probably lead to exposure to Swedish tax (see Table 1 above, under 'Recapture' heading and Example 15).

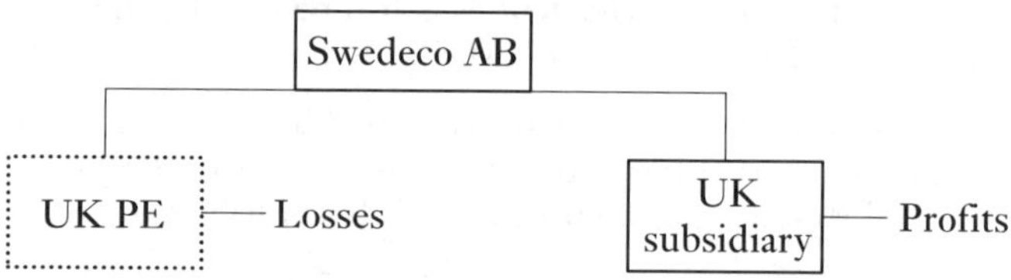

(e) Assuming that the PE's business is incorporated into a UK subsidiary at a later stage, its losses carried forward will be available to the UK subsidiary under ICTA 1988, s 343, provided the requisite 75% ownership is maintained. This may or may not result in a double deduction for the losses in both the UK and the foreign jurisdiction. Some jurisdictions, such as the USA, 'recapture' the losses when incorporation takes place (see Table 3 at paragraph **24.42**).

Example 17

Segovia SA, a Spanish company, opens a UK PE. In its first year of operation the PE incurs a loss of 100 which is offset against Spanish profits.

At the beginning of Year 2, the PE's business is transferred to a newly-incorporated UK company, Segovia Ltd, in return for shares. The subsidiary earns profits of 250 in Year 2. The PE's previous loss of 100 is carried over to the subsidiary so that its taxable profits are reduced to 150 on which corporation tax of 45 is payable. On payment of a dividend of 205 from Segovia Ltd's distributable profits, the dividend will be tax-exempt to Segovia SA (see Table 4 at paragraph **25.4**).

In this way the UK PE loss of 100 is deducted in both Spain and the UK. It is recaptured neither on incorporation (see Table 3 at paragraph **24.42**), nor on repatriation (see Table 4 at paragraph **25.4**).

The carryover of UK PE losses would be unavailable to a foreign individual transferring his or her UK branch to a UK company. ICTA

1988, s 343 applies only where the transferor of the UK PE is a home company, later transferring the PE to a UK company.

A foreign individual contemplating opening a UK PE should therefore consider the possibility of operating it through a home country company, later transferring the PE to a UK company.

(f) Depending upon the foreign jurisdiction concerned, profits earned by the UK PE may be exempt in the foreign country, either as a result of domestic legislation, such as France or the Netherlands, or as a result of a double tax treaty with the UK, such as Germany or Denmark (see OECD Model Convention article 23A(1), **Appendix 1** and paragraph **11.13** et seq). Exemption from foreign country tax similarly applies to capital gains realised by the UK PE, including the outright disposal of its business (see **Chapter 30**).

Table 2 below provides an overview of the taxability of the UK profits and gains in each of the selected jurisdictions. Some of the conditions are noted but the list is not exhaustive.

TABLE 2 UK PEs: taxability of UK profits and gains—foreign tax position

Company or individual resident in:	*Taxable with credit for UK tax*	*Exempt under treaty with UK(1)*	*Domestically exempt*
Australia			✓(2)
Austria	✓		
Belgium	–	✓	
Canada	✓		
Denmark	✓		
Finland	✓		
France	–	✓	✓
Germany	–	✓	
Greece	✓		
Hong Kong	–		✓
Ireland	✓		
Italy	✓		
Japan	✓		
Luxembourg	–	✓	
Netherlands	–	✓	✓
Portugal	✓		
Singapore	–		✓
Spain	–		✓(3)
Sweden	✓		

Company or individual resident in:	*Taxable with credit for UK tax*	*Exempt under treaty with UK*[(1)]	*Domestically exempt*
Switzerland	–	✓	✓
USA	✓		

Notes (not exhaustive)

(1) Although profits are exempt, an individual's tax rate may be arrived at by including the profits – ('exemption with progression'): OECD Model Tax Treaty article 23A.3 (see **Appendix 1** and paragraph **12.4**).

(2) Australian individual is taxable, with credit for UK tax.

(3) Election for exemption is required.

(g) In those foreign jurisdictions where the profits of the UK PE are taxable (see Table 2 above) the UK tax paid will normally be creditable against the local tax payable on the UK PE profits. In all these cases the credit for UK tax is provided for in the relevant country's double tax treaty with the UK (OECD Model Convention article 23B(1), **Appendix 1**)) even though in many cases the foreign country's domestic legislation similarly provides for a credit.

(h) Chargeable assets may be transferred tax-free between the PE and 75% or more owned UK subsidiaries of the foreign company [TCGA 1992, s 171(1A)].

(i) In a number of the selected jurisdictions, the foreign company may transfer assets into its UK PE without incurring any local tax liability on a deemed realisation of the assets. This is because the assets remain in the ownership of the foreign company. These jurisdictions include: Belgium, Canada, Denmark, Finland, Greece, Ireland and the USA. It should also be noted that capital equipment may be imported free of customs duty (see **Chapter 9** paragraph **(c)**)

Example 18

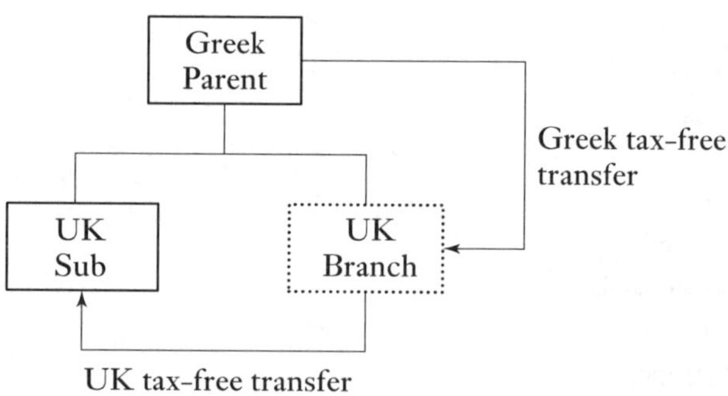

(j) A foreign individual's tax liability in his or her home country will normally be lower when profits are repatriated from a UK PE rather than from a UK company. The reason for this is that dividends received from a UK company will generally be subject to a further layer of taxes in the individual's country of residence (see Table 5 at paragraph **25.8** and Examples 36 to 41).

(k) If the PE is part of an existing foreign company, the small companies rate of corporation tax under ICTA 1988, s 13 is not reduced as a result of the addition of another company into the group.

(l) There is no Companies Act requirement for a PE to be subject to a UK audit.

(m) On the other hand, it will be necessary for tax returns of the PE to be prepared in both the UK and the foreign jurisdiction.

(n) But the main disadvantage to a PE structure is for foreign companies resident in a jurisdiction conferring a participation exemption on the sale of shares (see paragraph **25.3**). The sale of the PE business will attract UK corporation tax on the gains realised on disposal of the constituent assets [TCGA 1992, s 10B] (see **Chapter 30**). In contrast, the foreign company's sale of the shares of its UK subsidiary is normally exempt from UK tax [TCGA 1992, ss 2, 10] (see **Chapter 29**).

Example 19

A Belgian company wishes to set up a UK business. The Belgian and UK tax consequences of the ultimate sale of the business when operated as:

(a) a UK branch, or

(b) a UK subsidiary, are as follows:

Gain on sale of:	*UK PE*	*UK subsidiary*
Belgium	Exempt(1)	Exempt(2)
UK	Taxable(3)	Exempt(4)

Notes

(1) UK/Belgium tax treaty article 23(2)(a).

(2) Belgian participation exemption.

(3) TCGA 1992, s 10B.

(4) TCGA 1992, s 2.

Thus, a foreign company's gains on sale of a UK subsidiary are tax-exempt in both countries. However the purchaser of the UK subsidiary would wish to negotiate a discount in the share price to recognise inherent tax liabilities on the company's assets.

An important advantage of a UK PE is the ability to offset the UK losses against Belgian profits (see paragraph (b) above).

The situation may be different for foreign individuals as they do not benefit from a participation exemption and so will usually (but not always) be taxable on gains realised on disposal of their UK company (see Table 5 at paragraph **25.8**) as well as on gains realised from disposal of the UK PE (see Table 2 at paragraph **13.3(f)**).

(o) A possible alternative way of selling the UK PE's business would be for the shares of the foreign company to be sold. This assumes a UK purchaser willing to buy the shares of a foreign company. The foreign company would need to be a standalone company whose only activity was the UK PE. In that case the gain would not be liable to UK tax, being the sale of a foreign company by a non-resident.

Tax implications in the foreign jurisdiction

13.4 These have been discussed in each relevant paragraph above.

14 UK company: tax consequences

Overview

- Gains on eventual realisation of a UK company are free of UK tax to foreign seller. Where gains realised by home country company qualifying for participation exemption, gains also tax-free in home country.
- In most foreign countries, individuals liable to tax on gains realised from sale of shares in UK company. Therefore, consider ownership of UK company through local or foreign holding company.
- This could also achieve tax exemption on dividends received from UK company.
- UK business start-up through UK company *ab initio* avoids taxes otherwise payable in some home countries where business commences as PE with later transfer to UK company.

14.1 This Chapter discusses the tax consequences of a foreign company carrying on its UK business through a UK subsidiary, or a foreign individual trading in the UK through a UK company vehicle. It also compares the tax position with that of a UK permanent establishment as discussed in **Chapter 13**.

14.2 By reasons of its incorporation in the UK, the company will thereby be UK resident [FA 1988, s 66 and see paragraph **2.1**]. If the effective management of the UK company is abroad, then depending upon the jurisdiction, the company may be dually resident (see paragraph **2.9** et seq for the UK tax consequences).

Whether a foreign investor carries on a UK trade through a UK company or the UK permanent establishment of a foreign company, there is little or no difference in the UK tax consequences so far as the taxation of the ongoing profits and gains are concerned. However there are a number of other differences as noted below.

14.3 The UK and foreign tax consequences arising from the operation of a UK company are summarised at paragraphs (a) to (n) below:

(a) Profits of the company will be liable to corporation tax [ICTA 1988, s 8].

(b) The most significant advantage of operating through a UK company is that gains on eventual realisation of the shares will not be liable to UK tax [TCGA 1992, ss 2, 10] – see paragraph **29.1** – except in the rare event where the gain is taxable under ICTA 1988, s 776 as an indirect gain from the sale of UK land (see paragraph **33.23** et seq).

(c) In addition, in many foreign jurisdictions such as Austria, Denmark, Germany, Luxembourg, Spain and Switzerland, gains realised by resident companies will also be exempt from local tax under a 'participation exemption' (see Table 4 at paragraph **25.4**). Outside Europe the gain will be exempt in jurisdictions where there is no tax on capital gains, such as Hong Kong and Singapore.

Therefore, in the absence of UK tax, the only effective tax burden will be the discount in the share price which a purchaser will normally negotiate to take account of inherent tax liabilities in the shares of the UK company (see Example 19 above and paragraph **29.2**).

However, for foreign individuals resident in most of the jurisdictions surveyed, the gain on sale of the UK company will be liable to tax (see Table 5 at paragraph **25.8**). In such a case there will be an element of doubly taxing the gain. In this context, operating through a UK permanent establishment could be preferable (in respect of both gains and profits of the permanent establishment) (see Table 2 at paragraph **13.3(f)** and Example 36 at paragraph **25.9**).

An alternative solution might be to own the shares of the UK company through a holding company in a participation exemption jurisdiction which could be located in the foreign individual's home country (see Example 40 at paragraph **25.10**).

(d) In those foreign jurisdictions where profits of a UK permanent establishment would generally be liable to tax at a higher rate than in the UK, such as the USA and Canada, the UK company could retain profits taxable at the lower UK level as and until they were repatriated (see **Chapter 28**).

For shareholders in such jurisdictions, a UK company will also provide flexibility in timing repatriation of profits as well as the manner in which those profits are repatriated ie by way of dividend, share repurchase, liquidation or sale (see **Chapter 28**).

Retention of profits in the UK company is unlikely to create any problems in cases where there are controlled foreign company rules, or similar rules, in the foreign shareholder's jurisdiction. The UK company will be carrying on a trading activity and the rate of UK tax will not be low compared to tax rates in the jurisdictions where the controlled foreign company rules exist (see **Appendix 3**).

(e) In examining Table 2 at paragraph **13.3(f)** and Table 4 at paragraph **25.4**, it will be seen that in certain countries corporate shareholders are taxed on the profits of a UK permanent establishment (with a credit for corporation tax). The dividends they receive from UK subsidiaries are, however, tax-exempt. Those countries are Austria, Canada and Denmark.

Example 20

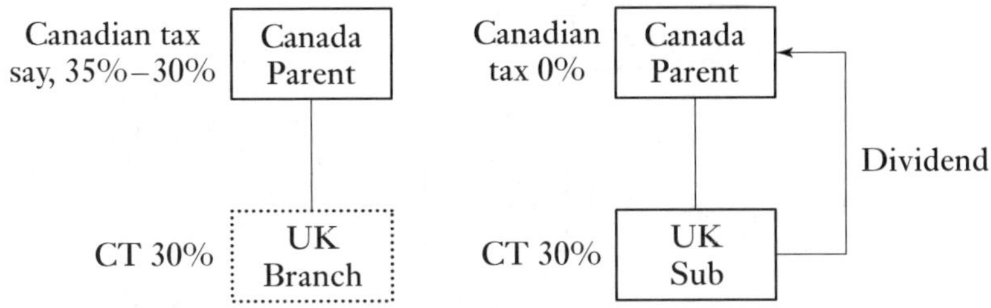

As corporate tax rates in these countries are generally higher than in the UK, it is clear that a UK subsidiary could achieve a permanent tax saving.

(f) Where a number of UK subsidiaries exist, a UK holding company with UK subsidiaries will allow for their debt/equity ratios to be measured on a consolidated basis (see paragraphs **19.4** and **19.5**).

(g) Foreign parent companies resident in an EU jurisdiction, whose domestic legislation provides for tax consolidation, may be in a position to claim that loss-making UK subsidiaries be included in the local tax consolidation.

This could therefore apply to parent companies in Austria, Denmark, Finland, France, Germany, Ireland, Italy (when proposed reforms are enacted), Luxembourg, the Netherlands, Portugal, Spain and Sweden. All these countries have, or soon will have, tax consolidation regimes.

In all these countries (with the exception of Denmark and, shortly, Italy, which allow or will allow consolidation of foreign subsidiaries), consolidation of foreign subsidiaries could follow a victory for Marks & Spencer in its pending appeal to the European Court of Justice, due for hearing in 2004. In this case Marks & Spencer plc claims that UK group relief legislation contravenes the freedom of establishment within article 43 of the EC Treaty in not allowing its non-UK EU subsidiaries in Belgium, France and Germany to be included in a group relief claim.

The Special Commissioners decided that Marks & Spencer was not entitled to group relief [*Marks & Spencer plc v Halsey* [2003] STC (SCD) 70, 17 December 2002]. However in a decision in the High Court on 3 May 2003, Mr Justice Andrew Park decided to refer the case to the European Court of Justice. The ECJ's decision will not be made until 2004. In the UK, the group relief claims are the subject of a Group Litigation Order.

Example 21

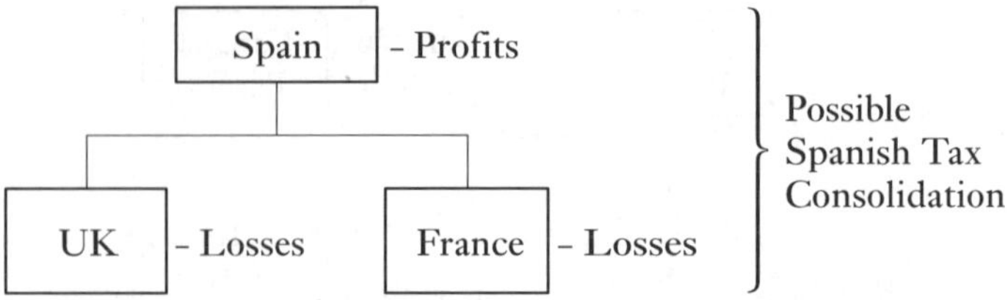

(h) Disclosure of results is limited to the activities of the UK company itself. If the foreign company sets up a UK permanent establishment but also has activities in the home country or other countries, details of these are likely to be questioned by the UK Revenue.

(i) A UK company generally provides a better local image and profile.

(j) If a foreign company acquires additional businesses in the UK (see **Chapter 27**), these may be more easily combined into a UK group with the facility for offsetting profits and losses in a group relief claim [ICTA 1988, s 402 et seq], and transferring assets inter-group [TCGA 1992, s 171]; although both facilities are also possible where a permanent establishment is used [ICTA 1988, s 403D and TCGA 1992, s 171(1A)].

(k) Royalties and interest paid by a UK company to its foreign affiliates are tax deductible insofar as they are on arm's length terms [ICTA 1988, s 770A, Sch 28AA] (see **Chapter 17**); whereas such payments are non-deductible when made by a UK permanent establishment to its foreign head office [ICTA 1988, Sch A1, paras 4 and 5] (see paragraph **11.6**).

(l) If a foreign individual or company subsequently transfers its UK permanent establishment to a UK company, tax may become payable abroad, and sometimes in the UK (see Table 3 at paragraph **24.42**). This problem is avoided if the operations are set up through a UK company *ab initio*.

(m) A UK company affords limited liability. Although this can also be achieved with a UK permanent establishment owned by a standalone foreign company.

(n) Duality of tax returns, in both the UK and the foreign jurisdiction, is avoided.

Foreign tax implications

14.4 These have been discussed in each relevant paragraph above.

15 UK partnership

Overview

- Same UK tax consequences as UK permanent establishment (see **Chapter 13**).
- But not the case if home country regards UK partnership as separate legal entity, for example limited liability partnership or Scottish partnership.
- Partnership structure often used for joint ventures (see **Chapter 16**).

15.1 An alternative to a UK permanent establishment or company would be a UK partnership with two or more foreign companies or individuals as its partners.

In most cases the UK tax implications are identical to those of a UK permanent establishment as discussed in **Chapter 13**. Each of the foreign partners will be trading in the UK through a permanent establishment and so will be liable to corporation tax or income tax on the partnership's profits and gains. This will be so whether the partnership is a general, limited, or limited liability, partnership [ICTA 1988, ss 11, 18(1)(a)(iii), 118ZA, and TCGA 1992, ss 10, 10B and 59A].

In general a partnership structure is of most interest for use in a joint venture between unrelated parties. Joint ventures are discussed in **Chapter 16**.

Tax implications in the foreign jurisdiction

15.2 By and large the foreign tax implications are identical to those of a UK permanent establishment discussed in **Chapter 13**. However, in some cases the foreign tax implications may be different. This is because of the possibility that the foreign jurisdiction may treat the UK partnership as an opaque entity rather than as transparent.

15.3 For example, because of its status as a separate legal entity [Limited Liability Partnership Act 2000, s 1(2)], an English Limited Liability partnership could be similarly treated in the foreign partner's home jurisdiction. Examples of potential treatment as a separate legal entity are Belgium, France and Ireland.

Limited liability partnerships are specifically treated as transparent for UK tax purposes provided that they carry on a trade or business [ICTA 1988, s 118ZA and TCGA 1992, s 59A].

15.4 Scottish partnerships (whether or not limited) are also separate legal entities and so could be treated as such for tax purposes in the foreign partner's home jurisdiction.

15.5 Then again, of the countries surveyed, Italy regards all types of foreign partnerships as separate legal entities.

15.6 And finally, US partners could elect to treat any type of UK partnership as a separate entity for US tax purposes under the US 'check the box' rules.

15.7 The broad results of the UK partnership being treated as a separate taxable entity in the foreign jurisdiction are as follows:

(a) Profits and gains retained in the partnership are only taxable in the foreign jurisdiction when distributed to the partners. The retained profits are unlikely to be subject to controlled foreign company rules in the foreign jurisdictions because the UK profits would be trading profits and the rate of UK tax is not unduly low (see **Appendix 3**).

(b) Partnership distributions received are taxed as dividends.

(c) Capital gains realised on sale of a share in the partnership are taxed as disposals of shares in the entity. In countries with a participation exemption for sales of shares (see Table 4 at paragraph **25.4** and **Appendix 5**) a foreign company's gains on the sale of a UK partnership share (in particular a share in a limited partnership) may or may not fall into that category.

15.8 For individual, as opposed to corporate, partners the treatment of a UK partnership as a taxable entity will normally be disadvantageous. Treatment of the partnership as a separate entity will generally attract an extra layer of taxes when distributions are received or partnership shares are sold. This compares unfavourably with the transparency of partnership treatment. (See the discussion at paragraph **25.8** et seq.)

Foreign individuals

15.9 See the comments in **Chapter 13** relative to foreign individuals.

16 Joint ventures

Overview

- UK joint ventures may be conducted through UK or foreign companies or partnerships.
- Partnership form generally allows greater flexibility and more easily facilitates individual requirements of each joint venturer.
- Tax liabilities may arise when each joint venturer transfers assets or businesses to joint venture vehicle.

16.1 A partnership entity would be an interesting alternative to a jointly owned UK company in the case of a joint venture between unrelated parties. Its tax transparency would permit the direct offset of losses and foreign tax credits for UK taxes paid. It would also allow for greater flexibility than a company in the sharing of profits, losses and capital gains – see 'Joint venture vehicle' below. (This assumes the partnership is not treated as a separate entity in the tax jurisdiction of the foreign partner.)

This Chapter deals with joint ventures conducted in the UK by non-resident companies, whether or not with UK joint venturers. It discusses the relevant tax aspects of the joint venture vehicle as either a partnership or a company. Most of the comments apply to joint ventures carrying on a trading business but see paragraph **16.18**, 'Joint venture investment vehicle'.

Joint venture vehicle

16.2 The joint venture vehicle could take one of the following forms:

(a) UK resident partnership;

(b) Non-UK resident partnership;

(c) UK resident company

(d) Non-UK resident company.

Scope of the joint venture

16.3 The joint venturers may decide to conduct every aspect of the profit-making venture, for example, from research and development, through to manufacturing, marketing and selling.

On the other hand, the joint venture may be limited in functional scope to, say, research and development, selling or purchasing. In such cases the rest of the operations will be carried out separately by each joint venturer which will buy in the services provided by the joint venture vehicle; and/or vice versa.

Example 22

Each joint venturer sells raw materials to the JV, which manufactures the product and sells it to third parties.

Example 23

One joint venturer provides finance, the other provides intellectual property. The JV uses the funds to develop the IP which, when developed, is licensed to each joint venturer.

16.4 Research and development and purchasing operations produce no profits in themselves. It should therefore be possible for a non-resident company or partnership to carry out these operations through a joint venture in the UK without incurring liability to UK tax provided that these functions were performed for the foreign head office (see **Chapter 10**).

16.5 On the other hand, if the joint venture performed these operations for its foreign joint venturers, the transfer pricing provisions of ICTA 1988, Sch 28AA would require an arm's length fee to be charged to any joint venturer having an at least 40% interest in the joint venture company or partnership [ICTA 1988, Sch 28AA para 4(2), (7)] (see paragraph **17.8**).

In these latter cases, and in the case of joint venture operations carrying out sales and manufacturing activities, the profits arising from the UK operations will be liable to UK corporation tax whichever of the four types of entity listed above conducts them.

16.6 The following topics relative to joint ventures are discussed elsewhere in relation to UK subsidiaries, permanent establishments and partnerships:

Chapter	
10	Non-revenue producing activities.
13–15	UK permanent establishments, companies and partnerships.
	The main advantage of a partnership vehicle will be the fact that losses incurred may be available for offset against profits of the non-resident joint venturer in its foreign jurisdiction. A partnership will also allow for greater flexibility than a company in the sharing of profits, losses and capital gains. While similar results could be achieved by including these factors into the rights of the shares issued by a UK joint venture company, this is a more complicated mechanism than a partnership profit-sharing arrangement.
19/20	Financing the UK subsidiary.

Chapter	
6/21	Licensing the UK subsidiary.
22	Leasing property to the UK subsidiary.
23	Management fees.
24	Transfer of UK permanent establishment to the UK company.
25	Ownership vehicle for UK company.
26	UK holding company.
28	Repatriation.
29	Sale of UK company.
30	Sale of UK permanent establishment.

Transfer of UK business to the joint venture

16.7 Each or some of the joint ventures may be transferring a UK business to the joint venture vehicle. Even though the transferors may be non-UK resident, UK taxes may arise on the transfer.

16.8 If the joint venture vehicle is a partnership, the transfer to it will be treated as a part disposal for UK tax purposes to the extent that third party partners now obtain an interest in the UK business [TCGA 1992, s 21(2)(a)].

16.9 The disposal value will normally be market value if only because that will be the valuation agreed upon by the unconnected parties. However it should be noted that for capital gains tax purposes the connected persons rules apply to transactions between partners except in relation to acquisitions or disposals of partnership assets pursuant to bona fide commercial arrangements [TCGA 1992, s 286(4)].

16.10 If the joint venture vehicle is a company, the transfer of a UK permanent establishment to it by its joint venture shareholders will be treated as an entire disposal for UK tax purposes [TCGA 1992, s 10(1)]. However, where the transferor is a company resident in an EU jurisdiction (other than the UK), the gain is deferred from UK tax under TCGA 1992, s 140A provided that the consideration is shares or loan stock issued by the joint venture company (see paragraph **24.3**). This legislation accords with the EC Merger Directive [90/434/EEC of 23 July 1990]. There is no requirement for any minimum shareholding relationship. In fact the deferral will normally amount to exemption because the transferor company will not be liable to UK tax on eventual disposal of the shares or loan stock [TCGA 1992, s 2(1)].

16.11 It is a peculiarity that a UK transferor cannot obtain deferral under s 140A in this situation. The only way in which deferral might be obtained would be under TCGA 1992, s 139. However, that is a less straightforward route as it would require the joint venture company to issue shares to the shareholders of the UK transferor company.

16.12 Exceptionally, any gain arising will also be exempt if the shareholder has a 75% or more shareholding interest in the joint venture company [TCGA 1992, s 171].

VAT

16.13 The transfer of the totality of the assets of a functioning UK business (or a part of a business capable of separate operation) from one entity to another where the transferee intends to continue the operation of that business is not treated as a taxable supply for VAT purposes [VAT (Special Provisions) Order, SI 1995/1268 art 5].

Transfer of single assets to the joint venture vehicle

16.14 The comments above relating to the transfer of a UK business similarly apply here with the exception that, for foreign tax purposes, any gain cannot qualify for exemption under the EC Merger Directive. The Directive applies only to the transfer of an entire business or the discrete division of a business.

VAT

16.15 In general, the VAT treatment of the transfer of a single asset to a joint venture vehicle by one of the venturers for a consideration will be subject to VAT in the usual way. However, in certain cases, it may be possible to introduce an asset by way of partnership contribution, which would render it outside the scope of VAT.

Consortium relief

16.16 If the joint venturers utilise a UK resident company, tax transparency will apply to a limited extent in that it will be possible to offset losses of the UK consortium company against profits of its UK shareholders, and vice versa, under the consortium rules.

However this facility will not extend to non-UK shareholders. But US shareholders could make a 'check the box' election which would have the effect of treating the UK company as a partnership for US tax purposes. This would allow a one-way US offset of the relevant proportion of consortium company losses against US shareholder profits.

16.17 A summary of the relevant consortium relief legislation is as follows:

(a) a UK company qualifies as consortium-owned if 75% or more of its ordinary share capital is held by companies, whether or not UK-resident, provided each shareholder owns at least 5% [ICTA 1988, s 413(6)];

(b) 'ordinary share capital' is all the capital other than that whose holders have a right to only a fixed rate, but no other right to share in the consortium company's profits [ICTA 1988, s 832(1)];

(c) the consortium company must be a trading company [ICTA 1988, s 402(3)(a)];

(d) alternatively it may be a 90% trading subsidiary of a holding company which is at least 75% owned by the consortium members [ICTA 1988, s 402(3)(b)]; or

(e) it may be a holding company which is at least 75% owned by the consortium members [ICTA 1988, s 402(3)(c)].

For these purposes, a holding company is a company whose business consists wholly or mainly in holding shares of companies which are its 90% trading subsidiaries. The trading subsidiaries can be resident in any jurisdiction [ICTA 1988, s 413(3)(b)].

Joint venture investment vehicle

16.18 For foreign investors into the UK, a partnership vehicle, particularly a limited partnership, is often used for investment into UK property (see paragraph **32.8**) and into shares in venture capital companies. The fact that the partnership is tax transparent makes it particularly suitable where the partners are resident in different tax jurisdictions, each with its own requirements, or where they are tax exempt, typically pension funds. The transparency will often permit the direct offset of losses, and of foreign tax credits for UK taxes paid. Most significantly, capital gains on realisation of the partnership investments will normally be exempt from UK tax to non-UK resident partners [TCGA 1992, s 2(1)].

Potential sources of income will be taxable to non-resident partners in the following manner:

Net rental income (paragraph **32.1**)	22%
Interest and royalties – often 0% under a tax treaty (**Appendix 2**)	
UK dividends (paragraph **28.3** et seq)	0%
Foreign source income and gains	0%

Foreign tax implications

16.19 In the case of foreign shareholders transferring the business of a UK permanent establishment to the joint venture company, it is likely that this will be a taxable disposal in the foreign jurisdiction. However, reference should be made to Table 3 at paragraph **24.42** as the gain may be exempt in the following circumstances:

(a) Where domestic legislation does not tax foreign permanent establishments.

(b) Under a double tax treaty with the UK.

(c) In the case of foreign shareholders resident in an EU jurisdiction, under the EC Merger Directive.

16.20 Where the shareholders in a joint venture company are resident in different jurisdictions so that none has shareholder control of the joint venture company, controlled foreign company rules are unlikely to apply in any of the jurisdictions (see **Appendix 3**). This may provide scope for minimising UK and foreign country taxes through the utilisation of low-tax companies owned by the joint venture shareholders.

Example 24

Each shareholder has a 33 1/3% interest.

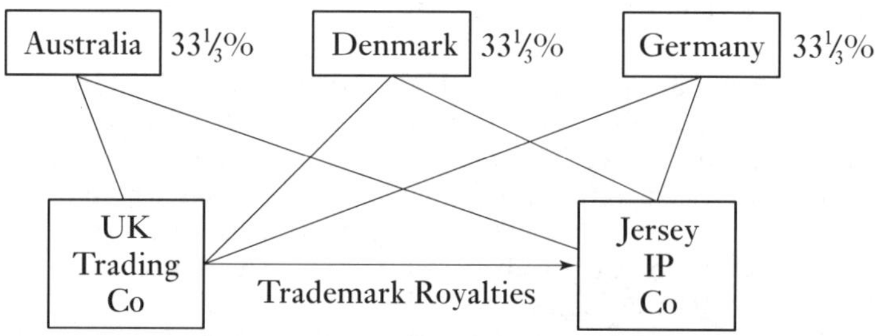

16.21 With regard to joint venture partnerships, it will need to be ascertained whether or not relief is available to a foreign partner in respect of the partnership's UK source income by virtue of a double tax treaty with the UK. The individual partner will be claiming relief as a resident of the foreign jurisdiction in respect of the share of the partnership income arising directly to the partner.

16.22 Obviously, in jurisdictions where the UK partnership is treated as a separate legal entity, this assertion will not be applicable. As mentioned above, Italy treats foreign partnerships as separate entities for tax purposes. In such cases the Italian partner's share of partnership income such as UK source interest will be fully liable to UK withholding tax [ICTA 1988, s 1B(1) and (2)].

17 Transfer pricing

Overview

- UK transfer pricing rules impact upon any transaction carried out between UK cntity and its foreign affiliate.
- Similarly, transfer pricing rules exist in most foreign jurisdictions.
- Resultant double taxation may be resolved by tax treaty mutual agreement procedure or EU Arbitration Convention.
- Rules may be challenged as EU discriminatory. They may be amended to avoid discrimination.

Introduction

17.1 Whenever a foreign-owned UK company or permanent establishment (including a property investment business) enters into transactions with foreign related parties, the price at which those transactions take place is subject to potential adjustment under UK transfer pricing rules. A detailed discussion is outside the scope of this book but this Chapter summarises the rules and their practical impact.

At the same time it is likely that the pricing of the transactions will be subject to potential adjustment in the foreign jurisdiction. This is discussed at paragraph **17.20** et seq.

It will therefore be seen that transfer pricing adjustments could affect the following transactions discussed in this book where reference to transfer pricing is usually made:

Chapter	
3	Exporting product to the UK (when the sale is made to a related UK purchaser).
4	Exporting services to the UK (as above).
19/20	Financing.
21	Licensing.
22	Leasing property.
23	Management fees.
32	UK property investment.
33	UK property trading.

Background

17.2 Transfer pricing provisions have been in place in UK legislation for over 40 years. However, the rules were significantly strengthened with the enactment of new legislation introduced in 1998 [ICTA 1988, s 770A, Sch 28AA].

Before the new rules came into force, the transfer pricing provisions were relatively brief. Essentially, the rules applied to situations where there were two parties to a transaction, the one party controlled the other, but both were under common control. If this situation existed, and the pricing for the transaction was above or below the market price such that there was a loss to the UK Exchequer, the price for the transaction could be adjusted to a market price for tax purposes.

Inevitably, because the transfer pricing provisions were brief and there was little or no guidance from the tax authorities to assist with their interpretation, there were a number of difficulties in the application of these rules. Furthermore, the system was reactive in that the onus on policing transfer pricing matters rested solely with the tax authorities. There was no requirement in the UK at that time to submit tax returns which included arm's length pricing. As a consequence no penalties could be levied by the Inland Revenue if an adjustment was in fact made.

Transfer pricing rules

17.3 The UK's new transfer pricing rules apply to accounting periods ended on or after 30 June 1999 and income tax years of assessment ended after 5 April 1999 [FA 1998, s 108(2), Sch 16]. Some key features of these new rules are as follows:

(a) The new regime applies where a non-arm's length provision exists between two persons in a prescribed relationship, one to the other, and that provision creates a potential UK tax advantage for one or both of those persons [ICTA 1988, Sch 28AA para 1]. There is no doubt that the Inland Revenue has thought carefully about these words. The reference to 'provision' is intended to allow offsetting transactions (but can only apply where the same two parties are involved). Equally, the term 'transaction' is given an extremely wide definition and will encompass any understanding, practice or arrangement. A potential UK tax advantage exists if the UK profits were less than would have been the case had the parties been acting on arm's length terms.

(b) The onus is now on UK taxpayers to confirm (when signing their self-assessment tax return) that all of their related party transactions are carried out on an arm's length basis. If the transactions are not carried out on an arm's length basis, taxpayers are expected to volunteer an adjustment within the return to correct those transactions that are not at arm's length. Any adjustment is made only to reverse profits which have for UK purposes been understated. No adjustment is to be included in respect of transactions where UK taxable profits may in fact be overstated.

(c) The rules introduce the OECD guidelines into UK law and it is clear that the intention is that the new UK rules are applied consistently with the detailed OECD transfer pricing guidelines, including any update of these guidelines [ICTA 1988, Sch 28AA para 2]. While this provides an element of guidance in relation to transfer pricing matters, it should be noted that there is still significant potential for disputes between companies and the UK tax authorities. The OECD guidelines themselves provide limited guidance in certain areas and they do not necessarily provide solutions to typical transfer pricing problems.

(d) The new rules introduce the requirement for taxpayers to keep records sufficient to enable them to deliver a return satisfying the arm's length standard [TMA 1970, s 12B]. Such documentation does not need to be submitted with the tax return but the documentation must be kept, as it may be called on by the Inland Revenue in the case of any enquiry. Some of the documentation requirements are straightforward in that they identify what would typically be part of a business's normal record keeping. However, some requirements are very specific to transfer pricing and these will include an analysis of market data, third party comparables and contemporaneous commercial agreements.

(e) Unlike the old regime, the new regime enables the Inland Revenue to levy a penalty of up to 100% of the tax due [TMA 1970, ss 95, 95A and FA 1998, Sch 18 para 20]. The Inland Revenue has made it clear that the penalty provisions have been used where, for example, the company's chosen method was deemed to be inappropriate.

17.4 In practice the new rules have changed the way in which transfer pricing enquiries are handled. The Inland Revenue has issued guidance in the Tax Bulletin (Issue 60) on how it approaches a detailed risk assessment as a precursor to a full scale transfer pricing enquiry. Factors that the Inland Revenue considers to be indicative of a high transfer pricing risk are set out in that Tax Bulletin and include such matters as the existence of tax haven entities that are profitable despite the absence of significant activities, mismatches between the scale of tax haven operations and the level of profits allocated to them, lower profit margins in the UK where there is reason to believe that this should not be the case, and other such matters.

17.5 For the regime to apply, one of the parties has to be directly or indirectly participating in the management, control or capital of the other, or the same person or persons has to be directly or indirectly participating in the management, control or capital of both parties [ICTA 1988, Sch 28AA para 1(1)(b)]. A person directly participates in the management, control or capital of another person if and only if that other person is a body corporate or a partnership and the first person controls the other person [ICTA 1988, Sch 28AA para 4(1)]. The definition of control follows the wording in ICTA 1988, s 840, which provides, inter alia, that control is the power of a person to secure that the affairs of a body corporate are conducted in accordance with that person's wishes (by means of the holding of shares, the possession of voting power, or by virtue of any powers conferred by the Articles of Association or other document regulating that or any other body corporate).

17.6 There are new concepts of 'potential participant' [ICTA 1988, Sch 28AA para 4(2)] and 'potential major participant' [ICTA 1988, Sch 28AA para 4(7)] to define the circumstances in which a party indirectly participates in the management, control or capital of the other party.

17.7 A potential participant is a person who is participating indirectly in the management, control or capital of another person in such a way that he would be considered to be directly participating by taking into account certain rights and powers. These include rights and powers that are required at a future date and rights and powers which may be exercised on the potential participant's behalf or by other connected persons [ICTA 1988, Sch 28AA para 4(2)–(6)].

17.8 A person can also be considered to be indirectly participating in the management, control or capital of another person, if he is one of a number of 'major participants' in that other person's enterprise. A person will be considered to be a major participant if he is a body corporate or a partnership and the so-called '40% test' is satisfied [ICTA 1988, Sch 28AA para 4(7)]. This test is satisfied where the potential major participant and a third person together control the body corporate or partnership, and where each of them has interests, rights and powers representing at least 40% of the holdings, rights and powers of the subordinate [ICTA 1988, Sch 28AA para 4(8), (9)].

17.9 It is intended that most transactions between UK taxpayers (including UK permanent establishments of non-residents) should be excluded from the application of the new rules [ICTA 1988, Sch 25 para 5(2) et seq]. There are therefore a number of tests which must be satisfied to give effect to this intention. The basic position is that there must be no overall loss of tax to the UK Exchequer.

However, following the European Court of Justice decision in *Lankhorst* (see paragraphs **17.25, 19.4 and 19.9**) there is an arguable case that the exclusion in para 5(2) is discriminatory in relation to all transactions with EU residents.

There is also a possible argument under the non-discrimination article of a tax treaty (see paragraph **19.10**).

Advance pricing agreements

17.10 The concept of advance pricing agreements (APAs) was introduced in FA 1999. There is a detailed Statement of Practice SP 3/99 that provides guidance about the APA programme.

17.11 APAs aim to assist businesses in determining complex transfer pricing issues. APAs allow transfer pricing issues to be resolved on a prospective basis for a minimum of three years and up to five years, although they can also provide assurance for past years. It is important that the issue is deemed to meet the complexity threshold required to be admitted to the programme as there are insufficient resources available to deal with more simple transfer pricing matters.

An APA can provide solutions to situations where there is considerable difficulty or doubt in determining the method by which the arm's length principle should be applied.

17.12 An example of an area where an APA may be used is in the area of intellectual property where a group decides to charge for its name or know-how. In this area, the amount of money involved in these transactions can be quite significant. Therefore businesses may want assurance that their transfer pricing policy chosen is deemed arm's length in nature.

17.13 An APA is a written agreement between a business and the Board of Inland Revenue which determines a method for resolving transfer pricing issues in advance of a return being made. When the terms of the agreement are complied with, they provide assurance that the treatment in accordance with the agreement of those transfer pricing issues will be accepted by both the Revenue and the business for the period covered by the agreement.

17.14 An APA may remain limited to a binding agreement between a UK business and the Inland Revenue known as a 'unilateral APA'. A unilateral APA is limited in use as it only confirms the tax treatment in the UK and does not determine how the issues are to be resolved in the other country involved. Therefore it is better to enter into a bilateral APA if there is a mutual agreement procedure contained in the double taxation treaty between the UK and the other country involved in the transaction, thus avoiding potential double taxation.

17.15 Businesses operating in several jurisdictions may wish to seek APAs that involve all the relevant tax administrations affected by the transfer pricing issues. The term, 'multilateral APA', has been used to describe such agreements, but in fact there is no mechanism for reaching multilateral agreements, and multilateral APAs in strictness are multiple, bilateral APAs.

Administration

17.16 An APA is dealt with by the Inland Revenue's International Division. Transfer pricing specialists and delegated competent authority officials from International Division, assisted by the tax office responsible for the business, will be responsible for assessing APA requests.

17.17 An APA comprises of four main stages:

(1) An expression of interest (which can be anonymous in the first instance to deal with basic issues, transactions and a proposal for how the taxpayer would like them dealt with).

(2) A formal submission for an application for the programme needs to include:

   (a) the identification of the parties and recent accounts (generally for the previous three years);

(b) a description of the transfer pricing issues proposed to be covered in the APA and analysis of the functions and risks of the parties and actual and projected financial data of the parties in relation to the issues;

(c) a description of the world-wide organisational structure, ownership, and business operations of the group to which the company in question belongs, the place or places where such operations are conducted, and all the major categories of transaction flows of the parties to whom the APA is intended to apply;

(d) a description of the records which will be maintained to support the transfer pricing method proposed for adoption in the APA and the information which it is proposed will be supplied each year to demonstrate that the tax return conforms to the terms of the APA;

(e) a description of any current tax enquiries or competent authority claims that are relevant to the issues covered by the proposed APA;

(f) the chargeable periods to be covered by the APA;

(g) the identification of assumptions made in developing the proposed transfer pricing method which are critical to the reliability of its application under the arm's length standard; and

(h) in the case of a cross-border transfer pricing issue, a request for competent authority assistance in reaching a bilateral APA (see paragraph **17.21** et seq).

(3) Evaluation (this is a flexible process of open dialogue between the taxpayer and the Inland Revenue with any overseas authority involved).

(4) Agreement (agreement binding on the parties, detailing the terms, conditions and critical assumptions involved).

Planning

17.18 Transfer pricing adjustments are made based on the factual conditions of the enterprises involved in the crossborder transaction.

It is therefore open to the foreign investor, within the constraints of commercial requirements, to increase or reduce the resources of the UK company or permanent establishment. Such resources would comprise the assets contributed into the UK, particularly cash and intellectual property, as well as the manpower resources. Obviously, the scale of the UK entity's resources and the functions and risks it undertakes will influence the determination of its profits on an arm's length basis (functional analysis).

17.19 Another planning possibility relating to intellectual property relates to cost-sharing arrangements for research and development expenditure on intellectual property. Such projects involve significant expenditures with the objective of creating a valuable intellectual property asset.

In order to locate the asset in the selected jurisdiction so as to avoid a taxable transfer to that jurisdiction or a royalty payment from that jurisdiction, a cost-sharing arrangement can be entered into. Briefly, this involves two or more group companies each contributing cash, assets or resources into the research project in return for partial ownership of the intellectual property ultimately developed, provided this is justified by the scale of each party's contribution to the project.

Example 25

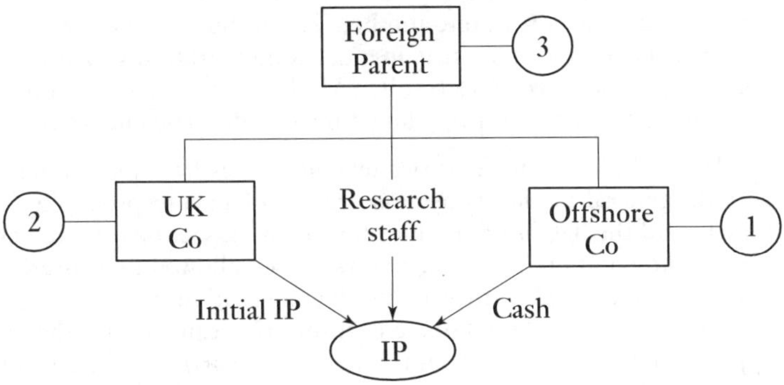

Division of rights – say:

(1) Americas;

(2) Europe;

(3) Rest of world.

Tax implications in the foreign jurisdiction

17.20 Apart from Hong Kong, Ireland, Luxembourg, Singapore and Switzerland, all of the selected jurisdictions have developed, or are developing, significant transfer pricing rules and documentation procedures. Transfer pricing adjustments in the UK and the foreign jurisdiction can lead to double taxation.

Mutual agreement procedure

17.21 Obviously, upward adjustments to UK taxable profits will result in double taxation if there is no corresponding reduction in the foreign jurisdiction. It is this position that is intended to be resolved by article 25 of the OECD Mutual Agreement Procedure of a tax treaty (see **Appendix 1**).

17.22 Where a taxpayer has an adjustment made by one tax authority and no corresponding adjustment from another tax authority, this will give rise to an instance of double taxation. Under article 9.2 of the OECD Model Convention (see **Appendix 1**) the taxpayer may invoke the mutual agreement procedure

('MAP') to attempt to get both tax authorities to resolve the instances of double taxation. This process will be carried out by the competent authorities of each tax jurisdiction.

17.23 In practice, the mutual agreement procedure has not been widely used for a number of reasons:

(1) MAPs are very time consuming and businesses wish to resolve transfer pricing issues quickly. The competent tax authorities of both countries must be convinced that a MAP is available and appropriate. They will then normally need extensive consultation with the taxpayer and require several rounds of talks with one another. Tax authorities tend to have only a few transfer pricing specialists in a tax administration which means that resources are strained. As a result, a MAP negotiation can last for several years' duration which is a very long time in today's business environment.

(2) A bilateral MAP means that two tax authorities have to become familiar with the general and local business strategy of an enterprise. They have to understand the details of complex business transactions and review complex documentation. As the taxpayers are not allowed to be present at the MAP itself, they have to provide documentation and prepare the tax authorities so that the competent authorities can discuss the case and appropriately represent the interests of the parties involved. This is a costly, burdensome and resource-consuming process.

(3) The tax authorities may not understand the business each of the affiliated entities is conducting and the complex business transactions that are the focus of the transfer pricing adjustments. There is also a concern that a solution will be agreed upon which is not in line with the transfer pricing guidelines and is the result of 'horse trading' between authorities.

(4) The MAP procedure does not oblige the tax authorities to reach a conclusion. Many enterprises are not willing to run the risks and costs of a MAP if they are not sure that double taxation will be eliminated at the end of the MAP.

EC Arbitration Convention

17.24 It is possible for EU transfer pricing issues to be resolved by the European Arbitration Convention ('EAC') [90/463/EC]. The benefit of the EAC is that it forces EU tax authorities to agree on issues of double taxation. Therefore, in practice, this could persuade tax authorities to agree an issue under the MAP procedure as they know that they will be forced to do so under the EAC. There are strict limits for making a claim under the EAC which is normally three years from the 'trigger' date (normally the time at which the action occurs which results in double taxation).

The EAC came into force on 1 January 1995 for an initial period of five years. The Convention only applies where both parties to the transactions in question are residents of EU Member States; or where an enterprise of one Member State carries on business through a permanent establishment in another Member State. The Convention is not currently in force because a 1999 Protocol extending its initial term has yet to be ratified by all EU Member States.

EU discrimination

17.25 Following the *Lankhorst* decision relating to German thin capitalisation rules, there is an arguable case that UK transfer pricing rules are discriminatory in relation to all transactions with residents of EU jurisdictions. That is because transactions with UK residents are excluded from the rules [ICTA 1988, Sch 25 para 5(2) et seq] – see paragraph **17.9**.

Anticipating this argument, the Inland Revenue Consultative Document of 12 August 2003 on Corporation Tax Reform proposed the extension of transfer pricing rules to all transactions with UK residents, thus removing the discrimination (see paragraph **19.9**).

18 Calculating profits and losses of the UK permanent establishment

Overview
• Transfer pricing rules require calculation of the taxable profits on arm's length terms where transactions are carried out with affiliates.
• This similarly applies to acquisitions of assets from foreign affiliates, with specific exceptions.

18.1 The comments in this Chapter apply to UK permanent establishments conducted by foreign companies or individuals.

In so far as the UK permanent establishment carries out transactions with its related entities outside the UK, its results for the purposes of Schedule D Case I are governed by the transfer pricing rules of ICTA 1988 s 770A and Sch 28AA (see **Chapter 17**).

18.2 To the extent transactions take place between the UK permanent establishment and its foreign head office, most modern tax treaties are based on article 7 of the OECD Model Convention (see **Appendix 1**). Article 7.3 provides that, in determining the profits of a permanent establishment, there shall be allowed as deductions, expenses which are incurred for the purposes of the permanent establishment including executive and general administrative expenses so incurred, whether in the State in which the permanent establishment is situated or elsewhere.

18.3 This allows for an allocation of head office expenses, including interest and royalties paid, to be deducted in arriving at the profits of the UK permanent establishment in so far as they can be clearly identified as appropriate to it. However, if the head office provides loans or intellectual property to the UK permanent establishment (for which the head office incurs no specific expense in view of its ownership of the cash or of the intellectual property), paragraphs 17 et seq of the commentary to the OECD Model Convention make it clear that any payments by the permanent establishment for these facilities should not be allowed as deductions in computing its profits (apart from the special case of financial enterprises such as banks). In relation to companies this treaty rule has now been given explicit statutory effect in UK domestic law by ICTA 1988, Sch A1 paras 4 and 5 inserted by FA 2003, s 149(3) (see paragraph **11.6**). It has always applied on general principles as payments made by a permanent establishment to its 'head office' are payments made by one part of the same legal entity to another, and hence not a deductible expense of the entity.

18.4 It can of course be ensured that the UK permanent establishment obtains deductions for the interest and royalties by arranging that the loans and intellectual property are provided, not by the foreign head office, but by a foreign affiliate. In that case, as the permanent establishment will be making payments to a separate entity, they will be deductible to the extent they are within arm's length parameters [ICTA 1988, s 770A, Sch 28AA] (see **Chapter 17**).

18.5 The UK permanent establishment may acquire various categories of asset from either its head office or from a foreign affiliate. The basis on which each category of asset enters the UK tax system is summarised below. It is assumed that the permanent establishment is charged the book value of the asset concerned in each case:

	Acquired from:	
	Head Office	*Foreign affiliate*
Plant and machinery	MV (ICTA 1988, s 337(1); CAA 2001, s 13)	Lowest of BV, MV and cost to sub (CAA 2001, s 218)
Industrial buildings/hotels	Notional TWDV (CAA 2001, s 339)	Notional TWDV (CAA 2001, s 339)
Patents (pre-1 April 2001)	Lowest of BV, MV and cost to sub (CAA 2001, s 481)	Lowest of BV, MV and cost to sub (CAA 2001, s 481)
Post-April 2002 intangible assets	BV	MV
Chargeable assets	AC	MV

Key: AC = actual cost; BV = book value; MV = market value; TWDV = tax written-down value.

Foreign tax implications

18.6 See **Chapter 17** 'Transfer Pricing' for the foreign transfer pricing implications of transactions between the UK permanent establishment and its foreign affiliates or related individuals.

18.7 The alternative strategies of paying interest or royalties to a foreign head office or to a foreign affiliate (see paragraphs **10.3** and **18.4**) may have different implications in the foreign jurisdiction. Most likely receipts by the head office will be non-taxable. Receipts by the foreign affiliate will certainly be taxable.

19 Financing the UK company or permanent establishment: loans

Overview

- Should borrowings be taken by UK company or foreign affiliates?
- Borrowings will normally be in sterling. However inter-company borrowings could be in foreign currency.
- Transfer pricing and debt/equity rules may restrict deductions for interest payable to foreign affiliates.
- Restrictions extend to interest paid to third parties where loan is secured or guaranteed by foreign affiliate.
- Restrictions may be overturned as being discriminatory in EU law or under tax treaties with other jurisdictions.
- UK withholding taxes generally deductible from interest but may be reduced as low as zero under tax treaty.
- Foreign investor may be able to utilise low-tax finance company to advance loans to UK entity.

19.1 This Chapter primarily discusses the financing of UK companies but most of the comments also apply to the financing of UK permanent establishments.

Basically, interest is deductible in accordance with the accounts [FA 1996, s 84], but this is subject to various exceptions discussed in this Chapter.

The general assumption is that borrowings from, or with the assistance of, a foreign affiliate are afforded by a related foreign company. However the tax implications that arise when the foreign lender, guarantor etc is an individual are also discussed.

Interest payable to a foreign affiliate must be paid within 12 months of the end of the accounting period in order to be deductible within it [FA 1996, s 84, Sch 9 para 2(1), (2)].

See paragraph **19.22** in relation to anti-avoidance.

Who should take on the borrowings?

19.2 Before deciding on whether or not the UK company should take on the burden of borrowings and the consequent financing costs, and leaving aside commercial considerations, it needs to be established whether it would be more tax-advantageous for the interest burden to be borne in the foreign jurisdiction or in the UK.

In view of the comparatively low rate of UK corporation tax it may be more beneficial for the foreign corporate affiliate or individual to take on the borrowings and to inject the funds as equity into the UK subsidiary provided the interest is tax-deductible in the foreign jurisdiction (see paragraph **19.23** et seq and Table 4 at paragraph **25.4**). In some cases, for example the US, it may be possible to obtain a deduction for interest in both jurisdictions.

Example 26

Marsalis Inc is a US company. It is making an acquisition of a UK company ('UK Target') partially funded by bank borrowings.

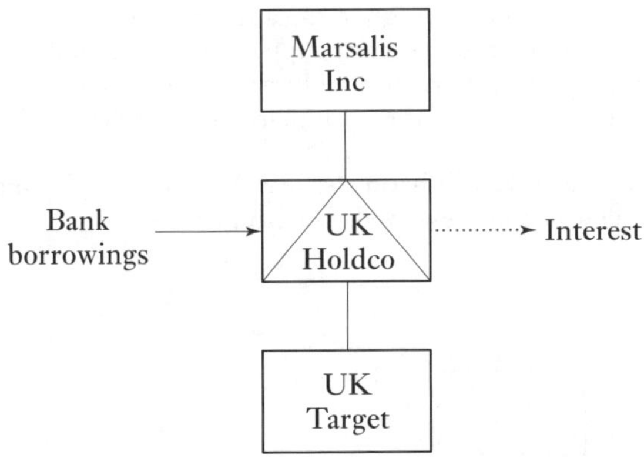

The interest payable by UK Holdco is group relievable against the profits of UK Target. The group relief anti-avoidance provisions of ICTA 1988, s 403D are inapplicable as UK Holdco is not a UK permanent establishment (see paragraph **13.3(d)**).

By 'checking the box' for US tax purposes, UK Holdco is treated as transparent so that the interest it pays is also deductible by Marsalis Inc.

Various factors need to be taken into account such as UK thin capitalisation rules (see paragraph **19.3** et seq), and the anti-avoidance provisions of FA 1996, Sch 9 para 13, as well as dual consolidated loss and foreign tax credit rules in the USA.

But subject to these factors, the bank interest paid is deductible in both the UK and the USA.

Collateralised borrowing: thin capitalisation and transfer pricing

19.3 In a situation where borrowings are taken in the UK, it can be assumed that the UK company or permanent establishment is able to obtain third party financing without any assistance from its foreign affiliates or related individuals (such as letters of comfort, guarantees or charges on their assets). In other words, the UK company has sufficient equity resources of its own to support third party borrowings. In this situation interest on borrowings utilised for the UK company's activities will be fully deductible.

19.4 However once third party borrowings are supported by guarantees, pledges etc from foreign affiliates or related individuals, interest deductibility will be restricted under UK domestic law as a result of transfer pricing rules [ICTA 1988, s 770A and Sch 28AA]. These rules arguably contravene EU law following the *Lankhorst* decision in Germany [*Lankhorst-Hohorst GmbH v Finanzamt Steinfurt* (Case C-324/00) [2003] STC 607] and may be challengeable under the non-discrimination article of a tax treaty. They are being challenged in the UK (see paragraphs **19.9** and **19.10**).

Account will be taken of debt/equity ratios, interest cover and similar risk factors that a bank would review in assessing the quantum and terms of loans that it was prepared to advance to a borrower without any support from shareholders in the form of guarantees etc. Such factors are invariably assessed on a group basis, but only if the group is headed by a UK holding company [ICTA 1988, s 209(8D)].

19.5 The Inland Revenue's Tax Bulletin (Issue 35) gives the following illustrations of permissible debt/equity reviewed on a group basis:

Example 27

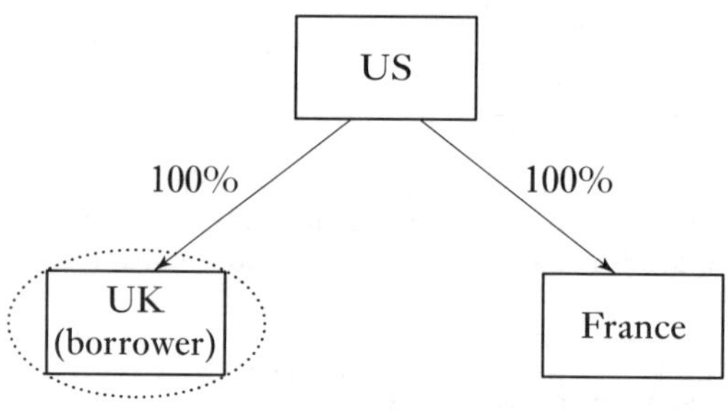

UK Grouping for purposes of legislation

Example 28

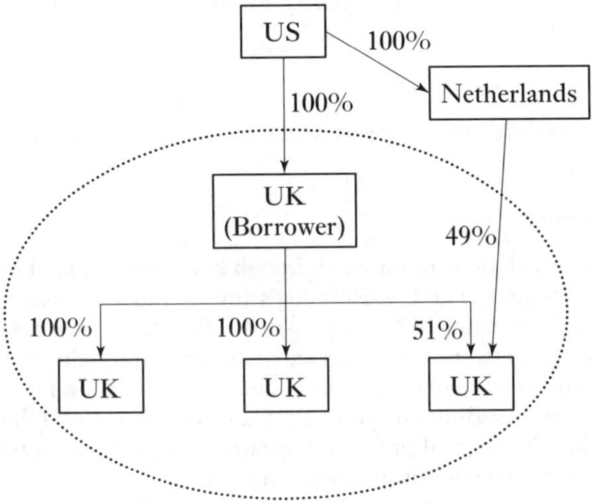

UK Grouping for purposes of legislation

Example 29

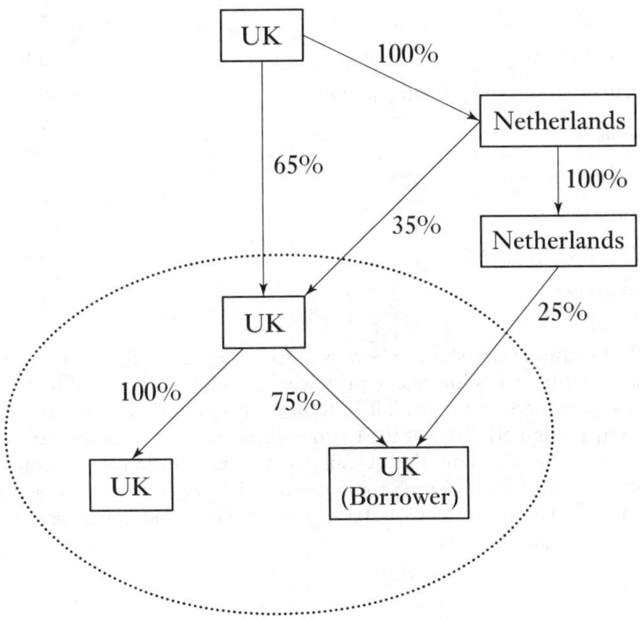

UK Grouping for purposes of legislation

19.5 *Financing the UK company or permanent establishment: loans*

In the June 1995 Tax Bulletin (which related to direct borrowings from foreign affiliates – see below – but is just as relevant to a collateralised borrowings), the Revenue stated that, apart from debt/equity ratios and interest cover, other relevant factors would be:

(a) the business sector concerned;

(b) the nature of, and title to, any assets which might provide security;

(c) cash flow; and

(d) the general state of the economy.

Quite obviously the calculations require a thorough knowledge of banking practice and lending techniques. The UK Revenue's International Division, which frequently reviews the financing of foreign-owned UK subsidiaries, has its own views on lending criteria etc, backed up by extensive data and field experience. International Division is prepared to discuss and negotiate funding arrangements in advance (see Tax Bulletins June 1995 and October 1998). This is a facility which has the advantage of providing certainty. See also paragraph **32.13** et seq in relation to borrowing for property investment.

Example 30

UK sub's balance sheet can be summarised as follows:

	£M
Fixed assets (value £6m)	5.0
Net current assets	3.0
Bank loan (guaranteed by foreign parent)	(6.5)
Net assets	1.5
Represented by	
Share capital	1.0
Reserves	0.5
Total reserves	1.5

The debt to equity ratio shown above is 4.3:1. The Inland Revenue's negotiating position would be that additional equity would need to be injected by the foreign parent company and for the bank loan to be correspondingly reduced. This has a positive impact on both sides of the balance sheet as it increases the net assets and the reserves of the company. The overall debt to equity ratio will be limited by the Revenue's general rule of thumb to a ratio of 1:1 (always subject to negotiation). The revised balance sheet below takes into account that the property can be revalued in the balance sheet.

Balance sheet with equity injection

	£M
Fixed assets (value £6m)	6.0
Net current assets	3.0
Bank loan (guaranteed by foreign parent)	(4.5)
Net assets	4.5
Represented by	
Additional equity	2.0
Share capital	1.0
Revaluation reserve	1.0
Reserves	0.5
Total reserves	4.5

It should also be noted that the general rule of thumb also provides that the level of interest cover should be at least 3:1 for the borrowing to be regarded as being on arm's length terms – again, subject to negotiation.

Note

Provided that a UK group of companies is headed by a UK holding company, the UK Revenue accepts that debt/equity ratios may be measured on a consolidated basis (see above).

Direct borrowing: thin capitalisation and transfer pricing

19.6 Similar comments to the above apply to direct loans made to the UK company or permanent establishment by foreign affiliates or related individuals. However, in the case of 75% related group corporate foreign lenders, restrictions can be applied under the distribution provisions of ICTA s 209(2)(da) as well as the transfer pricing rules of Sch 28AA. Interest on loans by other non-resident lenders, such as individuals, to a related UK company or permanent establishment will be restricted under Sch 28AA.

19.7 The quantum of the loans and the rate of the interest must adhere to arm's length arrangements [ICTA 1988, s 209(2)(da) and Sch 28AA para 1(2)]. However each of these two provisions is made inapplicable when the recipient of the interest is a company within the charge to corporation tax [ICTA 1988, s 212(1) and Sch 28AA para 5(3)].

19.8 Most of the interest articles in the UK's tax treaties allow for the debt/equity restrictions of s 209(2(da) or Sch 28AA to continue to apply.

The provisions of many of the UK's treaties are wider than article 11.6 of the OECD Model Tax Convention (see **Appendix 1**) which merely disallows excess interest, not excess debt.

However there is a need to distinguish which of the two sections applies and that is because of withholding tax on the excess interest paid. To reiterate:

(a) Section 209(2)(da) applies where a UK resident company, or the UK permanent establishment of a non-resident company, pays excessive interest to a 75% related group company. Section 209 applies to distributions made by any company (whether or not UK resident) for corporation tax purposes [ICTA 1988, s 209(2)].

However ICTA 1988, s 212(1) disapplies the section where the recipient of the interest is within the charge to corporation tax.

(b) Where section 209(2)(da) does not apply, the transfer pricing provisions of ICTA 1988, s 770A and Sch 28AA will restrict excess interest paid. Again, the section is disapplied where the recipient of the interest is within the charge to corporation tax [Sch 28AA para 5(3)].

Schedule 28AA could therefore apply, for example, in the following situations:

(i) The lender is a commonly controlled company outside the group.

(ii) The lender is a non-resident individual controlling the borrowing company.

(iii) The borrowing company is liable to income tax say; typically a non-resident company owning UK property (see paragraph **32.1**).

(iv) The lender is a third party whose loan is secured or guaranteed by a non-resident related party (see paragraphs **19.3** et seq).

If s 209(2)(da) applies, the excess interest is recharacterised as a distribution so there is no question of withholding tax. If Sch 28AA applies, the disallowed interest arguably retains its character and so could be subject to 20% withholding tax with no reduction under a tax treaty because of treaty thin capitalisation restrictions.

EU discrimination

19.9 Provisions similar to ICTA 1988, ss 209(2)(da) and 212(1) apply to thin capitalisation rules in German tax law. As a result the European Court of Justice, in *Lankhorst-Hohorst GmbH v Finanzamt Steinfurt* Case C-324/00, [2003] STC 607, has held that the principle of freedom of establishment set out in what is now article 43 of the EC Treaty had been contravened when the lending company was a resident of the EU (in that case, a Dutch company). It was held that the German thin-capitalisation rules involved a difference in treatment between German resident subsidiary companies according to whether or not their parent company was resident in Germany.

Following this decision the German tax authorities no longer apply thin capitalisation rules in the case of EU lenders. However the German government has published proposed changes to the current thin capitalisation rules, effective fiscal 2004 so that, if passed, they will apply both to German corporations with a domestic shareholder base and to those with a foreign shareholder base, thus removing the discriminatory effect of the rules.

As a result of the *Lankhorst* decision, UK companies are currently contending that ICTA 1988, s 209(2)(da)(ii) and Sch 28AA are inapplicable where the lender is EU resident. A Group Litigation Order against the UK Revenue was made in the High Court on 30 July 2003. On 12 August 2003 the Inland Revenue issued a Consultative Document on Corporation Tax Reform. It includes proposals to extend the thin capitalisation rules to UK lenders, thus removing the discriminatory effect. These proposals also extend to transfer pricing generally (see paragraph **17.25**). Following the above developments in Germany and the UK, it must be expected that other EU jurisdictions will similarly follow suit in changing their domestic thin capitalisation rules so as to block charges of discrimination.

Tax treaty discrimination

19.10 Additionally, where the lender is resident outside the EU, claims are being considered under the non-discrimination article of the relevant treaty (see paragraph **19.9** in relation to the Group Litigation Order of 30 July 2003). The argument is that the foreign-owned UK company is subjected to more burdensome taxation that a UK company owned by UK residents (see OECD Model Convention article 24.5, **Appendix 1**). The OECD commentary on this article states:

> 'This paragraph forbids a Contracting State to give less favourable treatment to an enterprise, the capital of which is owned or controlled, wholly or partly, directly or indirectly, by one or more residents of the other Contracting State. This provision, and the discrimination which it puts an end to, relates to the taxation only of enterprises and not of the persons owning or controlling their capital. Its object therefore is to ensure equal treatment for taxpayers residing in the same State, and not to subject foreign capital, in the hands of the partners or shareholders, to identical treatment to that applied to domestic capital.
>
> Paragraph 5, though relevant in principle to thin capitalisation, is worded in such general terms that it must take second place to more specific provisions in the Convention. Thus paragraph 4 (referring to paragraph 1 of Article 9 and paragraph 6 of Article 11) takes precedence over this paragraph in relation to the deduction of interest.
>
> In the case of transfer pricing enquiries, almost all Member countries consider that additional information requirements which would be more stringent than the normal requirements, or even a reversal of the burden of proof, would not constitute discrimination within the meaning of the Article.'

The Group Litigation Order referred to at paragraph **19.9** includes claims pursuant to article 24.5. The Corporation Tax Reform proposals would negate future claims.

An intriguing counter measure to this treaty discrimination argument is contained in the UK/Australia tax treaty dated 21 August 2003. It has yet to enter into force.

Article 25.6(a) make the non-discrimination article inapplicable to any domestic (UK or Australian) provisions designed to prevent tax avoidance or evasion. Paragraph 1 of the Exchange of Notes to the treaty states that these provisions include, inter alia, thin capitalisation, transfer pricing and controlled foreign company rules.

Withholding tax, tax treaties and the Interest and Royalties Directive

19.11 A 20% withholding tax is deductible at source from interest paid to a non-resident lender [ICTA 1988, ss 349(2), 4(1A) and 1A(1A)(c)].

There is an exception if the foreign lender trades in the UK through a permanent establishment and the interest it receives is liable to corporation tax [ICTA 1988, s 349B(2)]. Another exception applies in the case of interest on quoted Eurobonds [ICTA 1988, s 349(3)(c)].

In view of the non-resident status of the lender, withholding tax is only deductible if the interest is sourced in the UK. Since it is assumed that the payer of the interest is a UK company or permanent establishment, it is most likely that the interest will be sourced in the UK. Inland Revenue Tax Bulletin of November 1993 sets out the Revenue's views on the most important factors indicating where interest is sourced:

(a) the residence of the debtor, ie the place in which the debt will be enforced;

(b) the source from which interest is paid;

(c) where the interest is paid;

(d) nature and location of the security for the debt.

If all these are located in the UK then it is likely that the interest will have a UK source.

19.12 The UK has entered into tax treaties with many foreign jurisdictions under which the 20% withholding tax is reduced to 0% or a low rate (see **Appendix 2**). However, most of these treaties only apply the reduced withholding tax rate to arm's length interest, based on the amount of loan and/or rate of interest that would have been advanced or charged by a third party.

19.13 In cases where the disallowed interest arises under ICTA 1988, Sch 28AA, (see paragraph **19.8(b)**), this means that the full 20% withholding tax rate will arguably apply to interest disallowed by thin capitalisation rules and that the disallowed interest may be taxed in the foreign jurisdiction. In practice unnecessary payment of the excess interest can be avoided if the thin capitalisation position is agreed in advance with the UK Revenue International Division – see paragraph **19.5** – or possibly, when claiming the treaty relief with the Inland Revenue Centre for Non-Residents ('CNR').

Where relief under a tax treaty is being claimed it should be done in advance of the first interest payment by filing the appropriate forms with the CNR. Often reliance is placed on the double tax treaty and interest paid by reference to the treaty, with retrospective clearance applied for to the CNR. The Revenue take a very strict position on retrospective clearances. On the basis that interest has been paid without accounting for the 20% withholding tax that is due in the absence of advance clearance, the Revenue will charge interest on the 20% tax, running from the date of the interest payment to the date the treaty clearance is given.

19.14 However, it is arguable that the requirement to deduct tax at source (or to obtain treaty relief) is discriminatory in relation to EU resident corporate recipients following the *Lankhorst* decision discussed at paragraph **19.9**. The argument would be based on the fact that interest may be paid gross, outside the ambit of ICTA 1988, s 349(2), when paid to a UK resident company [ICTA 1988, s 349B(1)(a)].

19.15 In this context the European Council adopted the Interest and Royalties Directive (2003/49/EC) on 3 June 2003. It will eliminate withholding taxes on payments of interest and royalties between affiliated companies (25% shareholding relationships) in Member States. The Inland Revenue will be consulting on the legislative and practical changes needed to implement the Directive in the autumn of 2003, with the legislation promised for inclusion in the Finance Bill 2004. The Directive is due to be implemented by 1 January 2004, but this date may yet be set back unless disputes in the EC concerning the tax package of which the Directive is a part are settled quickly. At the time of writing, there are still difficulties to be resolved.

Foreign currency borrowings

19.16 Where a UK company or permanent establishment borrows funds in a foreign currency, the foreign exchange ('forex') tax treatment will be determined by the purpose for which the borrowings are taken.

19.17 To the extent the borrowings are for the purposes of a trade, the forex exchange profit or loss arising will be brought into accounts in computing the profits [FA 1996, s 80(2)].

At the end of the accounting period the forex borrowings are translated at the year end rate and the forex exchange profits and losses taken to the profit and loss account.

19.18 Alternatively, foreign currency funds may be borrowed for investment purposes, typically to finance the acquisition of shares in, or loans to, foreign subsidiaries. Under the original forex rules a company could elect to match the liability with an eligible asset, normally shares, and could calculate the exchange gain or loss using the alternative method. The effect was to match the forex exchange gain or loss with the underlying asset and bring it into account in the period the matched asset was disposed of. [Exchange Gains and Losses (Alternative Method of Calculation of Gain or Loss) Regulations, SI 1994/3227 para 4 et seq].

19.19 For accounting periods beginning after 30 September 2002, this method is abolished. New rules apply which extend the scope of matching and make it compulsory [FA 1996, s 84A]. In general where the forex exchange gain or loss is taken to reserves in the accounts then it will be matched. This means that borrowings may be matched with loan advances as well as shares when the loans are regarded as equity for accounting purposes.

19.20 Transitional provisions deal with forex exchange gains and losses under the old regime [Exchange Gains and Losses (Bringing into Account Gains or Losses) Regulations, SI 2002/1970].

19.21 Where borrowings are taken from a foreign affiliate, the currency of the loan is normally a matter of choice and will also influence the rate of interest. In most of the selected jurisdictions, the rules are broadly the same as in the UK; namely, the tax treatment follows the accounting treatment. Hong Kong and Singapore are exceptions in that they do not tax capital gains. Some leverage may therefore exist when funds are borrowed from affiliates in those jurisdictions. Similarly, when funds are borrowed from related individuals, their jurisdiction may not tax gains (see Table 5 at paragraph **25.8**), but if it does, any foreign currency gain will not usually be recognised until realisation.

Anti-avoidance

19.22 Interest deductions will be denied when borrowings are taken on for an unallowable purpose [FA 1996, Sch 9 para 13]. Since the UK company or permanent establishment will be borrowing funds to invest in a UK business, the anti-avoidance provisions are most unlikely to apply.

Tax implications in the foreign jurisdiction

Who should take on the borrowings?

19.23 In general, companies should do so as interest deductions are often denied to individuals (see Table 5 at paragraph **25.8**).

As mentioned at paragraph **19.2**, it needs to be reviewed whether it could be more advantageous for the foreign corporate affiliate or individual to take on the borrowings and to inject the funds as equity into the UK company. This assumes that interest on the borrowings will be tax-deductible in the foreign jurisdiction. It will be seen from Table 4 at paragraph **25.4** that, of the jurisdictions reviewed, this is the case in only Austria, Hong Kong, the Netherlands (but see the *Bosal* decision below) and Singapore would deny a tax deduction for interest payments.

As foreign corporate tax rates tend to be somewhat higher than in the UK, there should be a tendency for foreign parent companies in the rest of the selected jurisdictions to borrow the funds for subscription as equity into their UK subsidiaries.

19.24 The non-deductibility of interest in the Netherlands has been held to be discriminatory by the European Court of Justice in the case of *Bosal Holdings BV* Case C-168/01. The ECJ was of the view that this is discriminatory because the Netherlands permits deductions for interest on borrowings to finance the acquisition of Dutch companies but denies deductibility in relation to foreign (including EU) acquisitions. However it is likely that the Netherlands will amend its legislation to counteract the decision.

Interestingly, in his decision the Advocate General points out that Austria's tax system is not discriminatory in this regard because Austria denies deductibility for both Austrian and foreign acquisitions.

Guarantee fees and interest receivable

19.25 Turning to those cases where the UK company has obtained the borrowings with the collateral assistance of guarantees or pledges from its foreign affiliate, it would be normal to expect that transfer pricing rules in the foreign jurisdiction would require that an appropriate fee is received from the UK subsidiary, or is otherwise imputed for tax purposes (see paragraph **17.20** et seq).

Similarly, if a foreign corporate affiliate or related individual lends funds directly to the UK subsidiary, transfer pricing rules in the foreign jurisdiction will invariably require that an arm's length rate of interest be received.

19.26 Three exceptions to these transfer pricing requirements may apply in the foreign jurisdiction:

(a) Transfer pricing rules may not exist or may not be enforced. Ireland is a prime example. There are no general rules apart from those linked to local tax incentives.

(b) Although transfer pricing rules exist, they may not apply to loans or guarantees. This is the case in Canada when such facilities are afforded to a foreign subsidiary carrying on an active business.

(c) The loan to the UK subsidiary may be regarded as equity for tax purposes, typically where the subsidiary could not have obtained such a loan from a third party. Then, any interest received would generally be regarded as a dividend.

19.27 The majority of foreign tax jurisdictions will tax the interest received by the foreign affiliate on an accrual basis in accordance with the company's accounts. Thus, failure to pay the interest within 12 months will normally result in a disadvantageous timing mismatch in view of the need for the UK company or permanent establishment to do so in order to obtain a tax deduction in the period of accrual (see paragraph **19.1**).

19.28 In straightforward situations the corporate foreign affiliate receiving interest from the UK company will generally be taxable in the foreign jurisdiction on an accrual basis in accordance with the foreign affiliate's accounts. Any UK withholding tax deductible at source, depending on the relevant tax treaty with the UK (see **Appendix 2**) will normally be allowed as a credit or deduction in calculating tax on the interest income.

19.29 In less straightforward situations, interest paid by the UK company may be disallowed in the UK but taxed as interest received in the foreign jurisdiction (although some receiving countries will follow the UK recharacterisation of the interest as a dividend). In such cases the mismatch might be resolved under the mutual agreement procedure of article 25 of the OECD Model Convention (see paragraph **17.21** et seq). In practice, the ideal would be to endeavour to mutually agree the position in both jurisdictions in advance of implementing the borrowing arrangements.

Offshore finance company

19.30 In foreign jurisdictions where the interest received would be taxable at a comparatively high rate, a third country finance company could be considered.

Example 31

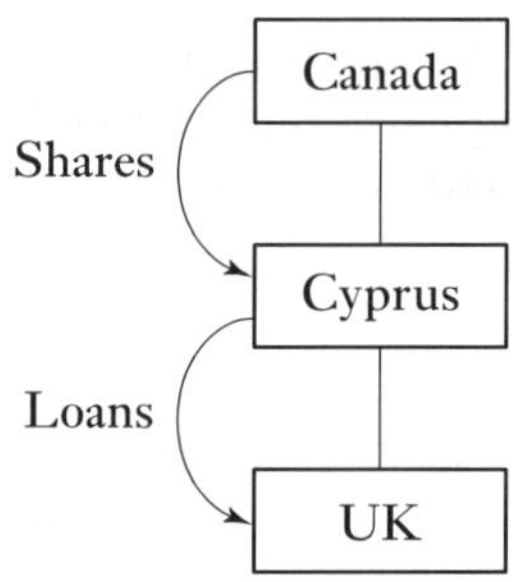

Apart from the question of UK withholding tax and debt/equity restrictions, the main factor requiring consideration is the question of controlled foreign company rules in the foreign jurisdiction, in this case, Canada (see **Appendix 3**). It would also need to be ensured that the Cyprus company was not resident in Canada or the UK (see paragraph **2.2** et seq).

Individuals

19.31 In general, most foreign jurisdictions tax interest received by individuals on a cash basis.

In a limited number of cases, the interest may not be taxable. Of the countries surveyed, Hong Kong taxes only local-source income. Interest receivable from a

UK subsidiary would normally be regarded as sourced outside Hong Kong. However, as there is no tax treaty with the UK, a 20% UK withholding tax would normally be suffered at source (see **Appendix 2**). No further UK tax would be payable [FA 1995, s 128(3)(a)].

19.32 Similarly, in Singapore the interest receivable would be taxable only insofar as remitted to Singapore. Unremitted interest would suffer a full 20% UK withholding tax because, as in the case of many UK tax treaties, article 24 of the UK/Singapore treaty has the effect that the unremitted interest is subject to the full 20% withholding tax:

> '24(1) Where under any provision of this Agreement any income is relieved from tax in a Contracting State and, under the law in force in the other Contracting State, a person in respect of that income, is subject to tax by reference to the amount thereof which is remitted to or received in that other Contracting State and not by reference to the full amount thereof, then the relief to be allowed under this Agreement in the first-mentioned Contracting State shall apply only to so much of the income as is taxed in the other Contracting State.'

In order to avoid the 20% withholding tax, the Singapore or Hong Kong loans might be channelled through a jurisdiction such as the Netherlands, although such a structure is open to challenge (see paragraph **6.16** et seq in relation to royalty income).

Instead of this, alternative financing methods should be considered in order to avoid the 20% withholding tax (see **Chapter 20**).

20 Alternative methods of financing the UK company or permanent establishment

Overview

- Instead of interest-bearing loans, foreign investor could provide finance in form of deep discount loans, debt factoring, property and equipment leasing, and licensing intellectual property.

20.1 Apart from normal interest-bearing loans, a number of other methods exist for financing a UK company, or permanent establishment, all of them subject to transfer pricing rules [ICTA 1988, s 765A and Sch 28AA] (see **Chapter 17**).

Deep discount loans

20.2 In principle, discounts are taxable under Schedule D Case III [ICTA 1988, s 18(3)(b)]. However withholding tax is not deductible at source and direct assessment is inapplicable [FA 1995, s 128(1), (2), (3)(a) and FA 2003, s 151(1), (2)]. This exemption is particularly beneficial when the lender cannot take advantage of a tax treaty. However this advantage must be reviewed in the light of the timing disadvantage to the UK company borrower in deducting the discount (see paragraph **20.6**).

Deep discount (or zero coupon) loan arrangements involve a UK company or permanent establishment borrowing funds, in this case from its foreign affiliate at a discount on issue (or premium on repayment), with a low or zero rate of interest.

20.3 A number of cases have distinguished discounts from interest. In *National Provident Institution v Brown* (1921) 8 TC 57, a discount was defined as:

> '. . . an abatement or deduction from the amount, or from the gross reckoning or value of anything and, as used in commerce is defined to mean (1) a deduction (usually) at a certain rate per cent, made for payment before it is due of a bill or account, or any deduction or abatement from the nominal value or price; (2) a deduction from the amount of a bill of exchange or promissory note by one who gives value for it before it is due.'

20.4 In other words, a discount is essentially any difference between a sum payable in the future and the same sum paid immediately. Although it represents interest in another form, it is not interest in the strict sense. It was said in

Willingale v International Commercial Bank Ltd (1977) 52 TC 242 that the essential difference between interest and a discount is that interest accrues from day to day but generally a discount does not.

20.5 In general terms the longer the period of the loan, the more the likelihood that the discount will be accepted as such, being consideration for the risk factor rather than a deferred payment of interest. The drafting of the loan documentation will also be an important factor.

20.6 Prima facie the corporate debt rules provide for the discount to be tax-deductible over the period of the loan in accordance with the UK company's or permanent establishment's accounts [FA 1996, s 82(2)]. However when the loan is from a connected party or close company, the discount cannot be accrued for tax purposes and is only tax-deductible on repayment at the end of the loan term [FA 1996, Sch 9 paras 17 and 18]. There is therefore a timing disadvantage compared to ordinary loan interest payable to a foreign affiliate although, as mentioned at paragraph **19.1**, that has to be paid within 12 months of the end of the accounting period in order to be deductible within it [FA 1996, s 84, Sch 8, para 2(1), (2)].

20.7 In short, in relation to the countries surveyed, deep discount loans are only likely to be advantageous where the lender is resident in Hong Kong or Singapore as the discount received may not be liable to tax in either jurisdiction (see paragraph **20.10**) while a UK deduction will be obtainable at the end of the loan term.

Example 32

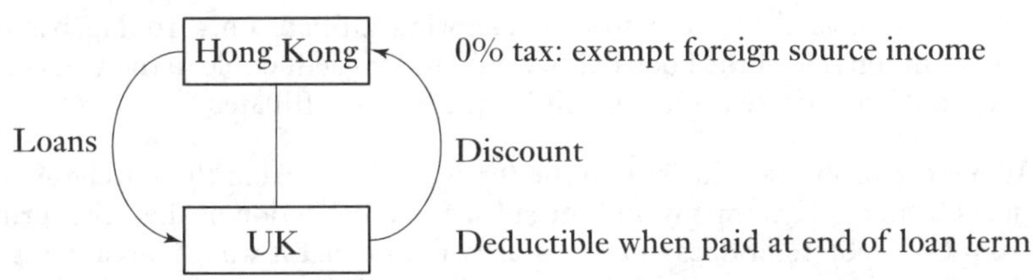

20.8 As with normal interest-bearing loans, any discount on 75% group foreign affliates' loans to a UK company or permanent establishment which is in excess of arm's length terms is a distribution within ICTA 1988, s 209(2)(da), as it relates to any interest or other distribution (see paragraph **19.8(a)**. In other circumstances the discount may be subject to transfer pricing restrictions [ICTA 1988, Sch 28AA] (see paragraph **19.8(b)**). (As mentioned at paragraph **20.2**, withholding tax does not apply to discounts.) These disallowances are challengeable when the discount is payable to EU lenders (see *Lankhorst* decision at paragraph **19.9**), and to tax treaty lenders (see OECD Model Tax Convention article 24.5 and paragraph **19.10** for a fuller discussion).

20.9 It should be noted that a deep discount borrowing would be inappropriate for a foreign individual operating a UK permanent establishment. The corporate debt rules discussed above relate to corporation tax only. For income tax purposes the discount would not be an admissible deduction in arriving at taxable profits under Schedule D Case I [ICTA 1988, s 74(1)(f)].

Tax implications in the foreign jurisdiction

20.10 The corporate foreign affiliate will generally be taxable on the discount on an accruals basis in accordance with its accounts. There will thus be a timing disadvantage as the UK company may only deduct the interest when the loan is repaid (see paragraph **20.6**).

However, provided that the loan to the UK company is regarded as foreign-sourced, the discount will be tax-exempt in Hong Kong. In Singapore it will be taxed only to the extent remitted.

In general most foreign jurisdictions tax discounts received by individuals on a cash basis. In Hong Kong and Singapore the potential exists for non-taxability or tax deferral (see above).

For foreign jurisdictions with a comparatively high rate of tax, a third country finance company might advance the deep discount loans, subject to controlled foreign company rules (see paragraph **19.30** and **Appendix 3**). It will need to be ensured that the finance company is resident in neither the UK nor the home country jurisdiction (see paragraph **2.2** et seq).

Debt factoring

20.11 The UK company or permanent establishment could obtain finance by selling its book debts to a foreign factoring affiliate on a rolling basis. The 'discount' on sale of the book debts would be tax-deductible to the UK company and would constitute trading profits of the foreign affiliate.

While the profits would arise to the foreign affiliate from the purchase of book debts from a UK company and the subsequent collection of the debts primarily from UK debtors, it does not necessarily follow that it would be carrying on its debt factoring trade in the UK, especially if all the operations of the business were carried out abroad (see paragraphs **3.1** and **4.1**).

Even if the purchase and sale of book debts constituted the carrying on of a trade in the UK, the profits would be exempted from UK tax in the absence of a UK permanent establishment or UK representative, typically a regular agent (see paragraphs **11.2** and **12.3**).

Tax implications in the foreign jurisdiction

20.12 In all the foreign jurisdictions surveyed, the debt factoring profits are likely to be fully taxable. The exact timing of the profit realisation may vary between the date on which the book debts are purchased and the date on which payment is collected.

In the case of Hong Kong and Singapore the factoring profits are likely to be regarded as sourced in the home territory if the foreign affiliate carries on the factoring business in its home jurisdiction. However if the business is operated entirely abroad by a foreign permanent establishment, the debt factoring profits will be exempt from tax in those jurisdictions indicated in Table 2 at paragraph **13.3(f)** whose domestic legislation exempts the profits of a foreign permanent establishment. Clearly the business should not be operated from the UK but from a jurisdiction that would not tax the factoring profits generated.

Instead of a foreign permanent establishment, a third country company in a low tax jurisdiction might be utilised for the debt factoring activities. If the home country jurisdiction legislates for controlled foreign company rules, these will require consideration (see paragraph **19.30** and **Appendix 3**). It will also need to be ensured that the debt factoring company is resident in neither the UK nor the home country jurisdiction (see paragraph **2.2** et seq).

Other financing methods

20.13 The foreign parent company or group could effectively finance the UK business by acquiring assets and leasing or licensing them to the business:

(a) Equipment leasing (see **Chapter 31**).

(b) Renting property (see **Chapter 32**).

(c) Licensing intellectual property (see **Chapters 6** and **21**).

21 Licensing or acquiring intellectual property

Overview

- New UK tax rules broadly align tax treatment of intellectual property with its accounting treatment.
- However, intellectual property acquired pre- 1 April 2002 continues under existing rules.

21.1 Often the foreign investor will be providing the UK permanent establishment or company with the benefit of intellectual property. In some cases this is obvious. For example the UK branch or company may be manufacturing a product with the benefit of a patent developed and registered by a foreign affiliate or related individual.

But in some cases the circumstances may not be so obvious. For example, the UK permanent establishment or company may have free access to its foreign affiliate's customer lists for UK marketing purposes; or may have access to professional experience, know-how, and supply chains of its foreign corporate affiliate or related individual.

21.2 Intellectual property is of increasing relevance for two main reasons. First, with present day emphasis on technology, branding and other intangibles, it constitutes a major business asset. Second, and partly as a response to this, most major fiscal authorities are steadily developing increasingly sophisticated transfer pricing rules designed to staunch the leakage of domestic tax revenues through the escape of intellectual property abroad (see **Chapter 17**).

21.3 Chapter 6 discusses the UK and foreign tax position of the licensor. This Chapter is concerned with the UK tax position of the UK company or permanent establishment that is using the intellectual property of its foreign affiliate.

21.4 However before proceeding it is first necessary to summarise the UK tax regime for intangible fixed assets which took effect from 1 April 2002, with particular emphasis on transactions with non-resident affiliates.

21.5 The detailed legislation is contained in FA 2002, Sch 29. A full discussion of the rules is inappropriate here but relevant aspects are summarised below:

(a) The new regime applies only for the purposes of corporation tax. Thus it applies only to UK companies and permanent establishments [FA 2002, Sch 29 para 1(1)] and not to foreign individuals.

(b) It applies to intangible property including goodwill (referred to hereupon as 'IP') acquired or created after 31 March 2002. Acquisitions from related parties, including those abroad, only fall within the new regime if the related party acquired or created the intellectual property after 31 March 2002 [FA 2002, Sch 29 paras 117, 118].

(c) Broadly speaking, all new regime IP is taxed according to its normal accounting treatment. So amortisation of most acquired IP is tax-deductible based on the accounts, which will amortise the IP over its expected useful life [FA 2002, Sch 29 paras 7–9]. Exceptionally, an election may be made to amortise IP at a fixed rate of 4% [FA 2002, Sch 29 para 10]. This is normally relevant to goodwill, and possibly brands, which may be justifiably amortised for accounting purposes at a slower or nil rate.

(d) Expenditure on internally generated IP is tax-deductible when charged to revenue.

(c) If, as a result of an impairment review, the book value of IP needs to be decreased in the accounts, the reduction is tax-deductible in the same way as accounts amortisation [FA 2002, Sch 29 para 9(1)(b)]. Similarly, but subject to limitations when IP is written up [FA 2002, Sch 29 para 13 et seq].

(f) Profits on sales of IP are taxed as income rather than as capital gains [FA 2002, Sch 29 para 20]. However, tax on the profits is deferrable if the proceeds are reinvested into other IP, broadly on the same lines as existing capital gains rollover rules [FA 2002, Sch 29 para 37]. The treatment is more generous in that all IP will qualify for reinvestment relief. (Rollover relief for capital gains purposes limits qualifying IP assets to goodwill.) The reinvestment relief applies on a group basis [FA 2002, Sch 29 para 56].

Under transitional rules, capital gains on realisation of pre-regime IP may be deferred by reinvestment into IP acquired after 31 March 2002 [FA 2002, Sch 29 para 130].

(g) In order to achieve neutrality between acquisitions in asset and share form, profits on IP may be rolled over against new regime IP owned by an acquired 75% subsidiary. The profits will be deducted from the written down values of the IP owned by the subsidiary at the time of its acquisition [FA 2002, Sch 29 para 57].

(h) The new regime applies to investment, as well as to trading, activities. Thus IP purchased to provide a flow of royalty income may be amortised for tax purposes.

(i) Gains arising on IP as a result of incorporation or merger, which are tax-deferred for capital gains purposes, may also be deferred under the new IP rules [FA 2002, Sch 29 para 84].

(j) Transfers of IP within a capital gains group are generally dealt with on a 'tax neutral' basis [FA 2002, Sch 29 para 55].

(k) Pre-regime IP continues to be taxed under existing rules. However post-regime gains on sale of pre-regime goodwill may be rolled into all classes of new regime IP [FA 2002, Sch 29 para 132]. They can no longer be rolled over, for example, into land or fixed plant and machinery [FA 2002, Sch 29 para 132].

(l) In following accounting principles, all royalties payable after 31 March 2002 are deductible on an accruals basis in accordance with the UK company's or permanent establishment's accounts. This is so, even if the IP in question was acquired or created before 1 April 2002 [FA 2002, Sch 29 para 119(1)(a)]. Royalties payable to foreign affiliates will be subject to transfer pricing rules (see **Chapter 17**).

(m) In general transactions with related parties are deemed to be at market value [FA 2002, Sch 29 para 92]. For example, the UK company's or permanent establishment's outright acquisition of UK territorial rights in brands owned by the foreign parent company.

However, as discussed above, if the foreign parent owned the brands before 1 April 2002, tax amortisation under the new regime is not available [FA 2002, Sch 29 para 122(3)].

21.6 Even if acquisition of the IP did not qualify for tax amortisation under FA 2002, it could qualify for UK capital allowances in the following circumstances. In all cases it is assumed that the IP is acquired from a foreign affiliate.

Computer software

21.7 Capital expenditure on computer software is treated as plant for capital allowance purposes and so qualifies for 25% writing down allowance [CAA 2001, s 71].

Specific to plant and machinery acquisitions, the anti avoidance provisions of CAA 2001, s 213 et seq are applicable. Because the UK permanent establishment or company and the foreign affiliate are connected persons within CAA 2001, s 214, section 218(3) applies because the foreign affiliate does not bring the disposal proceeds of the software into account for plant capital allowance purposes. The effect of this is that the acquisition price (the UK permanent establishment's or company's qualifying expenditure for capital allowance purposes) will be limited to the lowest of:

(a) its actual expenditure;

(b) market value;

(c) the foreign affiliate's capital expenditure on the software (so if its expenditure was of a revenue nature, the capital allowance cost will be nil);

(d) if a person connected with the foreign affiliate incurred capital expenditure on the software, the amount of that expenditure.

Research and development

21.8 If the IP acquired falls within this category, the expenditure will qualify for 100% capital allowances under CAA 2001, Part 6 provided it is incurred in carrying on a trade or in anticipation of carrying on a trade (CAA 2001, s 439(1)). Section 437(2)(a) specifies that the definition of 'research and development' follows the 'generally accepted accounting practice' definition in ICTA 1988, s 837A(2) (see **Appendix 6**).

21.9 CAA 2001, ss 567 and 568 require that the acquisition price for capital allowance purposes for transactions between connected persons be market value.

21.10 It should be noted that, if the acquisition arises in connection with the transfer of the business of a UK permanent establishment to a UK company by an EU affiliate under TCGA 1992, s 140, the UK company will instead take over the capital allowance basis in the research and development expenditure (which will be nil in view of the 100% allowance) [CAA 2001, ss 561, 567(5)]. This also follows from the provisions relating to the transfer of trades under 75% common ownership [ICTA 1988, s 343(2)] (see paragraph **24.18**).

Manufacturing know-how

21.11 Acquisition of know-how from a connected person is disqualified from capital allowances by CAA 2001, s 455(2).

Instead of acquiring the manufacturing know-how, it could instead be licensed from the foreign affiliate in return for a royalty. Transfer pricing legislation in most foreign jurisdictions will require that an arm's length royalty be charged.

Patents

21.12 Capital expenditure on patents qualifies for a 25% writing down allowance under CAA 2001, Part 8.

In view of the connected persons relationship, and the fact the foreign affiliate selling the patent rights will not bring the disposal proceeds into account for patent allowance purposes, the acquisition price will be limited in the same way as for the acquisition of computer software (see paragraph **21.7**) [CAA 2001, s 481(6)].

21.13 It should not be overlooked that, where the rights relate to a UK patent there is an obligation on the purchaser to deduct tax at 22% from the purchase price and to account for it to the UK Revenue [ICTA 1988, s 524(3)]. However, if the seller is resident in a jurisdiction having an appropriate tax treaty with the UK, the capital gains article of the treaty is likely to provide that gains from the alienation of all assets other than UK real estate and the assets of the UK permanent establishment are to be taxable only in the seller's state of residence. In such a case the 22% UK withholding tax will be inapplicable. This position should be cleared in advance with the CNR (see also paragraph **6.23**).

VAT

21.14 The supply of most types of intellectual property is covered by VATA 1994, Sch 5 para 1, which refers to 'Transfers and assignments of copyright, patents, licenses, trademarks and similar rights' (see paragraph **4.5(a)**).

21.15 Where supplies of this type are received by a person belonging in the UK for the purposes of a business carried on by him and the supplier belongs outside the UK, VATA 1994, s 8 requires the recipient to account for VAT under the 'reverse charge' provisions. In other words, it will need to account for output VAT on the royalty or capital cost of the intellectual property and will be able to recover as input VAT that proportion of the output VAT that the normal VAT rules allow (see paragraph **4.5(a)**).

Tax implications in the foreign jurisdiction

21.16 See paragraph **6.25**.

Where intellectual property is being developed, it is sometimes the case that various group companies share the burden of the development under a cost-sharing arrangement, by contributing cash or resources into the project in return for a share, usually geographic, in the intellectual property ultimately developed (see paragraph **17.19** and Example 25).

22 Leasing property

22.1 Instead of purchasing the property in which its business is carried on, the UK permanent establishment or company could lease it from a foreign affiliate. The rental payments would be tax-deductible within transfer pricing rules (see **Chapter 17**).

22.2 One of the main driving forces to having the property purchased by a foreign affiliate rather than the UK entity is the fact that as a non-UK resident, the foreign corporate affiliate or individual will not be liable to UK tax on the capital gain realised on eventual disposal of the property assuming, as is likely, that it is owned as an investment rather than as trading stock [TCGA 1992, ss 2(1), 10B] (see paragraph **32.2**).

22.3 See **Chapter 31** for a full discussion on the tax position of the foreign lessor. Withholding taxes are deductible from rent paid to non-residents unless there is prior clearance from the Inland Revenue (see paragraph **32.3** et seq).

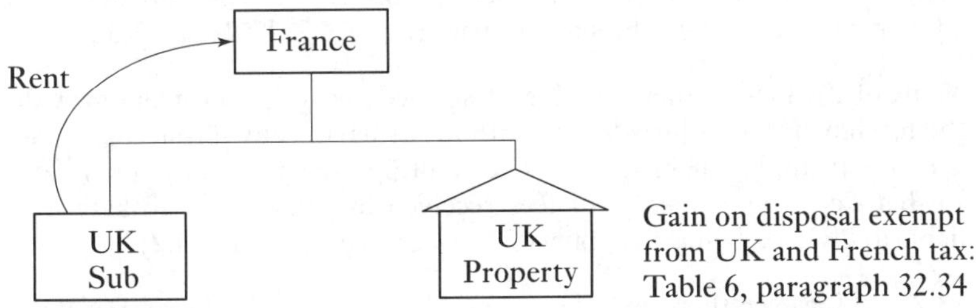

VAT

22.4 For VAT purposes, a lease of land situated in the UK is a supply made in the UK (see paragraph **8.4(a)**). The grant of a lease is an exempt supply [VATA 1994, Sch 9 Group 1], but the lessor may opt to waive the exemption, in which case the lease will be treated as a standard-rated supply, and VAT of 17.5% would be chargeable on the rent. The advantage of waiving the exemption is that it enables the lessor to recover any associated input VAT.

23 Management fees

Overview

- Foreign affiliates receiving management fees from UK entity will be liable to UK tax if fees are attributable to UK permanent establishment.
- Management fees require particular care from VAT viewpoint.

23.1 The foreign affiliate may provide the UK permanent establishment or company with management services such as accounting, legal advice, administrative services, debt collection, research etc. The quantum of the management fees paid will be subject to transfer pricing rules (see **Chapter 17**). Withholding taxes do not apply to the payment of such fees to non-residents.

Whether or not the foreign affiliate receiving the fees is liable to direct assessment in the UK on the fees received is dependent on whether these are derived through a UK permanent establishment (see paragraphs **4.2**, **11.2** and **12.3**).

Many of the management services described above are normally provided from the foreign affiliate's jurisdiction without its having any physical presence in the UK; for example, the provision of accounting information by email, fax or post. In that case, the management fees received by the foreign affiliate will not be liable to UK tax, being an export of services (see paragraph **4.2**).

23.2 However there may be situations in which the foreign affiliate's staff regularly visit the UK, or are even permanently stationed in the UK in order to fulfil its obligations under the management contract. This often occurs in the hotel industry when a foreign hotel operator manages a UK hotel. In this case it is perfectly possible that the foreign affiliate has a taxable UK permanent establishment, being the UK hotel premises at which its staff perform their work (see paragraph **11.2**). Similar situations occur where consultants regularly perform work at clients' premises in the UK.

23.3 Under FA 2003, s 148(1)(a), a fixed place of business through which the business of the non-resident company is wholly or partly carried on constitutes a permanent establishment (see paragraph **11.3**). Where a tax treaty is in place, paragraph 4 of the OECD commentary on article 5 of its Model Tax Convention (see **Appendix 1**) states that a fixed place of business may exist where a foreign enterprise has at its constant disposal certain premises owned by another enterprise. It can be assumed that the UK Revenue will make a similar assertion where no tax treaty exists and s 148(1)(a) is in point.

In these circumstances the foreign affiliate will be liable to UK tax on the profits arising through its UK permanent establishment, based on the management fees received less relevant expenses (see **Chapter 13**).

Given the UK tax exposure a decision needs to be made as to whether it would be more beneficial for the foreign affiliate to provide the management services through a UK company (see **Chapter 14**), rather than operate as a UK permanent establishment (see **Chapter 13**).

VAT

23.4 See paragraph **4.5** and **Chapter** 8.

From a VAT perspective, management fees require considerable care.

While 'management fees' may consist of accounting, legal, advisory and administrative services undertaken by a foreign affiliate for a UK company or permanent establishment, they may also comprise executive and managerial functions. There is an important distinction from a VAT perspective.

The provision of executive or management services is not seen as a consultancy or similar service. Accordingly, it is not seen as falling within VATA 1994, Sch 5 para 3 (see paragraph **4.5**). Therefore, for a management charge from an overseas affiliate to a UK business, it is likely that overseas VAT would be charged. Recovery of this VAT by the UK recipient could only be effected using the EC 8th (for EU-based businesses) or 13th (for non-EU businesses) Directive refund procedures.

23.5 Assuming that the management fee does not amount to an executive or management function, it is probable that the accounting, legal, advisory and similar services described above will fall within VATA 1994, Sch 5 para 3, namely:

> 'Services of consultants, engineers, consultancy bureaux, lawyers, accountants and other similar services; data processing and provision of information (but excluding . . . any services relating to land).'

Accordingly, charges for services of this type received in the UK will be subject to the 'reverse charge' procedure (see paragraph **4.3**).

Tax implications in the foreign jurisdiction

23.6 It is assumed that the foreign affiliate does not operate through a UK subsidiary but provides the management services itself.

If the foreign affiliate provides the services through a UK permanent establishment, so that the profits derived are liable to UK tax, the foreign tax implications are discussed in **Chapter 13**. In the case of a number of the jurisdictions surveyed, liability to UK tax results in the foreign affiliate being exempt from tax in the foreign jurisdiction (see Table 2 at paragraph **13.3(f)**).

23.6 *Management fees*

In the absence of a UK permanent establishment, the foreign affiliate will invariably be taxed in its home country. However it is possible that Hong Kong would consider the fees from the services to constitute foreign-source income even though there was no UK permanent establishment. If this was the case, Hong Kong would exempt the fee income from tax as it only taxes Hong Kong source income.

24 Transfer of UK permanent establishment to UK company

Overview

- PE can be transferred to UK company free of UK tax.
- Consideration needs to be given to tax position in foreign jurisdiction.
- PE's accumulated UK tax losses normally carry over into UK company. Double loss deduction may be possible.
- Stamp duty requires careful consideration.
- No VAT should arise.

24.1 While a foreign company or individual may initially operate in the UK through a permanent establishment ('PE') structure, it will often be the case that there is a desire to establish a firm local UK presence in the form of a UK limited company. This may also be driven by tax factors as will seen below. (The relevant tax consequences of operating as a UK PE or company are discussed in **Chapters 13** and **14**.)

This Chapter therefore considers the tax implications of the transfer of the initial PE to a UK company by a foreign company or individual.

Chargeable assets: foreign companies—group transfer

Example 34

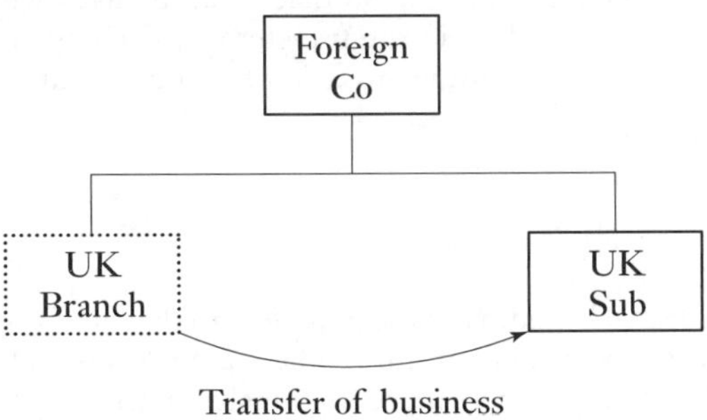

24.2 Now that companies are grouped on a worldwide basis for capital gains purposes, the transfer of chargeable assets from a foreign company's UK PE to a UK group member will be on a no gains/no loss basis [TCGA 1992, s 171(1A)].

Unlike the EU relief discussed at paragraph **24.3**, for relief under s 171, the consideration for the transfer can take any form, whether cash, loans or shares; and there is no anti-avoidance legislation to consider.

Chargeable assets: foreign companies—EC Merger Directive

24.3 A less flexible route for foreign companies to defer tax on capital gains is provided by TCGA 1992, s 140A. This section is enacted in accordance with the EC Merger Directive [90/434/EEC of 23 July 1990] and so applies only where the foreign company operating the UK PE is resident in an EU jurisdiction. Provided that the trade is transferred wholly in exchange for securities issued by the UK company, the assets of the PE are treated as disposed of on a no gains/no loss basis. There is an anti-avoidance requirement that the transfer must be for bona fide commercial reasons. A clearance procedure is available [TCGA 1992, s 140B].

24.4 TCGA 1992, s 140A(7) defines 'securities' as including shares. The consideration would therefore be limited to shares or loan stock, but certainly not cash.

24.5 Section 140A(4) disapplies TCGA 1992, s 25(3), which would otherwise deem the chargeable assets of the PE to be disposed of at market value on its ceasing to trade in the UK.

24.6 In contrast to a group transfer under s 171(1A), s 140B provides that s 140A will not apply unless the transfer of the trade is effected for bona fide commercial reasons and does not form part of a scheme to avoid UK income tax, corporation tax, or capital gains tax. Section 140B(2) provides a clearance procedure.

24.7 It is true that assets can be transferred on a no gain/no loss basis under s 171 without the restrictions that apply under s 140A. However s 140A does not require the existence of a capital gains group so that it can be used where the extent of the 'head office's' shareholding in the transferee UK company is less than 75%. This could be useful in setting up a joint venture company (see paragraph **16.10**).

Stamp duty

24.8 Before 1 December 2003, stamp duty is payable on a document transferring title to any asset, unless specifically exempt. There are various methods of minimising liability (see below), but where there is a transfer of property between companies within a group, as here, the relief under FA 1930, s 42 should apply.

24.9 Under FA 1930, s 42, transfers of property between associated 'bodies corporate' are exempt from stamp duty. A 'body corporate' is not defined in the legislation, but it is understood that it should have separate legal personality and be capable of perpetual succession. The expression is not limited to companies incorporated in the UK (*Canada Safeway Ltd v IRC* [1973] Ch 374). Bodies corporate are associated where one directly or indirectly owns not less than 75 per cent of the ordinary share capital of the other, or a third body corporate directly or indirectly owns at least 75 per cent of the share capital of both. At the same time, the ownership requirement also extends to the profits available for distribution and the assets available for distribution to equity holders on a winding-up [FA 1930, s 42(2A)-(7)]. There are rules that can result in a charge to stamp duty if the group relationship is broken within three years of the transfer of the property.

24.10 From 1 December 2003, stamp duty is abolished on documents transferring property other than stock or marketable securities and partnership interests (FA 2003, s 125, Sch 20). Stamp duty on land is reborn as stamp duty land tax, chargeable on all land transactions, whether or not there is any instrument effecting such a transaction. The new tax has a similar relief for transfers within a group.

Chargeable assets: foreign individuals

Example 35

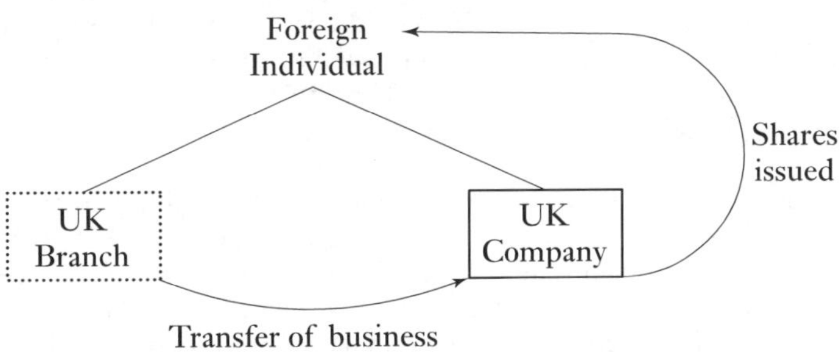

24.11 The transfer can be effected without incurring capital gains tax under TCGA 1992, s 10, provided that the consideration for the entire business (other than cash) consists of shares issued by the UK company [TCGA 1992, s 162].

24.12 The deferred gain is deducted from the capital gains tax cost of the shares issued to the foreign individual. However, as he or she will not normally be liable to UK capital gains tax on their disposal, the gain on transfer of the PE is permanently deferred [TCGA 1992, s 2(1)].

24.13 The chargeable assets acquired by the company will be treated as acquired at market value [TCGA 1992, s 18]. Thus, assuming the chargeable assets have increased in value since their acquisition date, a tax-free step-up of base costs will be achieved.

New-regime intangible property

24.14 Where part of the assets transferred by the UK PE of a foreign company consist of intangible property acquired or created after 31 March 2002 (see paragraph **21.5(i)**), provisions parallel to the inter-group and EU tax-free transfers discussed at paragraphs **24.2** and **24.3** similarly apply [FA 2002, Sch 29 paras 55, 85]. In the case of an EU merger under FA 2002, Sch 29 para 85, there is a similar bona fide requirement and clearance procedure [FA 2002, Sch 29 paras 85(4), 85(5)].

24.15 For a UK PE belonging to a foreign individual, the provisions of FA 2002 are inapplicable (see paragraph **21.5(a)**). In general, therefore, the intangible property transferred to the UK company will constitute a chargeable asset which can be transferred free of capital gains tax under TCGA 1992, s 162 (see paragraph **24.11**). As with chargeable assets, there is a similar tax-free step-up of the intangible property to the UK company (see paragraph **24.13**). Provided that the foreign individual created or acquired the intangible property after 31 March 2002, FA 2002 applies to the UK company and it can be amortised according to the accounts. There are exceptions, for example, goodwill might be amortisable at 4% (see paragraph **21.5(c)**).

24.16 There is an exception to the deferral process in the case of gains on transfer of a foreign individual's UK patent rights, and a foreign company's pre-1 April 2002 UK patent rights. These gains are taxable as income under Schedule D Case VI [ICTA 1988, s 524(3)] (see paragraph **6.23**). In the case of a foreign company transferor, the liability could be minimised by minimising the consideration. Transfer pricing adjustments will be inapplicable as the UK PE transferring the patent rights is within the charge to corporation tax [ICTA 1988, Sch 28AA para 5(3)(a)].

24.17 However a foreign individual's transfer will be subject to adjustment under Sch 28AA as he or she will not be a UK resident [ICTA 1988, Sch 28AA para 5(3)(c)]. This problem could be avoided if, *ab initio*, the non-resident individual arranged for the patent rights to be owned by a related company outside the UK from which he or she could take a licence at full royalty rates in order to use them in the UK PE when first established. The asset transferred would then be the licence, which would normally have a negligible capital value.

Capital allowance assets: foreign companies

24.18 In the case of a foreign company transferring its UK PE, the requisite 75% ownership will exist. All assets covered by CAA 2001 are treated as transferred to the UK subsidiary at tax written down value. This treatment applies to the full range of capital allowance assets, namely plant and machinery, industrial buildings and hotels, agricultural buildings, flat conversions, mineral assets, research and development assets, manufacturing know-how, patents, dredging works, and assured tenancies [ICTA 1988, s 343(1) and (2)].

Capital allowance assets: foreign individuals

24.19 Where the UK PE is being transferred by a foreign individual to the UK company, the treatment is as follows:

For plant and machinery, the foreign individual is treated as selling, and the transferee UK company as purchasing, the plant or machinery at its market value [CAA 2001, s 265(2)]. However, the foreign individual and the UK company may jointly elect to treat the plant or machinery as transferred at its tax written-down value [CAA 2001, s 267].

24.20 Capital expenditure on manufacturing know-how acquired by the UK company will not qualify for capital allowances as the transferor is a connected person [CAA 2001, s 455(2)]. Where a trade is being disposed of as here, consideration for know-how is treated as a payment for goodwill unless the parties elect otherwise [ICTA 1988, s 531(2)]. As no capital allowances are available to the UK company in this case, such an election is of no advantage. Moreover, even if the expenditure is incurred after 31 March 2002 and is treated as incurred on goodwill, the new rules of FA 2002, Sch 29 will not apply to it, and hence no amortisation will be deductible unless the trade commenced after 31 March 2002 [FA 2002, Sch 29 para 121].

24.21 For industrial buildings, agricultural buildings, flat conversions, mineral assets, R&D assets and assured tenancies, where there is a sale between connected persons, the assets are treated as sold and acquired at their market value unless the parties make an election under CAA 2001, s 569 for the assets to pass at their tax written-down value.

Transfer of losses

24.22 In the case of a foreign company transferring its UK PE, provided that it has a 75% interest in the UK company and relevant liabilities do not exceed relevant assets, any losses of the UK PE carried forward under ICTA 1988, s 393 will be available for carry-forward by the UK subsidiary [ICTA 1988, s 343(3)] (see Example 16 at paragraph **13.3(d)**). As discussed there, the carryover of losses may therefore achieve a double loss deduction but that depends upon the loss recapture rules in the foreign company's jurisdiction (see Table 3 at paragraph **24.42**).

The carry-over of UK PE losses would be unavailable to a foreign individual transferring his or her UK branch to a UK company. ICTA 1988, s 343 applies only where the transferor of the UK PE is a home company, later transferring the PE to a UK company.

A foreign individual contemplating opening a UK PE should therefore consider the possibility of operating it through a home country company, later transferring the PE to a UK company.

Stamp duty

24.23 Before 1 December 2003, stamp duty is payable on any document transferring title to an asset. In order to minimise the liability, assets that can legally be transferred by delivery (i.e. without the need for a written document), such as know-how, stock-in-trade and movable plant, should be transferred in this way. The sale of goodwill is specifically exempt from duty [FA 2002, s 116], as is the sale of other intellectual property [FA 2000, s 129]. This leaves chiefly land, debtors, bank deposits and any shares and securities held as investments. If the UK company assumes any liabilities from the PE, the amount of those liabilities is also liable to stamp duty.

24.24 Shares and securities are liable to duty at a rate of 0.5% [FA 1999, Sch 13 para 3]. The rate of duty on other dutiable assets, including land, varies with the consideration for transfer as follows:

No more than £60,000	nil
£60,001 – £250,000	1%
£250,001 – £500,000	3%
Over £500,000	4%

24.25 However, the transfer of commercial property in a 'disadvantaged area' is wholly exempt from stamp duty as from 10 April 2003 [FA 2001, s 92, SI 2003/861]. Between 30 November 2001 and 9 April 2003, exemption only applied if the consideration for the property was no more than £150,000. The transfer of residential property in a disadvantaged area continues to be exempt if valued at no more than £150,000 [FA 2001, s 92A].

24.26 Before 1 December 2003, it is possible to defer duty by executing and keeping the instrument of transfer outside the UK. However, in respect of UK land, penalties and interest are charged if the instrument is not stamped within 30 days of execution even if the instrument is kept abroad. The penalty is £300 (or the duty payable, if less) if duty is paid within one year of the 30-day deadline; and is the greater of £300 and the duty payable if payment is made after one year [Stamp Act 1891, s 15B]. If the stamp duty payable is very large, the interest and penalties may be considered worth paying in return for the cashflow benefit of the duty deferment, but this will vary from case to case. It ought to be pointed out that until the instrument has been stamped, the purchaser will not be able to prove title should any litigation arise.

24.27 If the land involved is situated outside the UK the conveyance or other instrument of transfer should be executed and kept abroad, so avoiding stamp duty. If it is executed in the UK or requires a matter or something to be done in the UK, stamp duty will become payable.

24.28 If property is transferred between connected persons (as in this case), it is of no benefit to fix the consideration at less than market value in an attempt to mitigate the duty payable, as such transfers are deemed to take place at market value [FA 2000, s 119].

24.29 Another avoidance device that was commonly used was to let the transfer of land 'rest on contract'. This involved concluding an agreement to sell land but not executing the actual conveyance for an indefinite period thereafter. Such an agreement to sell land is not *per se* liable to stamp duty. This device is still effective (until 1 December 2003) but only where the consideration is no more than £10 million [FA 2002, s 115].

24.30 It is possible to avoid duty on the transfer of debtors by in effect not transferring them but appointing the subsidiary as agent for the PE for collection of the sums due. A similar manoeuvre is possible in respect of liabilities. The PE would undertake to remain responsible for payment of the trade creditors, and the subsidiary would net those payments against the sums received by it from trade debtors.

24.31 From 1 December 2003 a fundamental change in the law relating to stamp duty takes place. Stamp duty is to be abolished on documents transferring any kind of property other than marketable securities and partnership interests [FA 2003, s 125, Sch 30]. A 'new' tax, stamp duty land tax, is to be levied on all land transactions, whether or not there is an instrument effecting the transaction [FA 2003, s 42]. Licences to occupy land, and certain other interests in land will be exempt [FA 2003, s 48, Sch 3]. The exemptions for land in disadvantaged areas remain [FA 2003, ss 55, 57, Sch 6]. Stamp duty land tax will be self-assessed and generally payable by the purchaser [FA 2003, s 85] on making the duty return.

VAT

24.32 In general, the transfer or sale of the totality of a business or a part of a business capable of separate operation, from one legal entity to another, will not be subject to VAT [VAT Special Provisions) Order, SI 1995/1268 art 5]. This provision applies throughout the EU as it stems from articles 5(8) and 6(5) of the EC 6th Directive. It is important to note that local provisions may vary from Member State to Member State.

Tax implications in the foreign jurisdiction

Generally

24.33 The character of the foreign company's or individual's investment into the UK will have changed, from the ownership of a foreign PE to the ownership of shares in a UK company. This change will have the following consequential effects in the foreign jurisdiction:

(a) Subject to local controlled foreign company rules, (which are unlikely to apply in the case of a UK trading operation (see **Appendix 3**), the UK profits will only be taxed when repatriated to the foreign parent company or foreign individual.

(b) The foreign company or individual will no longer derive profits and gains from a UK PE (see Table 2 at paragraph **13.3(f)**). Instead, dividends and gains will be derived from a UK company. The taxability of the UK dividends and gains in the selected foreign jurisdictions is summarised at Table 4 in paragraph **25.4** and Table 5 in paragraph **25.8**.

Foreign individuals

24.34

(a) The most significant change will occur in the case of foreign individuals. In the foreign jurisdiction, the foreign individual's profits from the UK PE will have either been exempted from local tax, under a tax treaty or by virtue of domestic rules; or taxed, with a credit for the UK income tax paid on the branch profits. Similarly, assuming the individual was to sell the business, the gains would either be exempt from UK tax; or taxed with a credit for the UK capital gains tax paid (see Table 2 at paragraph **13.3(f)**).

(b) In contrast, with the exception of Hong Kong and Singapore, the UK dividends received by the foreign individual post-incorporation will be fully taxed with no credit for the underlying corporation tax paid by the UK company (see Table 5 at paragraph **25.8**).

(c) Gains on ultimate disposal of the shares will be free of UK capital gains tax [TCGA 1992, s 2(1)] but will either be taxable in the foreign jurisdiction, or exempt if there is no tax on individual's capital gains – see Table 5 at paragraph **25.8**. Invariably the foreign jurisdiction's tax treaty with the UK will reserve the taxing rights to the foreign jurisdiction (see article 13.5 of the OECD Model Convention, **Appendix 1**).

(d) Ownership of the shares of a UK company rather than the assets of a UK PE may lead to changes in the foreign individual's liability to home country gift and estate taxes and net worth taxes.

(e) Ownership of shares will normally provide greater potential for flexibility in estate planning compared to ownership of a PE.

Foreign individual's transfer of UK shares to a company

24.35 As a result of the general taxability of dividends and gains arising from the foreign individual's ownership of shares in the UK company, it may be advantageous for the foreign individual to transfer them to a holding company in his or her home country, or in a suitable third country holding company jurisdiction (0.5% UK stamp duty will be payable on the value of the shares transferred).

24.36 The objective would be for the UK dividends and gains then received to be free of tax under a participation exemption. However this tactic would need to be considered in the light of the following tax factors applicable in the foreign jurisdiction:

(a) any taxes payable by the individual on transfer of the UK shares to the holding company;

(b) any controlled foreign company or similar rules that could immediately tax the individual on the dividends and gains realised by the holding company (see **Appendix 3**).

This topic is discussed in more detail at paragraph **25.8** et seq.

Foreign taxes arising on transfer of the permanent establishment: foreign companies and individuals

24.37 See Table 3 at paragraph **24.42** for an overview.

Some countries operate a territorial basis of taxation; namely, only profits and gains arising in the home jurisdiction are liable to tax. Examples of this are Hong Kong and France. In these cases the transfer of a UK PE to a UK company will be exempt from tax as it clearly takes place outside the home jurisdiction.

24.38 The same effect will occur where the foreign jurisdiction's double tax treaty with the UK provides for relief from double taxation by exempting profits and gains arising from a foreign PE (see article 23A(1) of the OECD Model Convention, **Appendix 1**). Examples of this are the treaties with Belgium and Germany. The transfer of the PE will be exempt from home country tax despite the fact that it will also be exempt from UK tax under TCGA 1992, ss 140A, 162 or 171(1A).

24.39 In the case of a foreign company resident in an EU jurisdiction, following the EC Merger Directive, the transfer of the UK PE in exchange for shares will be either exempt in the foreign jurisdiction; or will be taxed but with a credit for the hypothetical UK tax that would have been payable had the gain on transfer of the UK branch to the UK subsidiary not been exempted under TCGA 1992, s 140A (see Table 3 at paragraph **24.42**). The EU jurisdiction will have enacted the necessary legislation to allow for tax deferred transfers in this way. So again, the transfer of the PE will be broadly tax-exempt in both jurisdictions.

24.40 Finally, Austria, Portugal, Sweden and the USA, provide in their domestic legislation for the tax-free transfer of a foreign branch to a foreign company in exchange for an issue of shares (see Table 3 at paragraph **24.42**).

Recapture of losses

24.41 One of the main reasons for setting up a UK PE in the first place is to ensure that its start-up losses are deducted from taxable income in the home country of the head office (see paragraph **13.3(b)**). However the domestic tax legislation of a number of jurisdictions provides that, when the foreign PE (in this case, the UK) is transferred to a foreign (UK) subsidiary, those losses previously deducted are to be 'recaptured' by being taxed at the time the transfer takes place.

24.42 Table 3 below includes a summary of the loss recapture position in the countries surveyed. Namely, when UK PE losses have offset profits in the foreign jurisdiction head office. It will be noted that recapture occurs only in Denmark, Japan, the Netherlands (in due course), Portugal and the USA.

Table 3 provides an overview of the tax position in each of the selected jurisdictions when the UK PE is transferred to a UK company in exchange for shares. Some of the conditions required for tax exemption are noted but the list is not exhaustive.

TABLE 3 Transfer of UK PE to UK company: foreign tax position

		Exempt transfer			
Company or individual resident in:	*Taxable transfer*	*Domestic exemption*	*EC Merger Directive(1)*	*Treaty exemption(2)*	*PE loss recapture*
Australia	✓				X(7)
Austria	–	✓(3)	✓		X
Belgium	–		✓	✓	X
Canada	✓				X
Denmark(4)	–		✓		✓
Finland(4)	–		✓		X
France	–	✓	✓	✓	X(7)
Germany	–		✓	✓	X(7)
Greece(4)	–		✓		X(7)
Hong Kong	–	✓			X(7)
Ireland(4)	–		✓		X
Italy(4)	–		✓		X
Japan	✓				✓
Luxembourg	–		✓	✓	X(7)
Netherlands	–	✓	✓	✓	✓(5)
Portugal	–	✓(3)	✓		✓
Singapore	–	✓			X(7)
Spain(4)	–		✓		X
Sweden	–	✓(3)	✓		X
Switzerland	–	✓		✓	X(6)
USA	–	✓(3)			✓

Notes (not exhaustive)

(1) In accordance with the EC Merger Directive, gains of companies are either exempt, or taxed but with a credit for the UK tax that would have been payable had the gain on transfer of the UK PE to the UK subsidiary not been exempted under TCGA 1992, s 140A.

(2) Article 23A.1 of the OECD Model Convention (see **Appendix 1**). Exemption applies to companies and individuals.

(3) Austrian, Portuguese, Swedish and USA exemption applies when UK PE transferred in exchange for shares (certain US intangibles not exempted).

(4) Individuals taxable on transfer of branch.

(5) Where the UK PE has incurred losses which have been set against profits in the Netherlands, dividends from the UK subsidiary do not qualify for the participation exemption in the hands of the Dutch parent until they exceed in aggregate the total of those losses.

(6) Subject to tax avoidance.

(7) No recapture because losses non-deductible (see Table 1 at paragraph **13.3(b)**).

Foreign individuals

24.43 The EC Merger Directive does not apply to individuals. Table 3 at paragraph **24.42** indicates that in countries relying solely on the Merger Directive, individuals will be taxable on transferring the branch to a UK company. However in Austria, Portugal, Sweden and the US, tax deferral is available to individuals if the UK PE is transferred in exchange for shares.

Where the Table indicates a domestic or treaty exemption, this will also apply to individuals.

25 Ownership vehicle for UK company

Overview

- Ownership vehicle broadly neutral from UK tax viewpoint.
- But requires careful selection from foreign tax viewpoint, taking account of taxes on dividend repatriation and ultimate realisation, as well as ultimate extraction of funds.
- Selection of ownership vehicle also conditioned by which entity is best suited to bear interest costs.
- If third country holding company utilised, home country controlled foreign company rules require consideration.

25.1 As a result of the following factors, selection of the appropriate entity that is to own the shares of the UK company is broadly neutral from the UK tax viewpoint (but see paragraph **25.2**), and is therefore mainly dependent upon the tax implications in the jurisdiction of the foreign parent company or individual (see paragraph **25.3** et seq):

(a) Neither withholding tax nor advance corporation tax applies to distributions from the UK company.

(b) In general, UK tax is not payable on any gain which the foreign shareholder realises on disposal of the shares [TCGA 1992, ss 2 and 10B]; although a purchaser will normally seek a discount in the share price.

(c) Profits and losses of a 75% or more owned UK subsidiary may be group relieved against profits and losses of fellow UK subsidiaries or UK permanent establishments ultimately owned by the foreign company [ICTA 1988, ss 402 et seq and s 838(1)(b)].

(d) Chargeable assets may be transferred on a no gain/no loss basis between fellow UK 75% or more owned subsidiaries or permanent establishments of an ultimate foreign parent company [TCGA 1992, s 171(1) and (1A)].

25.2 There are two exceptions to the neutrality point:

(a) Where a number of UK subsidiaries exist, a UK holding company will allow for debt/equity ratios for measurement on a consolidated basis for interest deductibility purposes (see paragraph **19.4** and **Chapter 26**).

(b) Effective refund of half the tax credit attaching to the dividend paid by the UK subsidiary to a EU parent company resident in the appropriate jurisdiction will be available should the taxpayer succeed in the appeal before the European Court of Justice in the case of *Océ van der Grinten* that a 5% UK withholding tax should not be deducted. However a successful outcome seems unlikely (see paragraph **28.7**).

Tax implications in the foreign jurisdiction: companies

Participation exemption

25.3 In selecting the appropriate vehicle to own the UK company, the crucial question is whether the jurisdiction of the foreign parent company provides for a participation exemption that will exempt the dividends and gains flowing from ownership of the UK subsidiary from domestic taxes. In such cases the dividends and gains will be tax-free in both jurisdictions. This is subject to the fact that the ultimate purchaser of the shares of the UK company will invariably seek a discount in the price to take account of inherent capital gains taxes applicable to its underlying assets.

In discussing these factors this Chapter necessarily anticipates **Chapters 28** and **29**, relating to repatriation from, and sale of, the UK company.

25.4 The following table summarises the relevant information in the selected jurisdictions. More detailed information in relation to some of the selected jurisdictions is contained in **Appendix 5** 'BDO European Holding Companies Table'.

TABLE 4 Foreign parent company owns shares in UK company: key features

Parent company resident in:	*Tax-free dividends*(1)	*Tax-free gains on shares*	*Deductible interest*	*Parent Co distributions to non-resident Co Treaty WHT rates*	
				Dividends(2)	*Liquidation*(2)
Australia	✓	Taxable	✓	15–30	15–30
Austria	✓	✓	–	0–25	0(4)
Belgium	✓(3)	✓	✓	0–25	0–10(5)
Canada	✓	Taxable	✓	5–25	5–25
Denmark	✓	✓	✓	0–28	0(4)
Finland	✓(6)	Taxable	✓	0–29	0(4)
France	✓(3)	Taxable	✓	0–25	0–25
Germany	✓	✓	✓	0–20	0–20
Greece	Taxable	Taxable	✓	0(4)	0(4)
Hong Kong	✓	✓	–	0(4)	0(4)
Ireland	Taxable	Taxable	✓	0(4)	0(4)

Parent company resident in:	*Tax-free dividends*[1]	*Tax-free gains on shares*	*Deductible interest*	*Parent Co distributions to non-resident Co Treaty WHT rates*	
				Dividends[2]	*Liquidation*[2]
Italy	Taxable	Taxable	✓	0–27	0–27
Japan	Taxable	Taxable	✓	10–15	10–15
Luxembourg	✓	✓	✓[9]	0–20	0[4]
Netherlands	✓	✓	–[7]	0–25	0–25
Portugal	✓[8]	Taxable	✓	0–15	0–15
Singapore	✓	✓	–	0[4]	0[4]
Spain	✓	✓	✓	0–15	0–15
Sweden	✓	✓	✓	0[4]	0[4]
Switzerland	✓	✓	✓	0–35	0–35
USA	Taxable	Taxable	✓	0–30	0[4]

Notes (see also Appendix 5)

(1) Where dividends are taxable, the underlying corporation tax payable by the UK subsidiary will normally be allowed as a foreign tax credit (see article 23B of the OECD Model Convention, **Appendix 1**).

(2) 0% when payable to EU company owning 25% or more of shares - EC Parent/Subsidiary Directive [90/435/EEC article 5].

(3) 95% tax-free.

(4) In general, no withholding tax (Sweden as from 1.1.04).

(5) Special rate applicable to liquidation distributions.

(6) Exempt if received from EU, or generally tax treaty, subsidiary.

(7) Interest actually deductible following ECJ's decision in *Bosal* but counteracting legislation likely (see paragraph **19.24**).

(8) Exempt if dividend received from 25% or more EU-owned subsidiary.

(9) Interest only deductible to extent it exceeds tax-free dividend received. Will also be recaptured if subsequent tax-free gain.

As will be seen, the jurisdictions surveyed in which a participation exemption applies to both dividends and gains are Austria, Belgium, Denmark, Germany, Luxembourg, the Netherlands, Spain, Sweden and Switzerland. Hong Kong and Singapore do not tax foreign dividends and gains.

Controlled foreign company rules

25.5 The selected foreign investor jurisdictions in which a full participation exemption does not apply are Australia, Canada, Finland, France, Greece,

Ireland, Italy, Japan, Portugal and the USA. There are proposals for a full participation exemption in Australia and Italy.

The question then is whether controlled foreign company or similar anti-avoidance rules in non-participation exemption jurisdictions will make it ineffective for the foreign parent company to arrange for ownership of the UK subsidiary through an intermediate holding company in the above participation exemption jurisdictions, in order to defer home country tax on dividends and gains derived from the underlying UK subsidiary.

25.6 **Appendix 3** contains an overview of controlled foreign company rules. They apply in Australia, Canada, Denmark, France, Finland, Germany, Italy, Japan, Portugal, Spain, Sweden and the USA. In principle, passive income and gains of controlled foreign companies are taxable in all these jurisdictions which therefore tend to prevent the use of an intermediate holding company. However, it should be possible to successfully utilise an intermediate holding company for ownership of the UK subsidiary by an ultimate parent company resident in virtually all the above jurisdictions, namely:

(a) Australia (if current proposals are enacted);

(b) Canada;

(c) Finland;

(d) Greece (no CFC rules);

(e) Ireland (no CFC rules);

(f) Italy;

(g) Portugal.

For example:

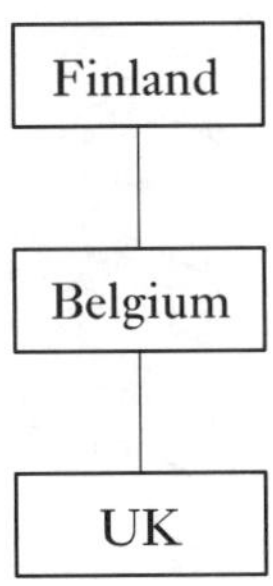

25.7 Other factors that will need to be taken into account before deciding on such an intermediate holding company are:

(a) registration and capital taxes in relation to the capital of the holding company;

(b) the deductibility in the holding company jurisdiction of interest on borrowings to acquire the UK subsidiary; and

(c) the rate of withholding tax on outward dividends paid by the holding company under a double tax treaty or under the EU Parent/Subsidiary Directive [90/435/EEC] – see Table 4 at paragraph **25.4** and **Appendix 5**.

It will also need to be ensured that the intermediate holding company is not resident in the home country or in the UK (see paragraph **2.2** et seq).

Tax implications in the foreign jurisdiction: individuals

25.8 The crucial question for foreign individuals is whether or not they should own the shares of the UK company directly or through an intermediate holding company. And if the latter whether it should be located in their jurisdiction of residence, in the UK, or in a third country.

In the case of direct ownership of the UK company, the key features are summarised in Table 5 below. It provides an overview of the position in each of the selected jurisdictions but the information should not be taken as exhaustive. The first column indicates whether or not controlled foreign company, or equivalent, rules apply to individuals owning shares in foreign companies.

TABLE 5 Foreign individual owns shares in UK company: key features

	CFC[(1)]	*Taxable dividends*[(2)]	*Taxable gains*[(3)]	*Deductible interest*
Australia	✓	✓	✓	✓
Austria	–	✓	✓	–
Belgium	✓[(7)]	✓	–	–
Canada	✓	✓	✓	✓
Denmark	✓	✓	✓	✓
Finland	✓	✓	✓	✓
France	✓	✓	✓	–
Germany	✓	✓	✓	✓[(5)]
Greece	–	✓	✓	–
Hong Kong	–	–	–	–
Ireland	✓[(8)]	✓	✓	✓
Italy	✓	✓	✓	–
Japan	✓	✓	✓	–
Luxembourg	–	✓	✓	✓[(5)]
Netherlands	✓[(7)]	✓	✓	–
Portugal	✓	✓	✓[(4)]	–
Singapore	–	–	–	–
Spain	✓	✓	✓	–
Sweden	✓	✓	✓	✓

	CFC(1)	*Taxable dividends*(2)	*Taxable gains* (3)	*Deductible interest*
Switzerland	–	✓	–	✓(5)
USA	✓	✓	✓	✓(6)

Notes (not exhaustive)

(1) CFC rules generally inapplicable if UK company's income is trading income.

(2) No credit available for underlying UK corporation tax.

(3) Purchaser will discount the share price re inherent gains. Gains often taxed at lower rates.

(4) Exempt if shares acquired before 1 January 2003.

(5) Limited to taxable dividends received.

(6) Limited to investment income.

(7) Limited type of CFC rules (see **Appendix 3**).

(8) CFC type rules apply to individuals only (see **Appendix 3**).

(9) Only where UK company carries on a trade and subject to detailed conditions.

25.9 Taking into account the factors above, as well as the implications of foreign holding companies discussed earlier in this Chapter and of UK holding companies discussed in **Chapter 26**, it may be useful to attempt to summarise the ownership vehicle options for foreign individuals.

What follows is necessarily an overview in relation to all jurisdictions rather than a case by case analysis. In all cases the individual's rate of tax in his or her home country is assumed to be 40%.

Example 36: Foreign individual owns UK business directly

UK branch profits	100
UK income tax	(40)
Home country tax – say 40% (less credit for UK tax)	–
Final net to foreign individual	60

It will be seen from the examples that follow that this structure achieves the lowest tax rate on profits as it avoids the cascading of taxes arising from multiple structures.

There are three possible disadvantages:

(a) Unlimited liability. That could possibly be resolved by operating as a limited liability partnership (LLP). An LLP would be transparent for UK tax purposes (see paragraph **15.3**). However it would also need to be accepted as transparent in the foreign individual's country of residence. As it is a separate legal entity, some foreign countries will treat it as such for their tax purposes so that transparency will not be achieved and extra taxes will therefore become payable when the foreign individual receives distributions from the partnership (see paragraph **15.7**). See also Example 38 at paragraph **25.10** for the special facility available to US individuals.

(b) UK capital gains tax will be payable when the foreign individual disposes of the UK permanent establishment although in most cases the rate of tax will be as low as 10% (see paragraph **30.2**). Payment of UK capital gains tax will be disadvantageous when it exceeds the capital gains tax payable in the individual's home country. (In contrast no tax will be payable if the foreign individual sells shares in a UK company operating the business but the purchaser will normally seek a discount in the share price for inherent taxes (see paragraph **29.2**.)

(c) Direct ownership of a UK business will expose the foreign individual to a potential liability to UK inheritance tax. However, business property relief will generally extinguish the liability [IHTA 1984, s 103].

25.10 The following corporate structures provide less attractive results in view of the fact that in all the selected jurisdictions, apart from Hong Kong (no tax on foreign dividends), and Singapore (no tax on unremitted foreign dividends), and the special option available to a US individual (see Example 38 below), there is a cascading effect of extra taxes arising from ultimate dividend distributions. However the additional factors at paragraph **25.11** et seq should also be referred to.

Example 37: Foreign individual owns UK company directly

UK profits	100
UK corporation tax	(30)
Dividend to foreign individual	70
Home country tax – say 40% (Hong Kong and Singapore: 0%)	(28)
Final net to foreign individual	42

Example 38

In the USA, the better result at Example 36 above could be achieved without the disadvantages summarised there. Under the US 'check the box' rules, the US individual can elect to treat the UK company as transparent for US tax purposes provided it is not a plc.

In this way limited liability and absence of UK capital gains tax on disposal would be achieved without the tax disadvantages of share ownership illustrated by Example 37. In addition, the UK tax rate on the profits is 30% compared to a marginal personal tax rate of 40%. This would benefit US individuals whose US tax rate was lower than 40%.

UK company:		
UK profits		100
UK corporation tax		(30)
Dividend to US individual		70
US individual:		
Profits of UK 'branch'	100	
US tax, say,	40	
Credit for UK tax	(30)	
US tax payable	10	(10)
Final net to US individual		60

Notes

(1) US state taxes ignored.

(2) The same result could be achieved by utilising a US corporation with a UK branch and the shareholders electing for S corporation status. The effect of this election (assuming the necessary conditions exist) is to make the US corporation transparent for US tax purposes.

However this structure has the disadvantage that a future UK purchaser may be unwilling to acquire the shares of a US company.

(3) As from 1 January 2004, US individuals are taxable at a maximum rate of 15% only, on dividends received from US companies; and on dividends received from foreign companies eligible to claim benefits under a comprehensive tax treaty with the US. In the example above, absent a 'check the box' election, the dividend of 70 from the UK company (whether or not a plc) taxed at 15% would result in a final net of just under 60.

Example 39: Foreign individual owns UK company through UK holding company

The same as Example 37 above (except for Hong Kong, Singapore and USA)	42

Example 40: Foreign individual owns UK company through home country company

	Participation exemption	*No participation exemption*
UK profits	100	100
UK corporation tax	(30)	(30)
Dividend to home company	70	70
Home company tax (less credit for UK tax)	–	(5)
Funds retained in home company	70	65

Ultimate dividend to foreign individual	70	65
Home country tax – say 40%	(28)	(26)
Final net to foreign individual (except for Hong Kong, Singapore and USA)	42	39

Example 41: Foreign individual owns UK company through third country company, say, the Netherlands

UK profits	100
UK corporation tax	(30)
Dividend to Nethco	70
Dutch tax	–
Dutch withholding tax on dividend paid, say 15%	(10)
	60
Home country tax – say 40% (less credit for Dutch WHT)	(18)
Final net to foreign individual (except for Hong Kong, Singapore and USA)	42

Additional factors

25.11 Table 5 at paragraph **25.8** indicates that a number of the selected jurisdictions do not permit resident individuals to deduct interest on borrowings for the acquisition of shares.

So when a UK company is to be acquired, the only possibility of obtaining an interest deduction will be for the foreign individual to make the acquisition through a company, principally a UK holding company (see **Chapter 26**), but possibly a home country or third country company for which interest is tax-deductible.

25.12 Table 5 at paragraph **25.8** identifies that in most of the selected jurisdictions a resident individual will be taxable on dividends and gains realised from the shares of a UK company. Tax on the dividends and gains could at least be deferred if the UK company was owned by:

(a) a UK holding company; or

(b) a company resident in one of the other jurisdictions indicated in Table 4 at paragraph **25.4** where dividends and gains would be tax-free.

25.13 It will be seen from Table 4 at paragraph **25.4** and Table 5 at paragraph **25.8** that jurisdictions that do not tax company dividends and gains do, in most but not all cases, tax dividends and gains of resident individuals. So in those jurisdictions, individuals will generally utilise a home country holding company to own local and foreign subsidiaries. In this way home country taxes on dividends and gains are deferred. As will be seen from Examples 37 and 40 (see paragraph **25.10**), this should be no more tax-expensive on ultimate repatriation to the individual. Until then, funds that have borne a lower tax rate are retained in the home country holding company for reinvestment.

In general there are no accumulated earnings taxes that would prevent retention of earnings in the home country holding company.

25.14 Utilisation of a home country holding company may be preferable to a third country holding company in a foreign jurisdiction. If the individual's home country has controlled foreign company rules these may tax the individual on the dividends or gains realised by the foreign holding company (see **Appendix 3** and discussion above in relation to companies).

25.15 For individuals resident in jurisdictions with no participation exemption for income and gains, a third country holding company in, say, Belgium, Luxembourg or the Netherlands could be considered. However if controlled foreign company rules exist in the individual's home country, they could negate any benefit by immediately taxing the individual on the dividends and gains realised by the foreign holding company, although not in all jurisdictions (see **Appendix 3** and Table 5 at paragraph **25.8**).

25.16 It will be appreciated that a holding company will simply defer home country taxes otherwise payable. Once the individual realises its accumulated income and gains (by way of dividend, liquidation distribution or disposal of the holding company's shares), home country taxes will be payable by the individual in most cases (see Table 5 at paragraph **25.8**).

25.17 However share sales, and liquidation distributions if taxed as capital gains, may be taxable at a lower rate than dividends or even tax-exempt as in Belgium, Hong Kong, Singapore and Switzerland (see Table 5 at paragraph **25.8**). In this way the UK profits might be ultimately repatriated to the foreign individual at a lower tax rate than through dividends.

26 UK holding company

Overview

- UK holding company less essential than previously in view of internationalisation of both group relief and inter-group asset transfers.
- However UK holding company will still achieve UK interest deductibility on acquisition of targets, debt/equity treatment on group basis, and substantial shareholding exemption for capital gains.

26.1 Even though they are not headed by a UK holding company, UK subsidiaries may now transfer assets between themselves tax-free [TCGA 1992, s 171] and surrender group relief between themselves [ICTA 1988, s 402 et seq]. However apart from commercial reasons, there still remain three main tax reasons for foreign investors to utilise a UK holding company.

26.2 First, interest payable by the UK holding company on borrowings raised to acquire or finance its UK subsidiaries will be group-relievable against their profits [ICTA 1988, s 403(1)(b)]. Interest on borrowings raised by a non-UK company cannot be offset against profits of its UK subsidiaries and, in relation to the jurisdictions surveyed, will not qualify for interest deductibility in Austria, Hong Kong or Singapore. With regard to the Netherlands, the European Court of Justice has ruled this to be discriminatory but counteracting legislation is likely (see Table 4 at paragraph **25.4**).

If any interest deductibility is to be achieved, at least for financing the acquisition of UK targets, borrowing through a UK holding company is the only solution for corporate investors in these four jurisdictions.

While the rest of the jurisdictions surveyed do allow domestic companies to deduct interest on acquisition financing, it may still be advantageous for the borrowings to be taken through a UK holding company. While UK corporate tax rates are generally lower (except in the case of Ireland and Finland), and so the tax benefit could be lower, there may be no local taxable profits to absorb the interest.

26.3 Second, for foreign investing companies in countries with a tax on capital gains and no participation exemption, gains realised on the sale of trading subsidiaries will generally be free of tax to the UK holding company following the substantial shareholdings legislation [TCGA 1992, s 192AA, Sch 7AC]. This could afford an advantage to investing companies from the following jurisdictions: Australia, Canada, Finland, France, Greece, Ireland, Italy, Japan, Portugal and the USA – see Table 4 at paragraph **25.4** – (although controlled foreign company rules may have the effect of taxing the gain in the hands of residents of some of these countries (see **Appendix 3** and the discussion at paragraph **25.5** et seq)).

26.4 However rather than owning the UK subsidiary through a UK holding company, or a holding company in a third country jurisdiction, it may be advantageous for the foreign investing company to own the UK subsidiary directly for all or any of the following reasons:

(a) A participation exemption may apply.

(b) Interest on the acquisition funding will be borne in the foreign jurisdiction. There may be situations where this is more advantageous than its being borne in the UK or in some third country jurisdiction.

(c) In some jurisdictions, relief for double taxation is limited where foreign subsidiaries, such as in the UK, are owned through a multiple tier of companies.

26.5 A third reason for a UK holding company is that where a number of UK subsidiaries exist, it will allow for debt/equity ratios to be measured on a consolidated basis (see paragraph **19.4**).

Tax implications in the foreign jurisdiction

26.6 These are included in the discussion above.

Foreign individuals

26.7 A foreign individual may be similarly motivated to utilise a UK holding company to acquire or hold UK subsidiaries for the same reasons as a foreign company; namely, deductibility of interest in the UK and freedom from tax on gains on realisation of its underlying trading subsidiaries.

27 Acquiring a UK business, including post-acquisition reorganisation

Overview

- Asset acquisitions generally preferable to share acquisitions.
- But vendors will usually prefer share disposals to asset disposals.
- Stamp duty on asset acquisitions higher than on share acquisitions.
- Consideration should be given to asset acquisitions being made by foreign, rather than UK, entity.
- Share acquisition effected by Spanish or US group company, could be treated as acquisition of underlying assets in those jurisdictions.
- Reorganisation of UK target post-acquisition may be desirable from tax and business viewpoints, with consequential UK and foreign tax implications.

27.1 Rather than starting a new UK business, many foreign investors acquire existing UK businesses.

Established foreign-owned UK groups may do so by having the acquisition made through their existing UK group. However it may be preferable to do so through the home country group or through a third country subsidiary. In closely owned businesses there may be circumstances in which the individual shareholders make the acquisition personally.

Reference should be made to **Chapters 25** and **26** for a detailed discussion of the UK and home country tax implications of these alternative acquisition vehicles. The main purpose of this Chapter is to discuss the UK tax implications of the acquisition.

The discussion focuses on the alternatives of acquiring the assets of the business or acquiring the shares. There then follows a section on post-acquisition structuring and planning.

In general the purchaser will wish to directly acquire the business and its constituent assets whereas the seller will wish to sell shares. This tension has recently increased as UK purchasers can now obtain amortisation deductions for intangible assets including goodwill (see paragraph **21.5(c)**).

Reference to the foreign tax implications is made where relevant.

Alternative acquisition vehicles

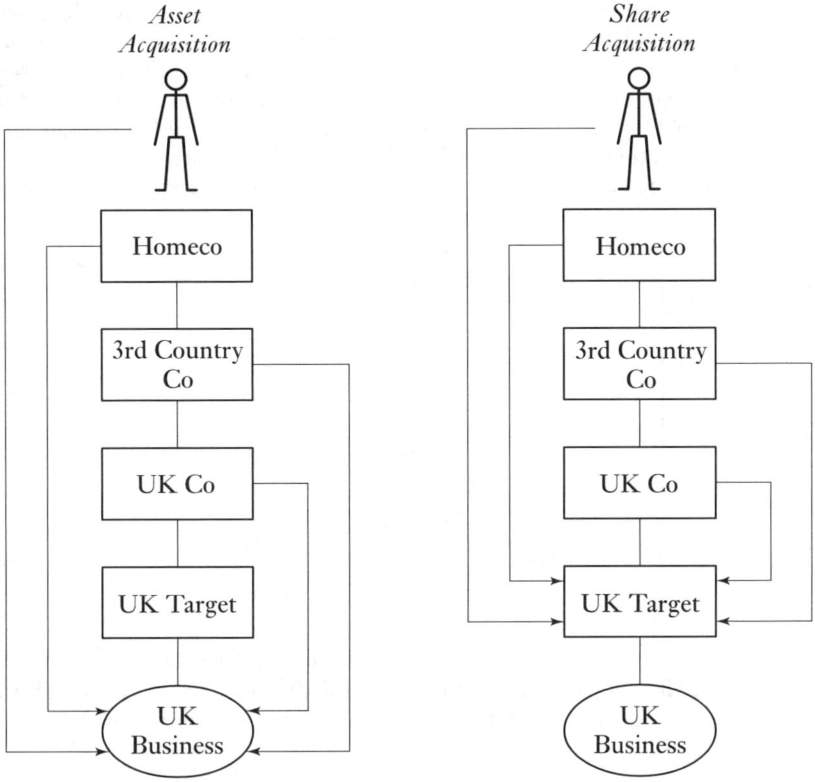

Acquisition of assets

27.2 The base tax cost of the assets will be the market value at which they are acquired from the vendor. In general this will be higher than the base cost of the assets underlying a share purchase although in present markets the reverse may sometimes be the case.

27.3 Now that the UK allows tax amortisation of intangible assets (see paragraph **21.5(c)**) it compares favourably with most other foreign jurisdictions in this regard. Broadly speaking all jurisdictions including the UK allow for amortisation over useful life, generally in accordance with accounting rules.

However there are exceptions. For example Japan and the Netherlands allow purchased goodwill to be amortised over 5 years. In the UK the norm would be 20 years.

In such cases it may be good tax planning policy for the business assets, or some of them, to be acquired by the foreign purchaser rather than by a UK company. The acquired assets could then be used by the foreign purchaser in a UK permanent establishment; or, in appropriate cases, rented or licensed to a UK subsidiary company that would carry on the UK business. While the ongoing profits would be liable to UK tax and the assets depreciated and amortised on UK tax lines, the amortisation costs in the foreign jurisdiction could create initial tax losses for offsetting against foreign profits. Obviously this technique would only be advantageous in jurisdictions which allowed the losses of the UK permanent establishment to be offset against home country profits (see Table 1 at paragraph **13.3(b)**).

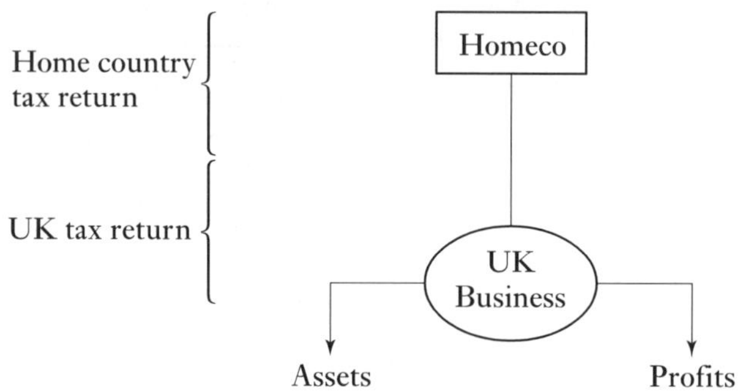

27.4 Leaving aside differences in amortisation or depreciation rates if, because of significant asset acquisitions, such deductions are large enough to create initial tax losses, these may be more valuable in the foreign jurisdiction than in the UK.

In that case the acquisition should be made by the foreign investor group which would operate the UK business through a UK permanent establishment.

27.5 Reverting to the situation where the business is acquired by a UK company or permanent establishment, it will be important for the purchaser to include the breakdown of the total purchase price in the purchase contract. While the UK Revenue has the statutory power to reallocate or apportion a consideration over the assets on a just and reasonable basis (see for example CAA 2001, s 562; TCGA 1992, s 52(4) and FA 2002, Sch 29 para 105), the Revenue is unlikely to interfere with any arm's length transaction between unconnected parties unless it is clearly artificial (eg see *EV Booth Holdings Ltd v Buckwell* [1980] STC 578).

27.6 Acquired assets qualifying as intangible property under FA 2002, Sch 29, may be rolled over against gains on intangible assets realised by the UK purchasing company or permanent establishment, or its UK group. This facility applies to gains on sale of both pre- and post- 31 March 2002 intangible property (see paragraph **21.5(f)**). However the rollover claim will reduce future amortisation deductions on the intangible property assets purchased.

27.7 In the case of property and fixed plant and machinery, their purchase price may be used in a rollover relief claim in respect of gains realised from a disposal of the same class of assets or of any assets qualifying for capital gains tax rollover relief under TCGA 1992, s 155.

27.8 In situations where the foreign investor acquires the business through a UK company with accumulated tax losses, the past losses may be available for offset against future profits from the acquired business [ICTA 1988, s 393(1)]. This will only be possible if the acquisition constitutes an expansion of the loss-making trade rather than a new business; for example see *Cannon Industries Ltd v Edwards* (1965) 42 TC 625 and *George Humphries & Co v Cook* (1934) 19 TC 121. (In fact the same loss offset could be achieved with a share purchase as the business underlying the purchase could be transferred to the UK group company with accumulated tax losses.)

Stamp duty

27.9 Until 1 December 2003, the purchaser will be liable to pay stamp duty on dutiable assets, typically, property, debts etc. It is also possible for know-how, stock and moveable plant to be transferred by delivery without stamp duty (see **Chapter 24**).

27.10 Where the purchaser assumes the vendor's liabilities, the amount of the assumed liabilities will be treated as consideration for stamp duty purposes, in addition to the actual cash consideration.

27.11 A number of fairly common assets are now exempt from duty. For example, goodwill transferred after 22 April 2002 and intellectual property from 28 March 2000. In appropriate cases, it may therefore be possible to achieve a useful stamp duty saving by justifiably reallocating the split of the total consideration in favour of goodwill etc. Knowhow is also exempt as it passes by delivery of the relevant documents, material, etc.

27.12 The amount allocated to intellectual property is required by statute to be made on a 'just and reasonable' basis [FA 2000, Sch 34]. The attribution of the total consideration to assets other than intellectual property should be made on a sensible basis, although not necessarily by reference to the market value of each asset. However, professional advisers should note the Court of Appeal decision in *Saunders v Edwards* [1987] 1 WLR 1116 which held that a solicitor involved in making a blatantly 'artificial' allocation was guilty of professional misconduct.

27.13 From 1 December 2003, stamp duty is abolished, except in relation to marketable securities and partnership interests. Transactions in land will be liable to stamp duty land tax, at the rates shown in **Chapter 24**. However, transfers of commercial property for a consideration of no more than £150,000 will be taxable at the zero rate, as will all commercial property within a disadvantaged area.

VAT

27.14 The acquisition of the business should not be subject to VAT, as a result of the transfer of going concern provisions [VAT (Special Provisions) Order, SI 1995/1268 art 5]. If let property (upon which the vendor has opted to tax) is to be transferred under these provisions without VAT, the purchaser must elect to opt to tax the property before the transfer (or any earlier tax point for VAT, eg the receipt of cash consideration).

27.15 Where the transfer of assets does not fall within these rules, the vendor should account for VAT on the purchase price. The recovery of this VAT would depend on the VAT status of the underlying business. Thus, for example, the VAT would be fully recoverable if the transferred business is fully taxable but only partly recoverable on the transfer of a partly exempt business.

Acquisition of shares (or loan accounts)

27.16 It needs to be determined whether the share (and, if relevant, loan) acquisition should be made by a UK or foreign company or, in the case of closely-owned groups, by a foreign individual. See **Chapters 25** and **26** for a discussion on ownership vehicles, and paragraph **27.1** above.

27.17 The tax base cost of the target company's assets is likely to be lower than the current market value had the assets been purchased directly.

27.18 The target company may have acquired intangible property post 31 March 2002 (or acquired it from a connected person who acquired it after that date). If so, profits on sales of intangible property realised by the acquiring UK company, or a member of its UK group, may be offset in a reinvestment relief claim, against the written down value of the intangible property owned by the target company provided that at least 75% of its ordinary shares are acquired [FA 2002, Sch 29 paras 56, 57] – see paragraph **21.5(g)**.

27.19 In a few cases it may be possible to treat the share purchase as an asset purchase in the foreign jurisdiction. For example:

USA

27.20 A US corporation or individual could treat the purchase of the UK company's shares as a purchase of the underlying assets by so electing under the 'check the box' rules, provided that the UK target is not a plc.

Spain

27.21 If a Spanish company acquires the UK target, it may amortise the goodwill underlying the share price, at the rate of 5% per year, provided that the target carries on an active business.

27.22 The target company's inherent liabilities, including actual and potential tax liabilities, will be assumed. As part of the contractual arrangements, tax warranties and indemnities should be obtained from the vendor.

27.23 Where the target has accumulated unutilised trading losses, Schedule D Case III deficits, capital losses, surplus ACT, and surplus foreign tax credits ('eligible unrelieved foreign tax' under ICTA 1988, s 806B), these may be available to the purchaser. However on a change of ownership some of these items are subject to potential disallowance under: ICTA 1988, s 768 (trading losses); Corporation Tax (Treatment of Unrelieved Surplus Advance Corporation Tax) Regulations, SI 1999/358 reg 16 (surplus ACT) and TCGA 1992, Sch 7A (capital losses).

27.24 The target company may own a US subsidiary or subsidiaries. Article 10.3 of the new UK/US tax treaty provides in certain circumstances for a 0% US withholding tax on dividends paid by a US subsidiary to its UK parent company. However, article 23 of the treaty contains extensive and complex limitation of benefits provisions. In particular the 0% rate is denied where the foreign purchaser's tax treaty with the US imposes a dividend withholding tax higher than the 0% US–UK rate. Apart from its treaty with Mexico, no other US treaty currently provides for a 0% rate although it is currently proposed or under discussion with tax treaty partners in Australia, Japan and the Netherlands. Nevertheless the 0% rate will still continue to be available if it can be demonstrated that the foreign purchaser's acquisition of the UK company did not have the obtaining of the 0% withholding rate as one of its principal purposes. In most cases the absence of this treaty shopping motive should be demonstrable. It will be necessary to apply to the US Internal Revenue Services for the 0% rate. It is understood that claims will be dealt with expeditiously.

27.25 Where the UK target owns French, German or Spanish subsidiaries, the 0% withholding tax applying on dividends flowing to the UK parent company under the EU Parent/Subsidiary Directive may be denied under domestic anti-treaty shopping provisions applying in each country. Broadly speaking this denial will not apply if the ultimate parent company is resident in an EU jurisdiction; or if it can be demonstrated that reduction of withholding tax was not the principal purpose of the acquisition.

27.26 For these reasons amongst others, it may be advantageous to transfer US, French, German or Spanish subsidiaries from the UK target to the foreign parent company or another foreign affiliate (see paragraph **27.28(a)**).

Stamp duty

27.27 Stamp duty at the rate of 0.5% will be payable on the purchase price of the UK company's shares. In effect the duty is payable on all of the company's assets less liabilities. This compares with a stamp duty at a maximum rate of 4% (see paragraph **24.24**) on the gross value of the dutiable assets when the assets are purchased directly. After 30 November 2003, the only dutiable assets will be land, marketable securities and partnership interests. Bearer instruments will, however, remain subject to stamp duty.

Post-acquisition reorganisation

27.28 The foreign purchaser may wish to remove assets or liabilities from the acquired UK target company following its acquisition for any of the following reasons. The tax consequences are discussed at paragraph **27.29** et seq:

(a) Reducing withholding taxes on dividend, interest or royalty income where the foreign purchaser's tax treaty with the source country provides for lower rates; for example, see paragraphs **27.24** and **27.25**.

(b) Lowering overall taxes by reducing the UK tax base of the target/increasing the tax base of the foreign parent or group.

(c) On ultimate disposal, the UK target's subsidiaries may not qualify for the substantial shareholdings exemption in the UK because, for example, they do not carry on a trading business; but will qualify in the foreign parent company's jurisdiction. For example, Belgium, Germany, Luxembourg or Switzerland (see **Appendix 5**).

(d) The UK target may own foreign subsidiaries that could be grouped in the tax jurisdiction of the foreign parent or its foreign subsidiaries. In most cases ownership under the UK group would disqualify the foreign subsidiary from tax consolidation in its own jurisdiction of residence; and it could not be included in a UK group relief claim except to the extent of any UK permanent establishment (see paragraph **13.3(d)**).

(e) The UK target may own foreign subsidiaries whose profits are subject to apportionment under UK controlled foreign company rules. The foreign parent company's jurisdiction may not legislate for controlled foreign companies, or may be more lenient towards them (see **Appendix 3**).

(f) The UK target's potential loss-making activities or loss-making subsidiaries (such as start-ups) may attract greater tax relief in the foreign jurisdiction than in the UK. In some circumstances the losses may be deductible in more than one jurisdiction.

(g) The UK target's potential profitable activities could be transferred to a foreign group company where the profits would be taxed at lower rate than in the UK, or where they could be offset by losses.

However there would be no point to this if the activities continued in the UK as invariably the foreign transferee would continue the trade in the UK through a taxable permanent establishment (see **Chapter 13**). To avoid this situation it would be necessary to move the management and staff (and any manufacturing facilities) out of the UK.

(h) Assets transferred to the foreign group could attract tax depreciation in the foreign jurisdiction based on current market values.

(i) Foreign currency loans or deposits may be taxed more leniently with regard to fluctuations. For example consideration could be given to transferring long-term assets expected to increase in value to a Hong Kong affiliate since Hong Kong does not tax capital gains (see paragraph **19.21**).

(j) It may be beneficial for borrowings of the UK target to be taken on by the foreign parent company or group if the consequent interest payments attract higher tax relief abroad than in the UK.

(k) Nevertheless consideration needs to be given to the funding of the repayments. For example it may be necessary for the UK company to pay dividends to its foreign parent so that it can service the borrowings. Receipt of the dividends may attract a tax liability in the foreign jurisdiction.

(l) It is also important to consider the foreign currency aspects of the borrowings (see paragraph **19.16** et seq):

  (i) to the UK target (if the borrowings are not in sterling) as the borrowings will be extinguished, and

  (ii) to the foreign affiliate if the currency of the borrowing is foreign to it.

(m) It is probable that repayment of the borrowings will be financed by new share capital of the UK target. Clearly this will increase the tax base of the UK group. However alternative funding possibilities could be new borrowings or asset sales (third party or inter-group).

Tax consequences: disposal of assets

27.29 The assets transferred by the UK target will normally attract a tax liability on disposal based on market value [TCGA 1992, s 17(1)(a)]. The transfer of qualifying trading subsidiaries may be exempt from tax under the substantial shareholdings exemption [TCGA 1992, Sch 7AC]. Gains may be deferred by rollover reliefs [TCGA 1992, s 155 and FA 2002, Sch 29 para 37], or capital losses [TCGA 1992 s 2(1)(a)].

27.30 Prior Treasury consent under ICTA 1988, s 765(1)(d) is required for the transfer by the UK company of a non-UK subsidiary unless the purchaser is a resident of an EU jurisdiction [ICTA 1988, ss 765(1)(d), 765A].

Tax consequences: the consideration

27.31 Thought needs to be given to the consideration received. Basically, this could take four forms:

(a) Cash:

  (i) There would be no direct tax consequences to the foreign purchaser apart from the ongoing interest cost. It would need to be ensured that interest on any borrowings was tax deductible in the foreign jurisdiction.

(b) Inter-company loans:

   (i) Similar to cash since UK transfer pricing rules would require the upstream loans to carry interest (see paragraph **19.23**). Depending on the currency of the loan, taxable exchange differences would normally arise in the UK (annual revaluation); or in the foreign borrowing jurisdiction (normally annually assuming differences are taxable and tax-deductible there) (see paragraph **19.16** et seq).

(c) Sales of assets to the UK target:

   (i) Depending on the nature of the assets, consideration would need to be given to the taxability of any gain to the foreign affiliate and the tax deductibility (capital allowances or amortisation) to the UK target.

   (ii) Future flows of income from the asset would also require consideration.

(d) Dividends paid by the UK target:

   (i) Cash dividends could be paid to the acquiring foreign parent company in order to remove assets and income from the UK or simply to furnish the foreign parent with cash resources. These will attract no UK tax. In the foreign jurisdiction the dividend may be tax-free as a result of a participation exemption (see paragraph **28.5** and Table 4 at paragraph **25.4**).

   (ii) In some jurisdictions, receipt of the dividend from profits accrued before the acquisition may be treated as a reduction in the purchase price of the shares and so free of tax; or the tax payable may be reduced by tax credits for the UK corporation tax previously paid on the underlying profits.

   (iii) The dividend could instead be paid in specie by transferring assets of the UK target company to the foreign parent. The tax ramifications would be the same as a cash dividend, but UK tax would generally arise based on the value of the assets transferred in specie (see paragraph **27.29**).

Transferring assets and liabilities from the target

27.32 It may be advantageous to remove assets or liabilities from underneath the target company and to transfer them directly to the UK acquirer for similar reasons to those summarised at paragraph **27.28**.

27.33 The tax consequences will be similar to those summarised at paragraph **27.29** et seq, albeit in the opposite direction.

27.34 However, two special features should be mentioned:

(a) It may be that the target group owns UK subsidiaries through a foreign parent company. There is no need to transfer these to the UK group to secure group relief which is now available outside the ownership of a UK holding company (see paragraph **26.1**).

(b) If the UK acquirer borrows funds to acquire the assets, it will need to be ensured that this is for an allowable purpose, otherwise the interest payable will be disallowed [FA 1996, Sch 9 para 13] – see paragraph **19.22**. The UK Revenue has issued guidance lines in its Manuals. In particular, CT12674(b) states that the anti-avoidance provisions will not normally apply where a company borrows to acquire shares in companies, whether in the UK or overseas, or to pay dividends, provided that the borrowings are not structured in an artificial way. CT12686(a) states that paragraph 13 will not normally be applied where relief for the interest is obtained in more than one jurisdiction ('double dipping') unless the structure has uncommercial features.

28 Repatriation from UK permanent establishments and companies

Overview

- UK taxes do not arise on repatriation of profits.
- Therefore consideration needs to be concentrated on foreign tax implications of alternatives such as dividends, repurchase of shares, upstream loans and liquidation distributions.

28.1 This Chapter discusses techniques for repatriating profits from a UK permanent establishment or company. It deals with the UK and foreign tax implications for foreign companies and individuals.

In general there are few UK tax implications in view of the absence of taxes on distributions. However it should be borne in mind that distributions, whether by dividend, repurchase of shares or liquidation, will remove assets, and the income they generate, from the UK permanent establishment or company and transfer those assets and consequent income to the foreign jurisdiction. This factor should be considered with regard to the respective tax positions in the UK and the foreign jurisdiction.

It is assumed that the UK permanent establishment or company is directly owned by the foreign company or individual. Reference should be made to **Chapters 25** and **26** for the repatriation consequences of indirect ownership through a UK, home country or third country holding company.

UK permanent establishments

28.2 Remittance of the UK permanent establishment's profits to the foreign head office will carry no tax consequences in either the UK or the foreign jurisdiction. The profits will have been taxed and no further UK taxes arise on their remittance.

The rest of this Chapter considers repatriation of the profits of UK companies.

Dividends payable to foreign shareholders

28.3 There is no withholding tax on outward UK dividends and advance corporation tax ('ACT') no longer applies. ICTA 1988, s 20 charges dividends and other distributions to income tax but FA 1995, s 128(1) and (3) limit the income tax liability of non-UK resident individuals with respect to Schedule F tax on UK dividends to the amount of the tax credit.

28.4 Dividends received by non-resident companies without a permanent establishment in the UK are similarly protected from income tax by FA 2003, s 150. ICTA 1988, s 208 exempts distributions from corporation tax. Those companies that had surplus unrelieved ACT at 6 April 1999 may continue to set it off against their corporation tax liability within the previous limits, but only to the extent that it exceeds the shadow ACT (the ACT that would have been payable on their distributions had ACT not been abolished).

28.5 Table 4 at paragraph **25.4** summarises the tax treatment of the dividends received by a foreign parent company in the jurisdictions surveyed.

28.6 The UK has negotiated certain tax treaties that provide for a refund of 50% of the tax credit attaching to the dividend when it is paid to a 10% or more corporate shareholder of the UK subsidiary. Those treaties are with: Belgium, Italy, Luxembourg, Netherlands, Norway, Sweden, Switzerland and USA (old treaty).

The treaties generally provide for a 5% UK tax to be deducted from the sum of the dividend and the tax credit refund. The effect of the 5% tax is to virtually cancel out the amount of the refund. In the case of Norway, the withholding tax is 10%, which does cancel out the whole of the credit. (The new US treaty, incidentally, withdraws entitlement to the tax credit refund and it is to be expected that the refund will also be withdrawn when new treaties are renegotiated with the above countries.)

	£	£
UK subsidiary's profits		100.00
UK corporation tax		(30.00)
Cash dividend		70.00
Tax credit reclaimable by overseas parent:		
Tax credit, 70 × 10/90	7.78	
50% thereof	3.89	
Less:		
5% UK withholding tax on (70 + 3.89)	(3.69)	0.20
Cash dividend + refund		70.20
Effective UK tax rate (approximately)		29.80

28.7 There is a case pending before the European Court of Justice, *Océ van der Grinten NV v IRC* (C-58/01) in which the Dutch appellant company asserts that the 5% tax contravenes the EU Parent/Subsidiary Directive (90/435/EEC). At the date of writing the Advocate-General has given his opinion, concluding that the 5% tax is not in breach of the Directive. It is likely that the European Court of Justice will follow this opinion. If so, the benefit of the tax credit refund is negligible, amounting to a net refund of 0.2% of the UK subsidiary's pre- tax profits.

Payment of ACT: foreign-owned UK companies

28.8 Before the abolition of ACT, UK subsidiaries of foreign parent companies were at a disadvantage to subsidiaries of UK-owned groups in that ACT was payable on dividends paid, whereas UK-owned subsidiaries could pay dividends free of ACT by virtue of a group election under the former ICTA 1988, s 247. Where the ACT could fully offset mainstream corporation tax this resulted in a cash flow disadvantage to foreign-owned UK subsidiaries as a result of the earlier payment of tax. Where the ACT could not fully offset mainstream corporation tax surplus ACT resulted and could constitute a permanent loss of tax.

28.9 The European Court of Justice ruled in March 2001 that the above disadvantages were discriminatory to EU-owned UK subsidiaries (*Hoechst AG and Hoechst UK Ltd v IRC and A-G* (Case C-410/98), and *Metallgeselschaft Ltd v IRC and A-G* (Case C-397/98)). Claims for compensation are being dealt with by way of a Group Litigation Order.

28.10 In those cases where the parent company was entitled to a refund of 50% of the tax credit attaching to the UK dividend under a tax treaty with the UK (see above) the Revenue had asserted that there was no loss of tax overall. However, this argument was rejected by Park J in the High Court in January 2003 in the case of *Pirelli Cable Holding NV v IRC* [2003] EWHC 32 (Ch), [2003] STC 250. The nub of the decision was that the ACT paid by the UK company is different from the tax credit attaching to the dividend. Furthermore, that the UK subsidiary and its parent company are two separate entities that cannot be viewed as one. The UK Revenue has appealed against the decision.

28.11 The decision so far relates to EU discrimination. Moreover, a similar argument is being made by parent companies resident in jurisdictions with which the UK has entered into a double tax treaty containing an appropriate non-discrimination article. The argument is that the UK subsidiary was subjected to a more burdensome tax requirement than a UK-owned company in having to pay ACT in advance of its mainstream corporation tax liability (see article 24.5 of the OECD Model Convention, **Appendix 1**). These treaty non-discrimination claims are also being dealt with under the same Group Litigation Order as mentioned at paragraph **28.9**.

Dividends payable to foreign individuals

28.12 Dividends receivable from UK-resident companies are chargeable to income tax under Schedule F [ICTA 1988, s 20(1)]. Subject to the terms of a double tax treaty between the UK and the individual's country of residence, the non-resident individual in receipt of a UK dividend is not entitled to the tax credit [ICTA 1988, s 231(1)]. Nonetheless, non-residents are treated as having paid income tax at the Schedule F ordinary rate of 10% [ICTA 1988, s 233(1)]. This amounts to the same thing. This deemed payment covers the individual's liability up to the higher-rate threshold but is not, however, refundable [ICTA 1988, s 233(1)(b)].

In principle non-resident individuals liable to income tax are chargeable at the lower, basic and higher rates of tax. An individual in receipt of sufficient UK dividend income would therefore be chargeable to additional income tax as soon as the higher-rate threshold was crossed.

28.13 However FA 1995, s 128 comes to the rescue here. It limits the non-resident's liability on Schedule F income to the amount of the tax credit.

> *Example 42*
>
> Thelonious is a non-resident with a wide portfolio of UK stocks. In the year 2003/04 he receives net UK dividends of £27,000. For income tax purposes, he is treated as having received £30,000 but as having paid £30,000 @ 10% = £3,000 of income tax. This corresponds exactly to the tax credit of £3,000 (£27,000 x 1/9) to which a UK resident would have been entitled. He is not liable to tax at the basic or higher rates on this income.
>
> This apparent generosity is no doubt due to the practical difficulties the Inland Revenue would have in collecting any additional liability.

There are two exceptions to the rule restricting tax credits to UK residents.

ICTA 1988, s 278

28.14 A non-resident individual who has claimed UK personal allowances under ICTA 1988, s 278 is thereby entitled to the same dividend tax credit as a UK-resident individual [ICTA 1988, s 232(1)].

28.15 Individuals who are entitled to claim personal allowances under s 278 are those falling into one or more of the following categories:

(a) Commonwealth citizens;

(b) EEA nationals;

(c) persons currently or formerly in the service of the Crown;

(d) persons employed in the service of a missionary society;

(e) persons employed in the service of a protected territory;

(f) residents of the Isle of Man or the Channel Islands;

(g) previous residents of the UK who are resident abroad for reasons of health (either their own or that of members of their family living with them); and

(h) widows or widowers of former Crown servants.

Treaty entitlements to tax credits

28.16 Approximately one-half of the UK's double tax treaties entitle a non-resident individual in receipt of a UK dividend to the actual payment of a tax credit. However each such treaty invariably reserves the UK's right to charge income tax at a rate of 15% (occasionally at 20% or 25%) on the total of the dividend and tax credit. Statutory authority for the charging of income tax in this situation is contained in FA 1995, s 128(1)(b) and (4)(a) and limits UK income tax on a non-resident's 'excluded income' [FA 1995, s 128(2) and (3)] (which includes Schedule F income), to the amount of the tax credit.

Set out below are the relevant double tax treaties providing for the tax-credit refund, together with a calculation demonstrating that the refund is in fact absorbed by the UK income tax liability. Where the UK withholding tax is not 15%, the appropriate rate is indicated.

Australia
Austria
Belgium (20%)
Belize
Bosnia and Herzegovina[2]
Brunei
Canada
Croatia[2]
Cyprus
Denmark
Fiji
France
Gambia
Iceland
India
Indonesia
Ireland
Italy
Jamaica
Japan
Kenya
Kiribati
Luxembourg
Macedonia[2]
Malawi
Malta
Mauritius
The Netherlands
New Zealand
Philippines (25%)
Poland
Romania
Serbia and Montenegro[2]
Slovenia[2]
Solomon Islands
Spain
Sudan
Sweden
Switzerland
Thailand
Trinidad and Tobago (20%)
Tuvalu
US (existing, but not new)[1]
Zambia
Zimbabwe (20%)

Notes

(1) The treaty signed on 24 July 2001, which is yet to take effect, does not allow for a tax-credit refund.

(2) The treaty with the former Yugoslavia applies. Negotiations are under way with Croatia, Slovenia and Serbia and Montenegro for replacement treaties.

Example 43

Schilperoort, who is a resident of the Netherlands, receives a dividend of £981 from a UK plc. He has no other income taxable in the UK. Under the

UK/Netherlands treaty, he is entitled to a refund of the associated tax credit, subject to tax of 15% on the sum of the dividend and credit.

Net dividend received	£981
Tax credit (one-ninth)	£109
Gross amount receivable	£1,090
Withholding tax @ 15%	£163.50

As the treaty cannot impose additional taxation, the net result is that the withholding tax is limited to the amount of the tax credit, thus negating the refund entirely.

Since the amount of the tax credit is 10% of the gross dividend, it is in fact self-evident that a withholding tax of 10% or more will render the refund ineffective. It is a moot point whether this last vestige of the imputation system is unlawful within the EC.

Foreign tax implications

Dividends received

28.17 In virtually all the jurisdictions surveyed, the dividend received by an individual will be fully liable to tax with no credit for the corporation tax paid by the UK company (see Table 5 at paragraph **25.8**).

This compares disadvantageously with a foreign corporate recipient in whose hands the dividend will either be tax exempt, or taxable but with a credit for the corporation tax paid by the UK company (see Table 4 at paragraph **25.4**). It is for this reason that foreign individuals will generally be in a better tax position if they own their shares in a UK company through a local or foreign holding company insofar as the repatriated funds are retained in the holding company (see paragraph **25.10**, Examples 40 and 41).

Repurchase or repayment of shares

28.18 To the extent that the payments by the UK subsidiary exceed its paid-up share capital, the excess will constitute a distribution [ICTA 1988, s 209(2)(b)]. (The provisions of ICTA 1988, s 219 under which the distribution treatment is negated are not relevant as the foreign parent company, being the vendor of the shares, will not qualify as a UK resident under ICTA 1988, s 220(1).) In any event, no UK tax will arise on the repurchase or repayment (see paragraph **28.1**).

The treatment of the share repurchase or repayment in the home country of the foreign investor requires separate study in each jurisdiction but in general it is treated as a dividend.

Liquidation distributions

28.19 ICTA 1988, s 209(1) provides that distributions in respect of share capital in a winding up do not constitute distributions for tax purposes. From the foreign tax viewpoint, however, the receipt of the liquidation distribution will generally constitute a disposal of the shares of the UK subsidiary.

Referring to Table 4 at paragraph **25.4**, in those jurisdictions where there is a participation exemption in respect of dividends and capital gains, the receipt of the liquidation distribution by a foreign company will be tax-free.

28.20 However in other jurisdictions the liquidation distribution will generally constitute a taxable disposal of the shares. Foreign tax credits will not attach to the distribution in respect of UK corporation tax paid on the profits underlying it, and this will also be the case for foreign individuals receiving liquidation distributions. (The USA is an exception in that liquidation distributions received are treated as a dividend to which foreign tax credits attach, to the extent the distributions represent accumulated earnings and profits of a US company's UK subsidiary. Several conditions need to be fulfilled to meet this treatment.)

28.21 In general, therefore, parent companies in non-participation exemption jurisdictions will be in a more advantageous position if they receive dividends rather than liquidation distributions as the former will normally attract foreign tax credits in respect of the underlying corporation tax paid by the UK subsidiary (see Table 4 at paragraph **25.4**).

Upstream loans

28.22 Under the transfer pricing rules of ICTA 1988, Sch 28AA it will be necessary for the UK subsidiary to receive an arm's length rate of interest. Before undertaking this transaction it will be important to ensure that the interest paid by the foreign parent company or individual will be tax deductible in its jurisdiction.

It will need to be reviewed whether the foreign jurisdiction would regard the loan as a dividend received. For example the USA treats loans that a US shareholder receives from a controlled foreign company as income to the recipient.

Some jurisdictions might treat the loan as being in substance a dividend.

Loan repayments

28.23 If the foreign company or individual has capitalised the UK company with sterling loans, its profits could be repatriated by repaying the loans. From a UK tax viewpoint the transaction would be neutral. In the foreign jurisdiction, any currency differences may be taxable or tax deductible. The reverse is the case if the loans are in the currency of the foreign company.

Sale of shares

28.24 See **Chapter 29**.

29 Sale of UK company's shares

29.1 In most cases the gain on sale of the UK company's shares will not be liable to UK capital gains tax as TCGA 1992, s 2(1) only charges UK residents to capital gains tax. Exceptions to this are where the gain on sale constitutes a taxable transaction in land under ICTA 1988, s 776 (see paragraph **33.23** et seq); or in the rare case where the UK company's shares constitute an asset held for the purposes of a UK permanent establishment's trade [TCGA 1992, s 10B(1)(b)].

29.2 Having said that, a purchaser will invariably negotiate a discount in the price of the shares to take account of the company's inherent tax liabilities.

29.3 But it is the foreign company or individual's tax position in the foreign jurisdiction that is most relevant. If the gain is taxable it will normally be advantageous to distribute the maximum pre-sale dividend to a foreign parent company before the sale takes place in order to reduce the potential gain at little or no tax cost. The dividend will either be tax-exempt; or taxable but with a credit for the corporation tax paid by the UK company (see Table 4 at paragraph **25.4**).

29.4 However the USA is a special case. Part of a US parent company's gain on sale of the shares is treated as a dividend to the extent of the UK subsidiary's earnings and profits. Several conditions need to be fulfilled to meet this treatment. In such a case there should be no need for the UK subsidiary to pay a pre-sale dividend to its US parent company.

29.5 In many cases the gain will not be taxable in the home country because of a participation exemption (see Table 4 at paragraph **25.4**). In this way the gain on sale of the UK company's shares will be completely free of tax, subject only to the discount in the price of the shares for inherent tax liabilities (see paragraph **29.2**).

Foreign individuals

29.6 Pre-sale dividends will not normally be advantageous to foreign individuals. Dividends are invariably fully taxable with no credit for the underlying UK corporation tax whereas gains from the sale of shares are sometimes taxable at a lower rate, or else exempt altogether (see Table 5 at paragraph **25.8**).

30 Sale of UK permanent establishment

30.1 UK tax will be payable on the gains arising on sale of the constituent assets, as follows:

Capital gains: goodwill, property etc

30.2 The gains will be taxable [TCGA 1992, ss 10, 10B].

Foreign companies will be liable to corporation tax at 30% [ICTA 1988, s 6(3)]. In view of taper relief, foreign individuals will be liable to tax at an effective rate of 10%, assuming the asset in question has been owned for at least two years [TCGA 1992, s 2A].

Gains on sale of post- 31.3.02 intangible assets

30.3 The gains will be taxed at 30% as part of the permanent establishment's trading profits [FA 2002, Sch 29, para 13 et seq] (see paragraph **21.5(f)**).

Individuals remain liable to capital gains tax. In view of taper relief, foreign individuals will be liable to tax at an effective rate of 10%, assuming the asset in question has been owned for at least two years [TCGA 1992, s 2A].

Gains on sale of patent rights

30.4 Gains of foreign individuals are taxable as income under Schedule D Case VI [ICTA 1988, s 524] (see paragraph **6.23**) as are gains of foreign companies where the patent rights were acquired or created pre- March 2002. Where the foreign company's permanent establishment acquired or created the patent rights after that date, the sale will come within the intangible property regime and so the gain will be liable to corporation tax as part of the trading profits [FA 2002, Sch 29 paras 1(1), 2(1) and 13 et seq] (see paragraph **21.5(f)**).

Gains on sale of capital allowance assets: plant and machinery, industrial buildings etc

30.5 To the extent that the disposal proceeds exceed the tax written-down value of the asset, a balancing adjustment will recoup the capital allowances granted. In the case of pooled assets, which include most plant and machinery, the disposal proceeds will reduce the pool of qualifying expenditure for writing-down allowances. Where the proceeds exceed the pool value, a balancing charge will recoup the excess as taxable income [CAA 2001, ss 55 and 56]. If disposal proceeds exceed cost, there may be a charge to capital gains tax or corporation tax [TCGA 1992, ss 37, 39].

Gains on sale of stock

30.6 These will be taxable as part of the branch's trading profits.

Tax implications in the foreign jurisdiction

30.7 See Table 2 at paragraph **13.3(f)** for the tax position of foreign companies and individuals in the selected foreign jurisdictions.

31 Leasing equipment in the UK: the foreign lessor

Overview

- Equipment rentals will be free of UK tax to a foreign lessor unless generated through a UK permanent establishment.

31.1 The equipment will be used in the UK. However if the foreign lessor company or individual does not perform any services in the UK, it is unlikely that a trade is being carried on (see paragraph **4.1**). On the other hand if the leasing contract is concluded in the UK, it could be argued that the leasing profits were earned in the UK, taking into account the fact that the equipment was located in the UK. It is unlikely that the mere presence of the leased equipment in the UK will by itself give rise to a taxable UK trade (see paragraph **31.2**).

31.2 As a guideline (whether or not a tax treaty exists with the lessor's country of residence), in relation to article 5 of its Model Convention (see **Appendix 1**) paragraph 8 of the OECD commentary states that the equipment itself will not constitute a permanent establishment of the foreign lessor. The commentary goes on to say that this remains the case even when, for example, the foreign lessor supplies personnel after installation to operate the equipment provided that their responsibility is limited solely to the operation or maintenance of the equipment under the direction, responsibility and control of the lessee. If the personnel have wider responsibilities, for example, participation in the decisions regarding the work for which the equipment is used, or if they operate, service, inspect and maintain the equipment under the responsibility and control of the lessor, the activity of the lessor may go beyond the mere leasing of equipment and may constitute an entrepreneurial activity. In such a case a permanent establishment could be deemed to exist if the criterion of permanence is met.

UK trade

31.3 Thus, even if the leasing activity constitutes the carrying on of a trade in the UK, the absence of a permanent establishment will avoid any corporation tax liability (see paragraph **11.2**). A Schedule D Case I income tax liability could still arise for both companies and individuals [ICTA 1988, s 18(3)]. However in the absence of a regular agent, on whom an assessment could be made, an actual tax assessment is unlikely (see paragraphs **12.2** and **12.3**).

Investment activity

31.4 If the leasing constitutes an investment activity rather than a trade, the net income could be taxable under Schedule D Case VI on the basis that it arises from property in the UK [ICTA 1988, s 18(1)(a)(iii), (3)]. Whether a UK source exists is debatable. Foreign companies, (as well as individuals), would be liable to income tax rather than corporation tax as no trade would be carried on in the UK [ICTA 1988, s 11(1)].

31.5 While a Case VI liability may exist (including a full income tax liability where there is no tax treaty), an actual liability is unlikely to be assessable if there is no regular UK agent on whom an income tax assessment could be made (see paragraphs **12.2** and **12.3**).

31.6 Where a UK tax treaty exists with the foreign lessor's country of residence, it will limit the UK tax payable on the leasing income. In a considerable number of the UK's tax treaties, equipment rentals are included in the definition of 'royalties'; for example, article 12(2) of the UK's treaties with France and the Netherlands (where the income remains taxable in the French or Dutch lessor's country only). Similarly, in the royalty article with Spain, for example, where UK tax would apply but at the limited rate of 10% (see **Appendix 2**).

31.7 Where equipment rentals are not specifically dealt with in the treaty they will fall within the 'Other Income' article which invariably restricts the taxing rights to the lessor's country of residence (see article 21.1 of the OECD Model Convention, **Appendix 1**).

Tax implications in the foreign jurisdiction

31.8 In the event that a UK permanent establishment exists, with a consequent liability to UK tax, the foreign tax consequences in the countries surveyed are discussed in **Chapter 13** (see in particular Table 2 at paragraph **13.3(f)**).

Assuming there is no liability to UK tax, or that the leasing constitutes an investment activity, the equipment rental profits will be taxable in the foreign jurisdiction. However in the case of Hong Kong and Singapore it might be possible to assert that the equipment rental income constitutes a foreign source. If so, it would not be taxable in Hong Kong, which taxes only Hong Kong source income. In Singapore only remitted rental income would be taxable.

32 UK property investment

Overview

- Foreign investors taxed at 22% on net rental income.
- Capital gains on realisation generally free of UK tax.
- Gains may also be free of tax in foreign jurisdiction.
- Corporate residence of foreign property investing company requires careful monitoring.
- Interest deductions for borrowings from foreign affiliates are subject to debt/equity restrictions including third party borrowings secured or guaranteed by foreign affiliates.

Rental income

32.1 A non-UK resident company or individual acquiring UK property as an investment for its rental return and long term capital appreciation will be liable to UK income tax on the net rental income from the property under Schedule A [ICTA 1988, s 21]. Non-UK resident companies are liable to corporation tax only on trading income derived through a UK permanent establishment [ICTA 1988, s 11(1)].

Individuals will be liable to income tax up to the marginal rate of 40%. However companies are not liable to higher-rate tax and so their rate of tax is limited to the basic rate of 22% [ICTA 1988, s 1(1), (2)(b)].That is one of the reasons why foreign individuals invariably invest in UK property through a non-UK company (see paragraph **32.9**).

In all of the double tax treaties concluded by the UK, it retains its right to tax the non-resident's rental income from ownership of UK property (see article 6.1 of the OECD Model Convention, **Appendix 1**).

Capital gains on realisation

32.2 Unusually amongst most jurisdictions, the UK does not tax capital gains accruing to non-resident investors from realisation of their UK property investments. Non-residents are only liable to tax on capital gains realised from property occupied by a UK permanent establishment, or from UK exploration or exploitation activities [TCGA 1992, s 2(1)]. In exceptional circumstances property gains may be taxable under ICTA 1988, s 776 (see paragraph **33.23** et seq).

In those circumstances where foreign investors are not taxable in their home country (as a result of domestic legislation or under a tax treaty with the UK), gains on UK property investments can thus be realised completely free of tax (see Table 6 at paragraph **32.34**).

Payment of tax

32.3 ICTA 1988, s 42A provides for the Inland Revenue to make regulations for assessing and collecting tax from non-residents under Schedule A. The regulations are contained in the Taxation of Income from Land (Non-residents) Regulations, SI 1995/2902. Inland Revenue Booklet IR40, 'Non-resident landlords, their agents and tenants', together with guidance notes for both tenants and letting agents, provides the following information:

> 'The letting agent, or the tenant where there is no letting agent, is required to pay basic rate tax each quarter on the UK property income of non-resident investors. Non-residents will be able to set the tax suffered by deduction from rent against their UK income tax liability. However, application may be made to the Inland Revenue for approval for non-resident investors to receive the UK property income gross provided:
>
> (a) their UK tax affairs are up to date; or
> (b) they have never had any obligations in relation to UK tax; or
> (c) they do not expect to be liable to UK tax; and
> (d) they undertake to comply with all their UK tax obligations in the future.'

32.4 The fact that tax is, or ought to be, deducted from rents by the letting agent or the tenant, as the case may be, does not free the non-resident landlord from the obligation to file a UK self-assessment return. At the end of every tax year, the letting agent, or the tenant, must provide the non-resident landlord with a certificate NRL6, that contains details of the rent paid in the year to 31 March, deductible expenses and the tax payable. Where approval to pay gross has been given, the last two items are replaced by the non-resident landlord's approval number.

It is in the non-resident landlord's interest to file a return, as the tax deducted will rarely match the landlord's actual liability.

32.5 Although the final liability for tax is the landlord's, the Inland Revenue's Centre for Non-Residents ('CNR') has the power to raise assessments on the letting agent or the tenant (on whoever should be operating the scheme and deducting tax) where it believes that an amount of tax should have been paid over but was not or that the quarterly return is incorrect. In such instances the assessment is issued by the tax office dealing with the agent or the tenant, on the instructions of the CNR.

Computation of property income

32.6 With specific exceptions that are not relevant here, the Schedule A profits are computed in the same way as the profits of a trader computed for the purposes of Case I of Schedule D Case I [ICTA 1988, s 21A]. It follows that all expenses incurred wholly and exclusively for the purpose of the property investment business are deductible provided that they are not of a capital nature [ICTA 1988, s 74(1)]. Typical deductible expenses would be:

(a) repairs;

(b) rent, rates and council taxes;

(c) insurance;

(d) rent collection expenses;

(e) most (but not all) costs of obtaining loan finance such as loan fees, commissions and guarantee fees [ICTA 1988, s 77];

(f) legal and professional costs that are not of a capital nature such as valuations for insurance, accountancy fees and legal costs for renewal of leases;

(g) bad debts for non-collectible rents;

(h) interest and certain (but not all) other financing costs (see paragraph **32.12** et seq).

Foreign pension funds and other exempt entities

32.7 Exempt entities will normally wish to make a direct investment into UK property. However that route will invariably attract 22% UK income tax on the rental income generated despite their tax-exempt status abroad.

For that reason, foreign exempt funds could consider investing into UK property through a foreign company into which they would advance interest-bearing loans. The objective would be for the interest to be deductible from the rental income. At the same time it should be free of UK tax to the exempt fund; either under a tax treaty, or because the interest is sourced outside the UK.

However pension and other exempt funds often obtain third party gearing for property investment and so may be constrained from introducing further borrowing.

Partnership

32.8 Joint investment into UK property is often effected through a partnership, including a UK limited partnership, in order to facilitate the different tax requirements of a variety of types of investor from different jurisdictions (see paragraph **16.18**).

Why invest through a foreign company?

32.9 Foreign individuals will find it invariably beneficial for the property investment to be made through a non-UK company whose shares are owned by the ultimate investor. This is because UK tax on the net rental income will be limited to the basic rate of 22% rather than the maximum of 40% applicable to individuals (see paragraph **32.1**). Furthermore, assuming he or she is non-UK domiciled, inheritance tax will be inapplicable as the foreign investor will own shares in a non-UK company rather than directly owning a UK property.

Foreign companies will also wish to invest through a non-UK company as capital gains will be free of UK tax and tax on the rental income will be limited to 22% (see paragraphs **32.1** and **32.2**).

Corporate residence

32.10 It will be essential to ensure that the foreign company is not UK resident for UK tax purposes. If it is resident, the net rental income and the gains on realisation of the property will be liable to corporation tax, generally at 30%.

Chapter 2 discusses the residence position of companies and paragraph **2.7** suggests the general disciplines for locating residence outside the UK. Specifically in relation to the UK property investment, great care is required to ensure that the following actions taken by the directors are taken outside the UK at fully minuted board meetings:

(a) Approval of properties for acquisition.

(b) Appointment and supervision of agents, builders, lawyers, surveyors, accountants etc.

(c) Borrowings arrangements.

(d) Acquisition of properties and signing of contracts.

(e) Applications for planning permission etc.

(f) Approval of tenants and tenancy agreements.

(g) Review and supervision of tenancies.

(h) Approval of alterations and repairs to properties.

(i) Sales of properties.

Obviously much of this work is usually undertaken by independent third parties, such as agents, surveyors and lawyers, and much of their liaison and supervision can be undertaken from outside the UK.

32.11 However there are numerous occasions when visits to the UK will be required. In these cases a single board member should do so and then report back to the board for its decisions. In this context the foreign company's articles of association, or equivalent, should specify that board decisions must be approved by the entire board and that, for specific major decisions, a single director cannot contractually bind the company.

In some cases the foreign investor forms a UK management company to perform any functions that need to be carried out in the UK.

Interest payable

32.12 As expenses in computing Schedule A income are deductible on Case I lines, interest paid in relation to the property business should be deductible from rental income. For example, interest on borrowings to acquire, improve, manage or maintain the property, or to finance income deficits.

Chapter 19 discusses the financing of a UK company or permanent establishment. However, where funds are borrowed by an investment company that is not resident in the UK the rules are subtly different and require separate consideration.

32.13 Where the non-UK company borrows funds from related persons, the amount of the interest payable that will be deductible for income tax purposes will be subject to thin capitalisation limitation under the transfer pricing provisions of ICTA 1988, s 770A and Sch 28AA (see **Chapter 17** and paragraph **19.3** et seq). The distribution provisions of ICTA 1988, s 209(2)(da) do not apply because the company is not liable to corporation tax [ICTA 1988, s 209(2)] (see paragraph **19.8(a)**).

(a) Schedule 28AA para 1(1) applies the transfer pricing rules where provision is made or imposed between the affected persons by means of a transaction or series of transactions.

(b) Schedule 28AA para 1(2) provides that, if the actual provision differs from the provision that would have been made between independent enterprises and confers a tax advantage, the actual provision is to be replaced by an arm's length provision. It is important to bear in mind that ICTA 1988, Sch 28AA para 2 provides that it is to be construed consistently with the transfer pricing guidelines contained in article 9 of the OECD Model Convention .

(c) Schedule 28AA para 4 contains detailed rules for construing whether or not the parties to the transaction are connected for transfer pricing purposes. Clearly interest on loans from companies which are commonly controlled or controlled by connected persons will be subject to adjustment under Sch 28AA.

32.14 As the legislation is concerned with provisions relating to loan transactions it can be applied by the Revenue to adjust not just the rate of interest on the actual loan, but also the amount of the loan provided. In other words, the interest will be limited to a market rate of interest on such an amount of loan that would have been advanced by an arm's length lender, based on factors such as security and interest cover. The calculations obviously require a thorough knowledge of banking practice and lending techniques in the property industry (see paragraph **19.3**). The UK Revenue has stated the following in its Tax Bulletin (Issue 46) of April 2000:

'How do I know what amount would have been lent at arm's length?

This will vary with the facts and circumstances of each case. If no other persons are involved, a third party lender will determine the amount it would lend by looking at the assets and income of the prospective borrower. In our experience third party lenders are primarily concerned with the value of the property they are being asked to lend against and currently offers of advances appear typically to be in the range of 65–80% if there is a satisfactory projected income stream. In reviewing projected rental streams a third party lender would have regard to both the quality of the tenant and the duration of the leases, and as always lending decisions are the result of the evaluation of a number of general economic and specific commercial factors.'

32.15 In many cases, instead of borrowing funds directly from a related company or individual, the property owning company will borrow funds from its bankers on the security of the property but with additional security provided by a connected company in the form of a back-to-back deposit, guarantee, or letter of comfort. The Revenue takes the position that such arrangements constitute a provision made between related parties by means of a series of transactions within the scope of ICTA 1988, Sch 28AA para 1(1) (see above and Tax Bulletin (Issue 37), October 1998 page 581). This attitude is subject to challenge. For example Sch 28AA is to be construed consistently with the OECD Model Convention. Article 9 of the Convention and the commentary on it, however, are confined to transactions between two related enterprises only and do not envisage such tripartite arrangements (see **Appendix 1**).

Nevertheless, it must be assumed that the Revenue will challenge any loan transactions secured by a related company as being within the transfer pricing provisions of Sch 28AA.

However following the European Court of Justice decision in *Lankhorst* (see paragraph **19.9**) there is an arguable case that the exclusion in relation to UK residents in Sch 28AA para 5(2) is discriminatory in relation to all transactions with EU residents; a tax treaty non-discrimination argument could also be made (see paragraph **19.10**).

32.16 As a contrary point it is certainly arguable that, had a third party guaranteed or otherwise assisted in securing the borrowing arrangements, it would have charged a guarantee fee for providing this facility. On this basis an arm's length guarantee fee could be paid by the property owning company to the related company or individual providing the guarantee. As the guarantee fee would be paid between two non-UK resident companies it is unlikely that it would be liable to UK income tax in the hands of the recipient as it would be sourced outside the UK.

32.17 Assuming the loans are from banks carrying on business in the UK, no withholding tax is deductible from the interest paid [ICTA 1988, s 349(3)(b)]. Otherwise, on the assumption that the loans paid by the non-UK company are sourced in the UK, a 20% withholding tax is deductible from the interest [ICTA 1988, ss 1A, 349(2)(a)]. This is often reducible to 0% under a double tax treaty between the lender's country of residence and the UK (see **Appendix 2**). Withholding tax is not deductible from interest on quoted Eurobonds [ICTA 1988, s 349(3)(c)].

32.18 However it would appear that, where the loan is from a non-UK lender, the interest paid by the non-UK company will not be regarded as sourced in the UK and so income tax will not be deductible at source [ICTA 1988, s 349(2)] (see paragraph **19.11**).

Deep discount loans

32.19 See paragraph **20.2** et seq. Discounts are not deductible for income tax purposes [ICTA 1988, s 64(1)(f)].

Capital allowances

32.20 Capital allowances may be available as deductions from the foreign investor's rental income, depending upon the category of asset as follows:

Plant and machinery in the building

32.21 Apart from moveable property and equipment in the building, this also extends to fixtures such as lifts, central heating and air conditioning. In this regard it is important that a separate valuation is attributed to these items when a building is constructed or purchased. The rate of writing down allowance is 25% calculated on the reducing balance basis [CAA 2001, ss15(1)(d), 56].

In most circumstances the purchaser and seller may elect to fix the sale price of the fixed plant and machinery in the building. However the price may not exceed the original cost to the seller [CAA 2001, s 198 et seq].

Industrial buildings and hotels

32.22 A 4% straight line writing down allowance is available, generally based on the historic construction cost [CAA 2001, ss 272, 279, 310(1)(b)].

Agricultural buildings and works

32.23 A 4% straight line writing down allowance is available (rebased on historic construction costs) [CAA 2001, ss 361, 373].

Flat conversion allowances

32.24 A 100% capital allowance (i.e. immediate write-off of the entire expenditure) is available for capital expenditure on certain residential conversions or on the renovation or conversion of empty or underused commercial premises for residential purposes [CAA 2001, s 393A et seq].

Assured tenancies

32.25 Residual capital allowances may still be available for capital expenditure on certain residential buildings let under assured tenancies. The original capital expenditure must have been incurred between 10 March 1982 and 1 April 1992 [CAA 2001, ss 490–531].

Commercial buildings in enterprise zones

32.26 An enterprise zone is a specially designated zone situated usually in a disadvantaged area, in which accelerated capital allowances, and other incentives such as relaxed planning controls, apply. The 100% initial allowance is available on capital expenditure on the construction of a commercial building within an enterprise zone. The definition of a commercial building is far wider than that of an industrial building and includes, for example, retail premises and office buildings, on which a capital allowance is not otherwise available at all. If the full 100% allowance is not claimed, the balance is depreciated for tax purposes at 25% per annum on a reducing-balance basis [CAA 2001, s 298 et seq]. The purchaser of such a building would be entitled to claim any residue of expenditure over the remaining 25-year term.

Enterprise zones are designated for a 10-year period and the expenditure on the construction of the building must, with certain exceptions, be incurred during the life of the zone. Enterprise zones whose designations have not yet lapsed are:

Name of zone	*Date designation lapses*
Dearne Valley	2 November 2005
East Midlands (North East Derbyshire)	2 November 2005
East Midlands (Bassetlaw)	15 November 2005
East Midlands (Ashfield)	20 November 2005
East Durham (Bracken Hill, Peterlee NW Industrial Estate, Peterlee SW Industrial Estate, Seaham Grange, Fox Cover and Dawdon)	28 November 2005
Tyne Riverside (North Tyneside)	18 February 2006
Tyne Riverside (North Tyneside No 2)	25 August 2006
Tyne Riverside (North Tyneside and South Tyneside)	20 October 2006

Environmentally beneficial plant machinery

32.27 Such plant and machinery qualifies for 100% first year allowances where the expenditure is incurred on or after 1 April 2003 [CAA 2001, ss 45H-45J].

VAT

32.28 For VAT purposes transactions in real property are always deemed to take place where the property is physically located [VAT (Place of Supply of

Services) Order, SI 1992/3121 article 5]. Therefore, a non-UK resident owning property in the UK will need to consider the UK VAT position.

With regard to the ownership of commercial investment property, the underlying VAT treatment is that the acquisition or grant of property, or of an interest in it, is exempt from VAT. However the UK VAT legislation enables this exemption to be waived (this procedure is commonly known as the 'option to tax'). Waiving exemption makes rents and the eventual sale of the property, or of a further grant of a major interest in it, subject to VAT. However, it enables the landlord to reclaim input VAT incurred on expenditure related to the property.

A property investment business would normally exercise and notify its election to waive exemption before acquiring a property that was subject to the vendor's election.

Residential property does not attract a similar option to tax. The only taxable transactions involving residential property are the sale or grant of a major interest (normally a lease exceeding 21 years) in a new dwelling.

[VATA 1994, Sch 10.]

Tax implications in the foreign jurisdiction

32.29 See Table 6 at paragraph **32.34**.

In principle the foreign investor will be liable to tax in the country of residence on the income and gains generated from the UK property investment.

However this depends upon the domestic tax rules as well as the terms of any double tax treaty between the country of residence and the UK. A Hong Kong investor would not be liable to tax as Hong Kong tax applies on a territorial basis so that income and gains arising from UK property are not taxed in Hong Kong.

In Singapore the UK rental income would only be taxed insofar as remitted to Singapore. There is no tax on capital gains.

32.30 Moreover, for example, articles 25(2)(a) and 22(2)(b) of the UK's tax treaties with Luxembourg and the Netherlands respectively exempt UK property income and gains from tax in the country of residence (see also article 23A(1) of the OECD Model Convention, **Appendix 1**). The exemption applies even though the UK does not actually tax non-residents' gains on realisation of UK property investments (see paragraph **32.2**). In contrast article 18(2)(a) of the UK's treaty with Germany requires the gains to be taxed in the UK if they are to be exempt in Germany.

32.31 Assuming the foreign investor's country of residence will fully tax UK property income and gains, a credit will normally be available for UK taxes paid on the rental income (see article 23B(1) of the OECD Model Convention,

Appendix 1). This will generally result in full home country tax on the gains (which are free of tax in the UK), and a balance of home country tax on the rental income.

32.32 In order to defer these taxes in the country of residence, the foreign investor may be able to utilise a company resident in one of the jurisdictions listed in Table 6 at paragraph **32.34** where UK property income and gains are exempt. Such a company would own the UK property and so avoid tax on capital gains and limit tax on rental income to the UK basic rate of 22%.

Consideration will also need to be given to withholding taxes on extraction of the accumulated profits and gains from the company by way of dividend or liquidation distribution, for example:

	Belgium %	*Luxembourg* %	*Netherlands* %
Dividends paid	0–25	0–20	0–25
Liquidation distributions	0–10	0	0–25

See Table 4 at paragraph **25.4**.

32.33 So, for example, a Portuguese investor might utilise a Luxembourg company, extracting the profits in due course by way of liquidation distribution. Subsequently, there is the question of taxability of the dividends or liquidation distributions in the recipient's country of residence (see Tables 4 and 5 at paragraphs **25.4** and **25.8** and the Examples in paragraph **25.8**).

Investors might wish to utilise a property-owning company in one of the above jurisdictions. The main problem, however, would be to overcome controlled foreign company rules, or their personal equivalent, in the country of residence (see **Appendix 3**).

32.34 Table 6 below provides an overview of the taxability of UK rental income and gains in each of the selected jurisdictions. It should not be taken as exhaustive.

TABLE 6 UK property investment: taxability of rental income and gains in foreign jurisdiction

Company or individual resident in:	*Taxable with credit for UK tax*	*Exempt under treaty with UK*[(1)]	*Domestically exempt*
Australia	✓		
Austria	✓[(2)]		
Belgium		✓	
Canada	✓		
Denmark	✓		
Finland	✓		

Company or individual resident in:	*Taxable with credit for UK tax*	*Exempt under treaty with UK*[1]	*Domestically exempt*
France		✓	✓
Germany		(3)	
Greece	✓		
Hong Kong			✓
Ireland	✓		
Italy	✓(4)		
Japan	✓		
Luxembourg		✓	
Netherlands		✓	✓
Portugal	✓		
Singapore	✓(5)		
Spain	✓		
Sweden	✓		
Switzerland		✓	
USA	✓		

Notes (not exhaustive)

(1) OECD Model Tax Convention article 23A.1 (see **Appendix 1**).

(2) Where UK property is not used in Austrian resident's or spouse's business and owned for at least 10 years, individual's gains are tax-free in Austria.

(3) Rental income exempt but gains from realisation of UK property are not exempt because article 18(2)(a) of the treaty requires them to be subject to UK tax.

(4) Where UK property owned for more than five years, individual's gains are tax-free in Italy.

(5) Rents taxable to extent remitted to Singapore. Gains exempt.

33 Property trading and gains of a capital nature

> **Overview**
>
> - In principle, foreign company can generate UK property dealing profits without creating taxable permanent establishment.
> - However, where construction activities take place, construction site will normally constitute taxable permanent establishment depending on its duration.
> - Assuming taxable profits arise, there are a number of techniques for minimising profits.
> - UK anti-avoidance rules of ICTA 1988 s 776 require consideration.

33.1 Assuming the non-resident is trading in UK property rather than owning the property as an investment for its rental return and long term capital appreciation, the profit arising on its disposal may be liable to UK income tax or corporation tax, as discussed below.

Is a trade being carried on?

33.2 It is a question of fact as to whether the property acquired constitutes trading stock or an investment. No overarching principle can be drawn from the line of cases in this area; every case has hinged on its own particular facts.

The question is simpler to determine where the person is a company as a company will have objects that may or may not include dealing in land. However even where a property-dealing company is concerned, a particular transaction may nevertheless be the realisation of an investment rather than a trading transaction. The presumption will, however, be that the sale is a trading transaction.

33.3 In *Parkstone Estates Ltd v Blair* (1966) 43 TC 246, a company acquired land under a long lease of 150 years, and then granted underleases for a rent and premium. The granting of the underleases was assessed as a trade. The company contended that the land was an investment and that the leasing activities were capital transactions. The assessments were upheld in the High Court. In *Eames v Stepnell Properties Ltd* (1967) 43 TC 698, the taxpayer company acquired land from another company while the latter was in negotiations with the local authority to sell the land for construction of a school. Assessment of the profits of the sale as a trading transaction was upheld by the Court of Appeal.

33.4 The mere fact that a property is treated in the accounts of a company as a fixed asset and not as trading stock will not by itself ensure investment status if the facts indicate otherwise (see *Shadford v H Fairweather & Co Ltd* (1966) 43 TC 291, *Bowie v Reg Dunn (Builders) Ltd* [1974] STC 234).

33.5 On the other hand, for trading to be found, there should be a clear intention to trade—a profit-seeking motive by itself is not enough (see, for example, *IRC v Reinhold* (1953) 34 TC 389). The acquisition of land in the knowledge that it will appreciate in value and may one day be sold at a profit, even where it does not in the meantime produce investment income, does not preclude its being acquired and held as an investment. However where the sale of a site is arranged prior to its acquisition, that is a clear pointer of an intention to trade.

33.6 In *Marson v Morton* [1986] STC 463, four brothers bought land for which planning permission had been granted, and sold it at a profit three months later following an unsolicited offer. The General Commissioners accepted the taxpayers' evidence that they had intended to hold the land as an investment and the High Court upheld their decision.

33.7 By contrast, in *Lynch v Edmondson* [1998] STC (SCD) 185, a bricklayer purchased a plot of land with a loan from a bank, and built two flats. When one flat was let at a premium and a peppercorn rent, the Revenue raised an assessment under Schedule D Case I (trading). The Special Commissioner rejected his appeal that the land had been an investment.

33.8 Land, when acquired, must be either an investment or trading stock. It cannot be both, nor can it have intermediate status. This was established in *Simmons v IRC* [1980] STC 350. In that case, a company and two of its subsidiaries, holding land, had gone into liquidation, and the land was sold. The liquidator's contention that the land had been acquired as an investment and its forced realisation did not transform it into trading stock succeeded in the House of Lords.

33.9 It can be the case, however, that land initially acquired and held as an investment becomes trading stock, if the owner forms the intention to trade with it. This is the concept of 'supervening trading'. The Inland Revenue's *Inspector's Manual* cites the example of the demolition of a warehouse and the construction for sale in its place of residential flats. In *Taylor v Good* [1974] STC 148, however, a taxpayer who had bought a large country estate with a view to living there, but had subsequently demolished it and built 90 houses for sale, following his wife's refusal to live there, was found not to be trading. In this unusual case, the Court of Appeal held that there was no evidence on the facts that the taxpayer had made an adventure in the nature of trade.

In contrast, in *New Angel Court Ltd v Adam* [2003] EWHC 1876 (Ch) a property dealing company acquired properties from a group investment company and subsequently sold them at a tax-adjusted loss but was held on the facts that the dealing company had continued to realise the properties held by the vendor as capital assets. It was merely a vehicle.

Trade carried on in the UK?

33.10 Assuming that a trade is being carried on, it then needs to be determined whether or not it is being carried on in the UK. However the very fact that the trading stock itself is located in the UK, and by its nature must be sold in the UK, points strongly towards the conduct of a trade in the UK. This is so even though, for example, contracts relating to purchase and sale are concluded abroad.

Invariably the activities relating to the trade will be carried out in the UK, for example negotiations and meetings with prospective purchasers and with solicitors, bankers and valuers. It is only in rare cases that no exposure to UK tax will arise, such as where the purchaser is not present in the UK and contracts are concluded outside the UK (see paragraph **3.10**).

Leaving aside for the moment the question of double tax treaties, the next question is whether the trade is being carried on in the UK through a permanent establishment. If it is, then a non-resident company will be liable to corporation tax on the profits generated [ICTA 1988, s 11(1)] (see paragraph **11.2**). A non-resident individual, and a non-resident company with no permanent establishment in the UK, will instead be liable to income tax on the profits generated [ICTA 1988, s 18(3)] (see paragraphs **12.1** and **12.3**).

No permanent establishment?

33.11 In principle it is possible for non-residents to conduct property trading activities without having a fixed place of business in the UK. The operation could be conducted through estate agents, property managers, valuers, contractors etc, all of whom are likely to be independent businesses with little risk of them being classified as dependent agents, UK representatives, or agents having habitual authority to do business on behalf of the non-resident (see paragraphs **11.3(b)**, **11.11** and **12.2**). For tax treaty purposes, persons in the above category having power to conclude contracts on behalf of the non-resident could certainly be considered agents for their non-resident principal. However, in normal cases the non-resident's business is unlikely to be a dominant part of the business of the agent, who would therefore be regarded as an agent of independent status and thus specifically exempted from being a permanent establishment of the non-resident [FA 2003, s 148(3)] (see article 5.5 of the OECD Model Convention, **Appendix 1**).

In these circumstances, in the absence of a permanent establishment, an income tax liability could arise for both companies and individuals [ICTA 1988, s 18(3)]. However, in the absence of a regular agent on whom an assessment could be made, an actual tax assessment is unlikely (see paragraphs **12.1**, **12.2** and **12.3**).

Nevertheless, it is understood that the UK Revenue regards development of a UK property as an indication that a permanent establishment exists.

Permanent establishment

33.12 If a foreign company maintains, or has regular use of, a UK office from which to carry on the property dealing trade, this will constitute a taxable UK permanent establishment (see paragraph **11.3**). This is the case under domestic law [ICTA 1988, s 11(1) and FA 2003, s 148(1)(a)]. It is also the case where a tax treaty applies [OECD Model Convention article 5.2(c), **Appendix 1**].

A non-resident individual with a UK permanent establishment will be similarly liable where a tax treaty applies. Where there is no tax treaty in force, income tax liability arises under ICTA 1988, s 18(1)(a)(iii), (3). The assessment will be made on the permanent establishment [FA 1995, s 126, Sch 23] (see paragraph **12.1**).

Dependent agent

33.13 For tax treaty purposes a non-resident company will be treated as having a taxable UK permanent establishment if there is a dependent agent in the UK with power to conclude contracts on its behalf (see paragraph **11.11** and OECD Model Convention article 5.5, **Appendix 1**).

33.14 If a tax treaty is inapplicable to a non-resident company, say, a Hong Kong resident company, it will be treated as having a taxable UK permanent establishment if it has an agent in the UK who habitually exercises an authority to do business on its behalf [FA 2003, s 148(1)] (see paragraph **11.3**).

33.15 If a tax treaty is inapplicable to a non-resident individual, say a Hong Kong resident, but the individual is carrying on a UK property dealing trade through a regular agent such as a dependent agent, an income tax liability will arise and will be assessable on the agent [ICTA 1988, s 18(3), FA 1995, s 126] (see paragraph **12.2**).

33.16 In the context of a UK property dealing trade where no development work is undertaken, it is unlikely that an independent property agent or lawyer could be classified as a dependent agent or an agent habitually exercising an authority to do business in view of the exclusions for independent agents in article 5.6 of the OECD Model Convention and FA 2003, s 148(3) respectively.

Construction and development

33.17 A taxable permanent establishment may also exist in cases in which the foreign property trader has the UK property or site constructed or developed.

FA 2003, s 148(2)(h) specifies that a foreign company has a taxable UK permanent establishment if it has a building site or construction or installation project in the UK (see paragraph **11.3**).

Although there is no such specific legislation relating to foreign individuals, it can be reasonably assumed that the same conditions apply to establish a taxable UK trade if a construction site exists.

33.18 In order to avoid this exposure, where the property dealing activity includes construction or development it should be conducted by a foreign company resident in a suitable tax treaty jurisdiction which may give protection from UK tax on the property trading profits through the permanent establishment article if the development site is within the time limit specified in the treaty. This will have the effect of confining taxability of the profits to the foreign jurisdiction. Foreign jurisdictions that have a double tax treaty with the UK and with a relatively low rate of tax are, for example, Cyprus (10%) and Ireland (12.5%).

33.19 Where a tax treaty applies, it will invariably specify that the construction site is a permanent establishment only if it exceeds a specific period of time, normally 6, 9 or 12 months depending upon the specific tax treaty. Article 5.3 of the OECD Model Convention specifies a 12 month period (see **Appendix 1**).

In this regard the commentary to the OECD Model Convention provides some useful guidelines as follows:

> '(a) If the site lasts for less than 12 months then offices or other workshops established at the site would not be regarded as a permanent establishment under any other definitions in the treaty because they represent a fixed place of business.
>
> (b) The term "building site or construction or installation project" includes not only construction of buildings but also the construction of roads, bridges, the laying of pipelines, excavating and dredging. Planning and supervision are also included if carried out by the building contractor. Planning and supervision are not, however, included if carried out by another enterprise whose activities in connection with the construction concerned are restricted to planning and supervision.
>
> (c) The 12 month test applies to each individual site or project. If there is one contract there is a presumption normally, at least as far as the UK Revenue is concerned, that separate sites completed within that contract are part of the same "project" with the result that their respective time periods are aggregated in determining whether a permanent establishment exists. The Commentary also states that a building site shall be regarded as a single unit even if it is based on several contracts provided it forms a coherent whole commercially and geographically.
>
> (d) In determining how long the site or project as existed, no account should be taken of the time previously spent by contractors concerned in other sites.
>
> (e) The site exists from the date on which the contractor begins his work, including any preparation work, and continues until the work is completed or permanently abandoned.'

It is interesting to note that the UK/Australia tax treaty of 21 August 2003 (yet to be ratified) contains a new provision relating to the duration of the construction period clearly designed to counteract avoidance devices. Article 5.4 provides, inter alia, that the construction period is to be determined by aggregating the periods during which connected activities are carried on in a Contracting State by associated enterprises.

A similar provision appears in the Exchange of Notes in relation to article 5(3) of the UK/Chile tax treaty of 12 July 2003. This treaty also awaits ratification.

Company residence

33.20 Leaving aside the question of a taxable permanent establishment, the foreign company will need to ensure that its UK property dealing activities do not result in it being managed and controlled, and thus tax resident, in the UK (see paragraphs **2.2** et seq and **32.10**).

Foreign individuals

33.21 Foreign individuals will not necessarily compromise their residence position by conducting property dealing activities in the UK unless they spend more than 183 days in the UK in a fiscal year, or an average of 90 days over a 4-year period [Revenue booklet IR20, paras 1.2, 3.3].

Minimising taxable profits

33.22 Leaving aside the question of double tax agreements, and assuming property dealing profits are liable to UK income or corporation tax, the following techniques could reduce the amount of taxable profits, depending upon the actual circumstances of each case:

(a) The company should be capitalised with the maximum supportable amount of borrowings, whether internal or external, with the interest payments being deductible from the trading profits within thin capitalisation limits (see paragraph **32.12** in relation to property investment).

(b) Work in relation to the project is often performed outside the UK. For example, planning and budgeting the project, making financial arrangements, corresponding and negotiating from abroad with agents and solicitors etc, finding the property, planning and arranging construction and selling the property. A management fee could be paid to a related company abroad for the provision of these services to the non-resident company carrying out the UK project. As the fee would be received for services performed outside the UK it would not constitute profits from a trade carried on in the UK (see paragraph **4.1**).

Anti-avoidance: gains of a capital nature

33.23 The anti-avoidance provisions of ICTA 1988, s 776 also require consideration. Under s 776(2) they are brought into play wherever:

(a) land, or any property deriving its value from land (which can include shares in a property owning company) is acquired with the sole or main object of realising a gain from disposing of the land as defined; or

(b) land is held as trading stock; or

(c) land is developed with the sole or main object of realising a gain from disposing of the land when developed

and any gain of a capital nature is obtained from disposal of the land as defined [ICTA 1988, s 777(2)]. A gain of a capital nature is defined as any gain which does not fall to be included in any computation of income for the purposes of the Tax Acts [ICTA 1988, s 777(13)].

33.24 Land is disposed of if, by any one or more transactions, or by any arrangement or scheme (whether concerning the land or property deriving its value from land), the property in the land, or control over the land, is effectively disposed of [ICTA 1988, s 777(4)]. So, for example, the disposal of shares in a company owning land will be treated as a disposal of the land.

33.25 A withholding tax procedure is provided for in s 777(9) where the Board of Inland Revenue makes a direction for it to apply in advance of the disposal.

33.26 In circumstances where there is a direct sale of the property, all of the circumstances detailed above in ICTA 1988, s 776(2) will normally be sufficient to give the Revenue grounds to tax the profit as a trading profit under Schedule D Case I. However, suppose that the Schedule D Case I profit is not liable to UK tax because, in the absence of a UK permanent establishment, it is exempted by a tax treaty. The key question is whether the gain realised is a gain of a capital nature on the basis that it does not fall to be included in a computation of income. It is arguable that the gain is first includible in a computation of income and is then excluded under the terms of the tax treaty. If so, it would not be a gain of a capital nature and so would be outside the ambit of ICTA 1988, s 776.

33.27 The clearest case in which the section might be applied would be where the property was disposed of indirectly by a sale of the shares in a non-resident company owning a UK property. A sale of the shares would invariably constitute a capital gain and thus a gain of a capital nature. If, for example, the company had acquired the property with the sole or main object of realising a gain from disposal in an indirect manner such as by the sale of its shares, the section would apply in principle. However any gain from the disposal of shares is exempt under ICTA 1988, s 776(10) where the land is held by the company as trading stock in the normal course of its trade. Thus, a gain on realisation of shares would normally be taxed under the section if shares in a property investment company were acquired with the sole or main object of indirectly realising a gain from the property by reselling the shares.

In such a case it is arguable that the taxable gain under ICTA 1988, s 776 could be negated by a tax treaty. Typically, suppose a foreign individual wishes to acquire the shares of a Gibraltar company owning UK property as an investment, solely to resell them at a profit. By making the acquisition through, say, a German company, it is arguable that the 'Capital Gains' or 'Other Income' articles, 8(3) and 15 of the Germany/UK tax treaty prevent the UK from assessing tax under s 776.

The gain would not be liable to German tax in view of the German participation exemption (see Table 4 at paragraph **25.4** and the Examples at paragraph **25.8**). Consideration would need to be given to the extraction of funds from the German company.

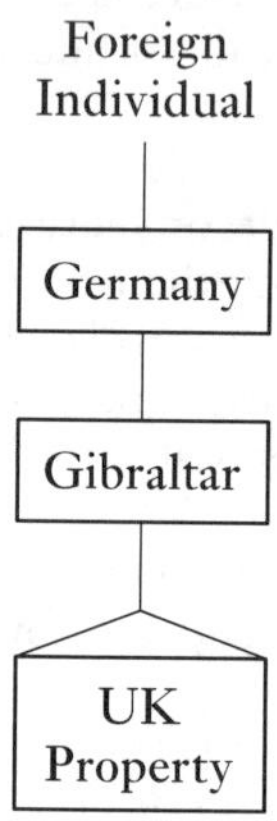

Tax implications in the foreign jurisdiction

33.28 In the case of straightforward property trading, the profits realised will generally be fully taxable in the foreign jurisdiction in the absence of a taxable UK permanent establishment.

However of the jurisdictions selected, Hong Kong and Singapore might regard the property trading profits as sourced in the UK. In that case, they would not be taxable in Hong Kong, which only taxes local source income. And in Singapore the profits would be exempt to the extent they were not remitted to Singapore.

Where the property trading profits arise through a UK permanent establishment, giving rise to taxable UK profits, the position in the selected jurisdictions is summarised in Table 2 at paragraph **13.3(f)**.

Depending upon controlled foreign company rules in the foreign company's or individual's jurisdiction of residence it might be possible to utilise a low-tax company in a third jurisdiction (Cyprus or Ireland were suggested at paragraph **33.18**), to carry out the property trading project and defer tax in the home country (see **Appendix 3**).

34 UK home ownership

34.1 This chapter discusses the tax implications and optimum structure for the non-resident owning a UK home. As in the rest of the book, the situation of a foreign investor who becomes resident or ordinarily resident in the UK is not covered.

There are several reasons why a foreign investor who is unlikely to spend enough time in the UK to acquire UK-residence status for tax purposes may nevertheless wish to have private accommodation available here. Saving on hotel or apartment bills, especially if the investor is accompanied by his or her family, greater privacy and the prospect of a tax-free gain once regular visits to the UK are no longer necessary, being just some.

34.2 The first question to be asked is does the sole fact of owning accommodation in the UK affect the foreign visitor's residence status? The law is silent on this point, but the Inland Revenue's booklet IR20 'Residents and non-residents' (1999), makes it clear that for longer-term visitors, the acquisition of accommodation can by itself make the individual ordinarily resident, but shorter-term visitors who do not become UK-resident under the 183-day rule or the 4-year 91-days average rule should not be affected.

34.3 The usual advice for non-residents is to own the home through the medium of an offshore company. That offshore company would in turn either be owned directly by the investor or through an offshore trust, thus providing shelter against inheritance tax. Capital gains tax is not in point as the investor is non-resident.

Before considering possible structures of ownership via some intermediate entity such as an offshore company, the advantages and disadvantages of direct ownership should first be discussed.

Direct ownership

34.4 There are two chief problems associated with direct ownership: the potential liability to UK inheritance tax ('IHT') and the question of UK withholding tax on loan interest.

34.5 Firstly, UK withholding tax may be deductible under ICTA 1988, s 349 on any interest payments on a loan to purchase the property, if a loan is necessary (or in fact advisable, as a means of reducing the IHT liability—see below). These provisions pose a problem, unlikely as it may seem, if the payments are made wholly abroad to a foreign lender. It was established in *IRC v Broome's Executors* (1935) 19 TC 667 and again in *Stokes v Bennett* (1953) 34 TC 337 that a non-resident is under an equal obligation to that of a resident to deduct tax under s 349 where the source of the payment is in the UK. The loan will be secured on

UK property, which is one item pointing towards a UK source. However, as the debtor will not be resident in the UK, the loan agreement will be executed under foreign law and the interest paid out of a non-UK source of funds, the balance of probability is that there is no UK source. A way of ensuring there is no liability under s 349, while paradoxically bringing things into the UK, would be for the loan to be made by the UK branch of a foreign bank. This would bring the exemption in ICTA 1988, s 349(3)(a) into play.

Alternatively, there would be no need to rely on the exemption under s 349(3)(a) if the lender was resident in a country with a suitable tax treaty with the UK which allows interest to be paid gross (on condition that prior clearance is obtained from the Inland Revenue—the dispensation with prior clearance permitted by ICTA 1988, s 349A does not apply to payments by individuals) (see paragraph **19.11** et seq).

34.6 Direct ownership does, of course, leave the investor with a potential exposure to UK IHT on death. The charge can be mitigated by obtaining a loan secured on the property, even where it is not strictly necessary from a cash point of view. Provided that the interest servicing is not a burden, this has the added advantage of releasing funds that would otherwise have been used for the purchase to be invested outside the UK. If the property were left to the investor's spouse, there would be no IHT charge, provided that the spouse was domiciled in the UK. In the likely event that the spouse was not UK-domiciled, exemption would be limited to £55,000 on the total estate transferred, if the transferor spouse was UK domiciled at death. Even with full exemption, there would at best be a deferral of IHT. Another avenue is to divide ownership of the property between several family members. Even with a property costing £1 million, four owners with equal shares would be sufficient to bring each person's share down to within the IHT nil-rate band. This need not cause problems as to beneficial ownership or right to occupy, as the parents could register the property in their name and make a declaration of trust in favour of the children. This route does, however, require that the owners each purchase their respective share of the property. If the investor alone or the investor and the investor's spouse purchase the property in their names and then gift an interest to the other family members, the transfer may be ineffective on the grounds of a reservation of benefit under FA 1986, s 102.

34.7 Finally, it would be possible simply to insure against the IHT liability. If this were done by a policy on the life of the investor, written on trust for the intended heirs, the value would fall outside the investor's estate at death and so outside the ambit of IHT.

34.8 A further practical complication against direct ownership is the need to obtain probate in the UK on the deceased investor's estate before ownership of the property can legally pass. Proof of the investor's non-UK domicile would have to be provided by the personal representatives and the normal probate formalities would have to be observed. A way round this would be for the property to be owned by an offshore company as nominee. This is not thought to create a benefit charge under ITEPA 2003, s 102.

Indirect ownership

34.9 All of this still argues for indirect ownership through an offshore vehicle. The alternative structures are illustrated diagrammatically as follows:

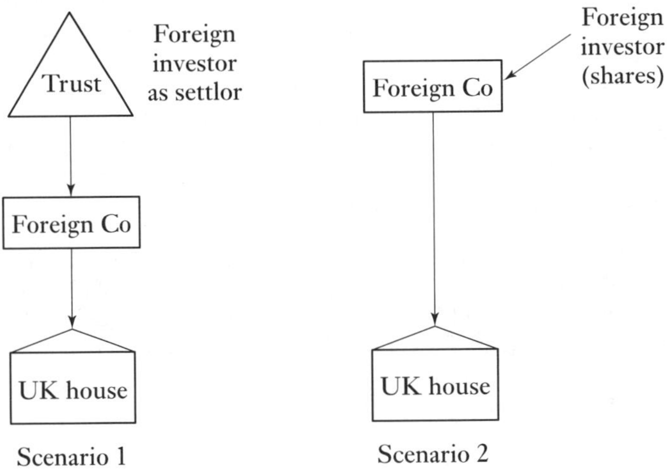

Foreign company

34.10 By contrast to the position with non-domiciled but resident individuals, the potential income tax charge on the investor for the benefit in kind represented by the living accommodation provided by the company to the investor is almost certainly not in point for the following reasons.

34.11 A non-resident individual is liable to UK income tax on earnings in respect of duties performed in the UK [ITEPA 2003, s 27(1)(a)]. Under ITEPA 2003, s 102, the cash equivalent of living accommodation provided for an employee by an employer constitutes taxable earnings of the employee. Under ITEPA 2003, s 66(3), an 'employee' includes a director of a company. A 'director' in turn includes any person in accordance with whose directions or instructions the formal directors are accustomed to act [ITEPA 2003, s 67(1)]. Such people are commonly referred to as 'shadow directors'. It was confirmed beyond doubt in *Regina v Allen (No 2)* [2001] STC 1537 that a shadow director who received no other remuneration from the company was nevertheless within the scope of the charge under s 102 (strictly speaking, its predecessor, ICTA 1988, ss 145, 146 (now repealed).

34.12 The amount of the benefit charge can be quite considerable. If the cost of the property to the employer exceeds £75,000 (which it almost certainly will), ITEPA 2003, s 106 provides that the employee (the foreign investor as shadow director, in this case) is liable every year to a charge on the rental value of the property plus an amount equal to a prescribed percentage of the amount by which its cost exceeds £75,000. By way of example, the prescribed percentage has been set at 5% for 2003/04. On a property costing £500,000, this is equivalent to £21,250 (or to additional tax of £8,500 for higher-rate taxpayers), on the excess over £75,000.

34.13 However for the benefit to be taxable, it must still be provided in respect of duties performed in the UK. If the company is nothing other than a holding entity for the home, and the non-resident investor does not carry out any activities in the UK which could be construed as duties of the deemed employment, it would be difficult for the Inland Revenue to establish that the home was provided in respect of UK duties, and the non-resident investor should thus escape the charge under s 102. But it is essential that the directors of the foreign company make decisions abroad in relation to the property (see paragraph **32.10**). Otherwise a taxable benefit may arise.

34.14 The chief reason for interposing an offshore company and/or trust lies in the IHT advantages. Capital gains tax does not arise [TCGA 1992, s 2(1)]. Owning the property through an offshore company avoids a possible IHT charge on the investor in the event of his or her death while the property remained in his or her ownership. Shares in a foreign company are foreign property, provided that the share register is not kept in the UK.

Foreign trust

34.15 A third possible structure would be for the property to be owned by a foreign trust, in which the investor, as well as being the settlor, owned an interest in possession. There is no question of a benefit charge under s 102, as no company is involved. For the reasons discussed above, there is little likelihood of a withholding tax obligation on interest payments. Non-residence also exempts a sale of the property from capital gains tax [TCGA 1992, s 2(1)], without having to rely on a sole or main residence exemption in the case of direct ownership. The only problem here is with IHT. A person with an interest in possession in a trust is treated for IHT purposes as if he or she directly held the property in which the interest in possession subsists [IHTA 1984, s 49(1)]. Such a charge cannot be avoided but can be mitigated or provided against by the same means as discussed under direct ownership (i.e. by borrowing against the property, by dividing ownership or by insurance directly – see paragraph **34.6**).

35 Foreign entertainers and athletes

Overview

- Foreign entertainers and athletes invariably liable to UK tax on income from performances in UK.
- Tax withheld at source and supervised by Inland Revenue Foreign Entertainers' Unit.
- Royalty income dealt with separately. UK tax generally minimised under tax treaty.

Liability to UK tax

35.1 Foreign entertainers and athletes often make appearances in the UK that generate significant amounts of income for them from their appearance in the entertainment or sports event.

Unlike other foreign entrepreneurs, the absence of a UK permanent establishment, dependent agent or permanent regular agency will not prevent a UK tax liability from arising under Schedule D Case II, from the carrying on of the entertainer's or athlete's profession in the UK [ICTA 1988, s 18(1)(a)(iii), (3)] (see paragraph **12.1** et seq).

Double tax treaties: entertainers and athletes article

35.2 Invariably, a double tax treaty between the UK and the foreign entertainer or athlete's state of residence will allow the UK to tax the net income arising to the individual from his or her personal activities in the UK, based on article 17 of the OECD Model Convention (see **Appendix 1**). It should be noted that the income in question is that generated from the performance itself. As such, income that does not arise from the UK performance, typically merchandising or record royalties, is not taxed in this category (see paragraph **35.29** et seq).

Most, although not all, of the UK's treaties contain a similar entertainers and athletes article. The various treaties can be classified into the five categories summarised in Table 7 at paragraph **35.8**.

35.3 The first category has an article similar to that in the OECD Model Convention, which allows the host country (the UK) to tax both payments made directly to the entertainer or athlete for his or her UK activities as such (article 17.1 of the OECD Model Convention), and payments to third parties (article 17.2). The third party would normally be a loanout company owned by the entertainer or athlete. Many treaties, such as the new US/UK treaty (article 16.2), effectively specify this. This is the most common category of article in the UK's tax treaty network (see paragraph **35.20** et seq).

35.4 A second category limits the UK's taxing rights to payments made to the entertainer or athlete, but not to third parties.

35.5 A third category has no special article but excludes entertainers and athletes from the personal services article (article 14 of the OECD Model Convention, now deleted). As a result, the UK may tax payments made to the entertainer or athlete even though he or she has no permanent establishment in the UK, nor works in the UK for more than 183 days in a fiscal year.

35.6 A fourth category is limited to the old USSR treaty in which taxing rights are reserved to the entertainer's or athlete's country of residence. This treaty is now in force between the UK and Belarus only.

35.7 Finally, the fifth category comprises the treaty with Gambia alone. This has no specific entertainers or athletes article. As a result a foreign entertainer or athlete resident in Gambia will be exempt from UK tax unless he or she has a permanent establishment in the UK or works in the UK for more than 183 days in any fiscal year.

35.8 It should be added that, while on the face of it, treaties in categories 2 and 3 limit the UK's taxing rights to payments to the entertainer alone, it is the Inland Revenue's opinion that paragraph 8 of the commentary on article 17 of the OECD Model Convention allows it to 'look through' the arrangement and to also tax payments made to certain connected parties, typically loanout companies.

TABLE 7 Entertainers and athletes: types of treaty article

Category 1	*Category 2*	*Category 3*	*Category 4*	*Category 5*
Argentina	Australia	Antigua	Belarus	Gambia
Austria	Barbados	Belize		
Azerbaijan	Botswana	Brunei		
Bangladesh	Cyprus	Greece		
Bolivia	Fiji	Grenada		
Canada	Finland	Guernsey		
China	France	Isle of Man		
Croatia	Germany	Jersey		
Czech Republic	Hungary	Kiribati		
Denmark	Israel	Malawi		
Egypt	Jamaica	Montserrat		
Estonia	Japan	Myanmar		
Falkland Islands	Kazakhstan	St Kitts		

Category 1	*Category 2*	*Category 3*	*Category 4*	*Category 5*
Ghana	Kenya	Sierra Leone		
Guyana	Luxembourg	Solomon Islands		
Iceland	Namibia	Tuvalu		
India	Portugal			
Indonesia	Romania			
Ireland	Sudan			
Italy	Swaziland			
Ivory Coast	Tajikistan			
Jordan	Turkmenistan			
Korea	Zambia			
Kuwait				
Latvia				
Lesotho				
Lithuania				
Macedonia				
Malaysia				
Malta				
Mauritius				
Mexico				
Mongolia				
Morocco				
Netherlands				
New Zealand				
Nigeria				
Norway				
Oman				
Pakistan				
Papua New Guinea				
Philippines				
Poland				
Russia				
Singapore				
Slovakia				
Slovenia				
South Africa				
Spain				
Sri Lanka				
Sweden				

Category 1	*Category 2*	*Category 3*	*Category 4*	*Category 5*
Switzerland				
Taiwan				
Thailand				
Trinidad and Tobago				
Tunisia				
Turkey				
Uganda				
Ukraine				
United States				
Uzbekistan				
Venezuela				
Vietnam				
Zimbabwe				

Notes

(1) Many treaties in categories 1 and 2 exempt entertainers taking part in a state-sponsored event or cultural exchange; some (eg that with the US) set a *de minimis* limit for application of taxing rights (USD 20,000 in the case of the US treaty).

(2) Until they repudiated the USSR treaty with effect from 6 April 2002, Armenia, Georgia, Kyrgyzstan and Moldova were also in category 4.

Collection of UK tax: The Foreign Entertainers' Unit ('FEU')

35.9 Foreign entertainers and athletes pose particular problems for national tax authorities due to their brief appearances in the host country and the often large sums involved. In many countries, therefore, there is a special scheme to withhold tax from foreign entertainers' and athletes' earnings, either on account of a final liability or as a final, non-mitigable tax.

The UK's scheme was introduced in 1987 and, apart from changes in the basic rate of tax, is largely unamended. It is a scheme for the collection of tax rather than a basis for assessing tax. It is contained in ICTA 1988, ss 555–558 and the Income Tax (Entertainers and Sportsmen) Regulations, SI 1987/530. The commentary below is based on this legislation.

35.10 The scheme is managed by the Foreign Entertainers' Unit ('FEU') of the Inland Revenue's Special Compliance Office. It deals with all aspects of the tax affairs of overseas entertainers and athletes other than cases where PAYE operates, eg a foreign rugby league player would normally have PAYE deducted by his club. The PAYE aspect is usually dealt with at local district level. The FEU is thus the office that administers and enforces the withholding tax levied under the regulations themselves and is responsible for determining the entertainer's or athlete's eventual liability to UK tax including nearly all investigations work. The address of FEU is:

Inland Revenue
Special Compliance Office
Foreign Entertainers' Unit
Royal House
Prince's Gate
2–6 Homer Road
Solihull
West Midlands B91 3WG
Tel: +44 (0)121 712 8600 Fax: +44 (0)121 712 8662
E-mail: sco.ir.birm@gtnet.gov.uk

35.11 The scheme applies to 'any description of individuals (and whether performing alone or with others) who give performances in their character as entertainers or sportsmen in any kind of entertainment or sport'. 'Entertainment or sport' in this context includes 'any activity of a physical kind, performed by such an individual, which is or may be made available to the public or any section of the public and whether for payment or not'. *Individuals answering this description are referred to in the legislation and here simply as 'entertainers'.*

35.12 The activities to which the scheme applies are either activities performed in the UK by an entertainer in his or her capacity as entertainer on a commercial occasion or event or an activity performed in the UK by an entertainer in his or her character as such in connection with a commercial occasion or event. Specifically included in the scope of the scheme are:

(a) appearances by the entertainer in, or in connection, with a promotion of a commercial event or occasion;

(b) participation in a sound recording, film or video, or in a live or recorded radio, television or other similar transmission.

35.13 It is therefore clear that there must be a *physical activity* and that it must be performed in or in connection with a commercial occasion or event. Examples of commercial occasions or events specified by the legislation are occasions or events:

(a) for which any person might receive or become entitled to receive cash or any other form of property by virtue of the entertainer's performance; or

(b) which are designed to promote commercial sales or activity by advertising, the endorsement of goods or services, sponsorship or other promotional means.

35.14 The tax must be withheld or otherwise accounted for by any payer who makes a payment, to any person, which in any way arises directly or indirectly from a UK appearance by a non-resident entertainer. Thus, payments made to an agent or management company in connection with the entertainer's UK performance are within this ambit (see Example 44 at paragraph **35.19**).

35.15 The legislation applies to payments and transfers. A payment includes a loan of money. A transfer may be a payment or loan in kind, such as the award of a car or the provision of airline tickets.

35.16 No tax needs to be deducted where the total of connected payments and connected transfers made or to be made in the tax year to the entertainer, an associate or a connected party is no more than £1,000. The Inland Revenue interprets this *de minimis* limit as applying separately to each unconnected payer.

35.17 Tax is deducted from the amount of the payment or transfer at the basic rate (22%). For transfers, the net value must be grossed up to arrive at the amount treated as paid. The value of the asset transferred is the cost of providing it, less any amount reimbursed by the entertainer. Where there is a chain of payments, tax previously withheld in the chain may in certain circumstances be taken into account in computing what (if any) further tax needs to be deducted. Alternatively, on application, some payments in the chain may be made gross. These so-called 'middleman applications' seem to be limited in practice to the music industry.

35.18 As the entertainer's eventual liability will, in many cases, be less than the tax deducted (after taking into account allowable expenses), an application for a reduced rate of withholding tax ('an RTP application') is often made to the FEU. Such applications may be accepted from the entertainer, the entertainer's adviser, the payer or the person who receives the payment on the entertainer's behalf. Applications are usually made on a form FEU8 and take the form of a *pro forma* computation of the entertainer's liability to UK tax in respect of the performance. Certain specific documents and information must be submitted with the application, which must be made at least 30 days before the payment or transfer needs to be made. Late applications may be rejected. The Revenue is under no obligation to agree to an application and there is no right of appeal against a refusal or the designation of a rate other than that applied for. In practice, however, provided that the documentation is satisfactory, the Revenue will normally agree, by means of a form FEU4. This may specify a percentage rate or a lump sum. It is possible for zero to be specified. Until the payer has received the Revenue's agreement, he or she is obliged to deduct tax at the full rate of 22%.

35.19 As mentioned above, payments will frequently be made, not directly to the entertainer, but to some other person on the entertainer's behalf. Provided that these third parties have the prescribed connection with the entertainer, the payments will be attributed to the entertainer and deduction of tax has to be made in the normal way. Persons with the prescribed connection include loanout companies and other persons under the control of the entertainer and persons in a contractual relationship with the entertainer such that it can reasonably be supposed that the entertainer or an associate will receive amounts not substantially less than the appropriate amount of profits and gains arising from the payment. This sort of arrangement is typically one in which an intermediate management company receives the payment for the performance, deducts a fee and then passes on the balance to the entertainer or connected parties. In these circumstances the payment is treated as the entertainer's income and the tax withheld may be credited by him or her.

Example 44

A concert promoter arranges with Gold Ltd, a UK based management company, for Crawl, a Canadian jazz singer/pianist, to play two dates in the UK on her forthcoming tour of Europe. The promoter pays Gold Ltd £300,000 less tax. Gold deducts commission and expenses of £30,000 and pays the balance to Crawl.

The promoter must deduct tax from the payment to Gold Ltd, as it is connected with Crawl's appearance in the UK and does not fall within any of the exemptions. In turn, Gold is obliged to deduct tax from its payment to Crawl.

Tax deducted by promoter: £300,000 x 22% = £66,000

Sums received by Gold Ltd: £234,000

Gross sum payable to Crawl: £204,000

Tax due from Gold Ltd: £204,000 x 22% = £44,880

As the promoter's £66,000 exceeds the £44,880 due from Gold, Gold can treat its withholding tax as paid.

Loanout companies

35.20 Where the services in the UK have been provided by the performer's loanout company, he or she will normally receive a salary from the company. Invariably the employer loanout company will be incorporated and resident outside the UK.

35.21 Insofar as the salary relates to the foreign performer's UK activities, it is taxable as the UK-based earnings of an employee not resident in the UK [ITEPA 2003, s 27].

35.22 In situations other than live performers the salary would invariably be exempt from UK tax provided that the employee spent less than 183 days in the UK in the fiscal year in question and the salary was not borne by the foreign employer company's UK permanent establishment (see OECD Model Convention article 15, **Appendix 1**).

However the entertainer's and athlete's article in the UK treaty will invariably override the article 15 exemption, thus allowing the UK to tax the salary as earnings (see OECD Model Convention article 17, **Appendix 1**).

35.23 Whether or not the foreign employer company must operate PAYE is a complex question. In practice this is normally resolved by the fact that the fees received by the loanout company will have been subjected to withholding tax in relation to the employee's UK performance under the FEU procedures discussed above.

National insurance contributions

35.24 Entertainers who are employees of a company having its original place of business outside the UK and whose employment is carried out mainly outside the UK will not normally be liable to pay employee's (primary) Class 1 national insurance contributions until they have been present in the UK for a minimum of 52 consecutive contribution weeks. [Social Security (Contributions) Regulations, SI 2001/1004 reg 145(2)]. If the employer has no UK tax presence and the employee is not under the general control and management of some other person with a UK tax presence, then no employer's (secondary) Class 1 NIC will be due, even after 52 weeks.

35.25 Self-employed entertainers (the deeming provisions of ICTA 1988, s 556 and the regulations have no effect here) who are not ordinarily resident have no liability to pay Class 2 (flat rate) national insurance contributions until they have been resident in the UK for at least 26 out of the preceding 52 contribution weeks [SI 2001/1004 reg 145(1)(d)]. They are entitled to pay Class 2 contributions, should they wish to do so, for any contribution week in which they are 'present' in the UK [SI 2001/1004 reg 145(1)(c)]. The term 'present' is not defined, but simply means physically present. Non-residents are not liable to pay Class 4 contributions [SI 2001/1004 reg 91(b)].

VAT

35.26 A supply of services made in the UK in the course of a business is a taxable supply. Services are treated as supplied in the UK where the person supplying them 'belongs' in the UK. Belonging is determined by the location of the supplier's business establishment or main business establishment; failing that, by his usual place of residence (see paragraph **4.3**).

35.27 Therefore, a non-resident entertainer will not generally be required to register for VAT if he or she has no business establishment in the UK. However if the entertainer has business establishments both in the UK and abroad, there will be a VAT liability (provided always the turnover threshold is reached) if the UK establishment is the one most directly concerned with the supply. Customs and Excise have made it clear that they regard a theatre to be a business establishment. Thus, a non-resident entertainer may well come within the VAT net if he or she hires a theatre in the UK in which to give a performance [VAT Leaflet No 700/4/87 (now withdrawn) paragraph 3]. If it is considered necessary to avoid registration for VAT, it is therefore best for UK resident and VAT registered companies to hire venues etc. On the other hand, if the inconvenience of registration and accounting for VAT is acceptable, registration will enable the entertainer to recoup the VAT suffered on business expenditure.

35.28 It should be noted that a branch or agency through which a person carries on a trade in the UK is regarded as a business establishment. A UK based theatrical agent, who arranges an entertainer's UK appearances almost certainly constitutes a branch or agency, so a liability to VAT may well arise by this means.

Royalties

35.29 It is important to distinguish between genuine royalties and payments for services, as the term tends to be loosely used in the industry.

In the context of this chapter, royalties are payments for the use of copyright. An entertainer will receive royalties only where at some time he or she owns the copyright in the finished product of a performance (eg a compact disc released after a studio recording or live performance). It follows that where, as is usually the case, the agreement stipulates that the copyright belongs not to the entertainer but to a third party (eg the record company or, in the case of a film, the film company), payments received by the entertainer, albeit based on sales or box office takings, are a payment for services and not royalties.

35.30 The distinction is important because where copyright royalties are payable to a person whose 'usual place of abode' is outside the UK, there has always been a requirement to deduct basic rate tax [ICTA 1988, s 536] (see paragraph **6.5** et seq). Copyright royalties for this purpose do not extend to rights in a cinematograph film or video recording or to the accompanying soundtrack, as long as it is not separately exploited. Nor is deduction of tax required where the work has been exported from the UK for distribution abroad [ICTA 1988, s 536(2)].

35.31 Payments already subject to deduction of tax are exempt from the special withholding tax [Income Tax (Entertainers and Sportsmen) Regulations, SI 1987/530 reg 3(3)(a)] as are payments made in respect of sales of records which the entertainer makes in the UK [SI 1987/530 reg 3(3)(c)].

35.32 As mentioned at paragraph **35.29** copyright in the recording does not normally vest in the artiste, so, strictly speaking, deduction of tax under ICTA 1988, s 536 is not appropriate and payments, unless falling within the specific exemption in SI 1987/530 reg 3(3)(c) (see paragraph **35.31**), would be subject to the withholding tax. However it is normal practice in the industry to deduct tax under ICTA 1988, s 536 regardless (but subject to a reduced rate of tax under a treaty).

See **Chapter 6** for a fuller discussion on the taxation of royalties.

Minimising UK tax liabilities

35.33 This section suggests a number of possible strategies that may be utilised to properly minimise the foreign entertainer's or athlete's exposure to UK tax.

35.34 In most circumstances, liability to UK tax under Schedule D Case II is restricted to personal performance in the UK. The time that is spent abroad in rehearsing and preparing for the UK appearance is not a performance in the UK. Ideally, the best arrangement is for the promoter to make a separate payment for these non-UK services and, wherever possible, to make it not to the entertainer or to the loanout company providing the UK services, but rather to a separate entity owned by the entertainer or athlete.

If the rehearsals and pre-performance work take place outside the performer's country of residence it may be possible for tax to be avoided altogether on the fees for the work, provided the country of residence does not impose tax on income from services performed outside its jurisdiction.

A considerable income is often generated by the sale of merchandised products containing the entertainer's or athlete's image, in return for a royalty payable by the merchandiser to the entertainer or athlete. Again, these payments do not arise from any personal performance in the UK.

However where any payments made for endorsing sportswear or for any other use of the entertainer's or athlete's name or image are linked directly or indirectly to performances in the UK, a recent decision of the Special Commissioners (*Set, Ball and Deuce v Robinson*, unreported) indicates that a proportion relating to UK appearances will be taxable in the UK, even where the payments are made by a non-resident person to a non-resident loanout company. Great care should therefore be taken to draft contracts so that exposure to such a charge is minimised.

It is a separate legal question as to whether the royalty is or is not a copyright or design royalty. If it is, a 22% UK withholding tax will normally apply subject to reduction under a tax treaty. If copyright or design is inapplicable, withholding tax will not be deductible except in the unlikely case that the royalty is an annual payment. See **Chapter 6** for a discussion on the UK and foreign tax position relating to royalties.

Again, it is advisable that a separate entity own the relevant rights and receive the royalties, rather than the entertainer or his or her loanout company.

35.35 Anyone attending a pop concert will be aware of the enormously expensive technical equipment and scenery involved in the performance. This equipment may be owned and financed by the artist's own organisation.

Again, a separate entity owned by the artist could rent the equipment to the promoter in return for a hiring fee. Depending upon the duration of the UK tour and the number of locations, it is perfectly possible that the foreign entity will have no UK permanent establishment to which the equipment rents can be attributed. As a result, it is arguable that UK tax will not be payable on the net income from the hiring activity (see paragraph **31.1** et seq).

Tax implications in the foreign jurisdiction

35.36 Reference should be made to Table 2 at paragraph **13.3(f)**. Foreign entertainers and athletes liable to UK tax from their performances in the UK will either be taxable in the relevant foreign jurisdiction with a credit for the UK tax paid; or alternatively will be exempt from tax in their home jurisdiction (see paragraphs **11.13**, **11.14** and article 23 of the OECD Model Convention, **Appendix 1**). In this latter case, as the UK tax will constitute a final tax, any UK tax saving will also constitute a real tax saving. It will be seen from Note 1 to the Table that, although the UK earnings may be exempt in the home country as a result of a tax treaty with the UK, the foreign entertainer or athlete's tax rate in his or her home jurisdiction is usually arrived at by including the UK income in his or her total income for the purposes of arriving at the relevant rate of tax in his or her jurisdiction of residence.

In cases where the foreign entertainer or athlete receives a salary from his or her loanout company for the services performed in the UK, UK tax will be payable on the salary as discussed at paragraph **35.20** et seq.

Depending on the domestic tax legislation in the foreign individual's country of residence and the terms of the double tax treaty with the UK, the salary will either be exempt from tax in the home country or taxable with a credit for the UK tax paid (see paragraphs **11.13**, **11.14** and the OECD Model Convention, **Appendix 1**).

For the treatment of royalty income and equipment rents in the foreign jurisdiction, see **Chapters 6** and **31**.

Appendix 1

Articles of the Model Convention with respect to taxes on income and on capital

[as they read on 28 January 2003]

Summary of the Convention

Title of the Convention

Convention between (State A) and (State B) with respect to taxes on income and on capital[1]

Preamble to the Convention[2]

1. States wishing to do so may follow the widespread practice of including in the title a reference to either the avoidance of double taxation or to both the avoidance of double taxation and the prevention of fiscal evasion.
2. The Preamble of the Convention shall be drafted in accordance with the constitutional procedure of both Contracting States.

Chapter I
Scope Of The Convention

Article 1
Persons covered

This Convention shall apply to persons who are residents of one or both of the Contracting States.

Article 2
Taxes covered

1. This Convention shall apply to taxes on income and on capital imposed on behalf of a Contracting State or of its political subdivisions or local authorities, irrespective of the manner in which they are levied.
2. There shall be regarded as taxes on income and on capital all taxes imposed on total income, on total capital, or on elements of income or of capital, including taxes on gains from the alienation of movable or immovable property, taxes on the total amounts of wages or salaries paid by enterprises, as well as taxes on capital appreciation.
3. The existing taxes to which the Convention shall apply are in particular:
   a) (in State A): . . . .
   b) (in State B): . . . .
4. The Convention shall apply also to any identical or substantially similar taxes that are imposed after the date of signature of the Convention in addition to, or in place of, the existing taxes. The competent authorities of the Contracting States shall notify each other of any significant changes that have been made in their taxation laws.

Chapter II
Definitions

Article 3
General definitions

1. For the purposes of this Convention, unless the context otherwise requires:

a) the term 'person' includes an individual, a company and any other body of persons;

b) the term 'company' means any body corporate or any entity that is treated as a body corporate for tax purposes;

c) the term 'enterprise' applies to the carrying on of any business;

d) the terms 'enterprise of a Contracting State' and 'enterprise of the other Contracting State' mean respectively an enterprise carried on by a resident of a Contracting State and an enterprise carried on by a resident of the other Contracting State;

e) the term 'international traffic' means any transport by a ship or aircraft operated by an enterprise that has its place of effective management in a Contracting State, except when the ship or aircraft is operated solely between places in the other Contracting State;

f) the term 'competent authority' means:

(*i*) (in State A): . . . .

(*ii*) (in State B): . . . .

g) the term 'national', in relation to a Contracting State, means:

(*i*) any individual possessing the nationality or citizenship of that Contracting State; and

(*ii*) any legal person, partnership or association deriving its status as such from the laws in force in that Contracting State;

h) the term 'business' includes the performance of professional services and of other activities of an independent character.

2. As regards the application of the Convention at any time by a Contracting State, any term not defined therein shall, unless the context otherwise requires, have the meaning that it has at that time under the law of that State for the purposes of the taxes to which the Convention applies, any meaning under the applicable tax laws of that State prevailing over a meaning given to the term under other laws of that State.

Article 4
Resident

1. For the purposes of this Convention, the term 'resident of a Contracting State' means any person who, under the laws of that State, is liable to tax therein by reason of his domicile, residence, place of management or any other criterion of a similar nature, and also includes that State and any political subdivision or local authority thereof. This term, however, does not include any person who is liable to tax in that State in respect only of income from sources in that State or capital situated therein.

2. Where by reason of the provisions of paragraph 1 an individual is a resident of both Contracting States, then his status shall be determined as follows:

a) he shall be deemed to be a resident only of the State in which he has a permanent home available to him; if he has a permanent home available to him in both States, he shall be deemed to be a resident only of the State with which his personal and economic relations are closer (centre of vital interests);

b) if the State in which he has his centre of vital interests cannot be determined, or if he has not a permanent home available to him in either State, he shall be deemed to be a resident only of the State in which he has an habitual abode;

c) if he has an habitual abode in both States or in neither of them, he shall be deemed to be a resident only of the State of which he is a national;

d) if he is a national of both States or of neither of them, the competent authorities of the Contracting States shall settle the question by mutual agreement.

3. Where by reason of the provisions of paragraph 1 a person other than an individual is a resident of both Contracting States, then it shall be deemed to be a resident only of the State in which its place of effective management is situated.

Article 5
Permanent establishment

1. For the purposes of this Convention, the term 'permanent establishment' means a fixed place of business through which the business of an enterprise is wholly or partly carried on.

2. The term 'permanent establishment' includes especially:

a) a place of management;

b) a branch;

c) an office;

d) a factory;

e) a workshop, and

f) a mine, an oil or gas well, a quarry or any other place of extraction of natural resources.

3. A building site or construction or installation project constitutes a permanent establishment only if it lasts more than twelve months.

4. Notwithstanding the preceding provisions of this Article, the term 'permanent establishment' shall be deemed not to include:

a) the use of facilities solely for the purpose of storage, display or delivery of goods or merchandise belonging to the enterprise;

b) the maintenance of a stock of goods or merchandise belonging to the enterprise solely for the purpose of storage, display or delivery;

c) the maintenance of a stock of goods or merchandise belonging to the enterprise solely for the purpose of processing by another enterprise;

d) the maintenance of a fixed place of business solely for the purpose of purchasing goods or merchandise or of collecting information, for the enterprise;

e) the maintenance of a fixed place of business solely for the purpose of carrying on, for the enterprise, any other activity of a preparatory or auxiliary character;

f) the maintenance of a fixed place of business solely for any combination of activities mentioned in subparagraphs *a*) to *e*), provided that the overall activity of the fixed place of business resulting from this combination is of a preparatory or auxiliary character.

5. Notwithstanding the provisions of paragraphs 1 and 2, where a person — other than an agent of an independent status to whom paragraph 6 applies — is acting on behalf of an enterprise and has, and habitually exercises, in a Contracting State an authority to conclude contracts in the name of the enterprise, that enterprise shall be deemed to have a permanent establishment in that State in respect of any activities which that person undertakes for the enterprise, unless the activities of such person are limited to those mentioned in paragraph 4 which, if exercised through a fixed place of business, would not make this fixed place of business a permanent establishment under the provisions of that paragraph.

6. An enterprise shall not be deemed to have a permanent establishment in a Contracting State merely because it carries on business in that State through a broker, general commission agent or any other agent of an independent status, provided that such persons are acting in the ordinary course of their business.

7. The fact that a company which is a resident of a Contracting State controls or is controlled by a company which is a resident of the other Contracting State, or which carries on business in that other State (whether through a permanent establishment or otherwise), shall not of itself constitute either company a permanent establishment of the other.

Chapter III
Taxation of income

Article 6
Income from immovable property

1. Income derived by a resident of a Contracting State from immovable property (including income from agriculture or forestry) situated in the other Contracting State may be taxed in that other State.

2. The term 'immovable property' shall have the meaning which it has under the law of the Contracting State in which the property in question is

situated. The term shall in any case include property accessory to immovable property, livestock and equipment used in agriculture and forestry, rights to which the provisions of general law respecting landed property apply, usufruct of immovable property and rights to variable or fixed payments as consideration for the working of, or the right to work, mineral deposits, sources and other natural resources; ships, boats and aircraft shall not be regarded as immovable property.

3. The provisions of paragraph 1 shall apply to income derived from the direct use, letting, or use in any other form of immovable property.

4. The provisions of paragraphs 1 and 3 shall also apply to the income from immovable property of an enterprise.

Article 7
Business profits

1. The profits of an enterprise of a Contracting State shall be taxable only in that State unless the enterprise carries on business in the other Contracting State through a permanent establishment situated therein. If the enterprise carries on business as aforesaid, the profits of the enterprise may be taxed in the other State but only so much of them as is attributable to that permanent establishment.

2. Subject to the provisions of paragraph 3, where an enterprise of a Contracting State carries on business in the other Contracting State through a permanent establishment situated therein, there shall in each Contracting State be attributed to that permanent establishment the profits which it might be expected to make if it were a distinct and separate enterprise engaged in the same or similar activities under the same or similar conditions and dealing wholly independently with the enterprise of which it is a permanent establishment.

3. In determining the profits of a permanent establishment, there shall be allowed as deductions expenses which are incurred for the purposes of the permanent establishment, including executive and general administrative expenses so incurred, whether in the State in which the permanent establishment is situated or elsewhere.

4. Insofar as it has been customary in a Contracting State to determine the profits to be attributed to a permanent establishment on the basis of an apportionment of the total profits of the enterprise to its various parts, nothing in paragraph 2 shall preclude that Contracting State from determining the profits to be taxed by such an apportionment as may be customary; the method of apportionment adopted shall, however, be such that the result shall be in accordance with the principles contained in this Article.

5. No profits shall be attributed to a permanent establishment by reason of the mere purchase by that permanent establishment of goods or merchandise for the enterprise.

6. For the purposes of the preceding paragraphs, the profits to be attributed to the permanent establishment shall be determined by the same method year by year unless there is good and sufficient reason to the contrary.

7. Where profits include items of income which are dealt with separately in other Articles of this Convention, then the provisions of those Articles shall not be affected by the provisions of this Article.

Article 8
Shipping, inland waterways transport and air transport

1. Profits from the operation of ships or aircraft in international traffic shall be taxable only in the Contracting State in which the place of effective management of the enterprise is situated.

2. Profits from the operation of boats engaged in inland waterways transport shall be taxable only in the Contracting State in which the place of effective management of the enterprise is situated.

3. If the place of effective management of a shipping enterprise or of an inland waterways transport enterprise is aboard a ship or boat, then it shall be deemed to be situated in the Contracting State in which the home harbour of the ship or boat is situated, or, if there is no such home harbour, in the Contracting State of which the operator of the ship or boat is a resident.

4. The provisions of paragraph 1 shall also apply to profits from the participation in a pool, a joint business or an international operating agency.

Article 9
Associated enterprises

1. Where

   a) an enterprise of a Contracting State participates directly or indirectly in the management, control or capital of an enterprise of the other Contracting State, or

   b) the same persons participate directly or indirectly in the management, control or capital of an enterprise of a Contracting State and an enterprise of the other Contracting State, and in either case conditions are made or imposed between the two enterprises in their commercial or financial relations which differ from those which would be made between independent enterprises, then any profits which would, but for those conditions, have accrued to one of the enterprises, but, by reason of those conditions, have not so accrued, may be included in the profits of that enterprise and taxed accordingly.

2. Where a Contracting State includes in the profits of an enterprise of that State — and taxes accordingly — profits on which an enterprise of the other Contracting State has been charged to tax in that other State and the profits so included are profits which would have accrued to the enterprise

of the first-mentioned State if the conditions made between the two enterprises had been those which would have been made between independent enterprises, then that other State shall make an appropriate adjustment to the amount of the tax charged therein on those profits. In determining such adjustment, due regard shall be had to the other provisions of this Convention and the competent authorities of the Contracting States shall if necessary consult each other.

Article 10
Dividends

1. Dividends paid by a company which is a resident of a Contracting State to a resident of the other Contracting State may be taxed in that other State.

2. However, such dividends may also be taxed in the Contracting State of which the company paying the dividends is a resident and according to the laws of that State, but if the beneficial owner of the dividends is a resident of the other Contracting State, the tax so charged shall not exceed:

   a) 5 per cent of the gross amount of the dividends if the beneficial owner is a company (other than a partnership) which holds directly at least 25 per cent of the capital of the company paying the dividends;

   b) 15 per cent of the gross amount of the dividends in all other cases. The competent authorities of the Contracting States shall by mutual agreement settle the mode of application of these limitations. This paragraph shall not affect the taxation of the company in respect of the profits out of which the dividends are paid. 3. The term 'dividends' as used in this Article means income from shares, 'jouissance' shares or 'jouissance' rights, mining shares, founders' shares or other rights, not being debt-claims, participating in profits, as well as income from other corporate rights which is subjected to the same taxation treatment as income from shares by the laws of the State of which the company making the distribution is a resident.

4. The provisions of paragraphs 1 and 2 shall not apply if the beneficial owner of the dividends, being a resident of a Contracting State, carries on business in the other Contracting State of which the company paying the dividends is a resident through a permanent establishment situated therein and the holding in respect of which the dividends are paid is effectively connected with such permanent establishment. In such case the provisions of Article 7 shall apply.

5. Where a company which is a resident of a Contracting State derives profits or income from the other Contracting State, that other State may not impose any tax on the dividends paid by the company, except insofar as such dividends are paid to a resident of that other State or insofar as the holding in respect of which the dividends are paid is effectively connected with a permanent establishment situated in that other State, nor subject the company's undistributed profits to a tax on the company's undistributed

profits, even if the dividends paid or the undistributed profits consist wholly or partly of profits or income arising in such other State.

Article 11
Interest

1. Interest arising in a Contracting State and paid to a resident of the other Contracting State may be taxed in that other State.

2. However, such interest may also be taxed in the Contracting State in which it arises and according to the laws of that State, but if the beneficial owner of the interest is a resident of the other Contracting State, the tax so charged shall not exceed 10 per cent of the gross amount of the interest. The competent authorities of the Contracting States shall by mutual agreement settle the mode of application of this limitation.

3. The term 'interest' as used in this Article means income from debt-claims of every kind, whether or not secured by mortgage and whether or not carrying a right to participate in the debtor's profits, and in particular, income from government securities and income from bonds or debentures, including premiums and prizes attaching to such securities, bonds or debentures. Penalty charges for late payment shall not be regarded as interest for the purpose of this Article.

4. The provisions of paragraphs 1 and 2 shall not apply if the beneficial owner of the interest, being a resident of a Contracting State, carries on business in the other Contracting State in which the interest arises through a permanent establishment situated therein and the debt-claim in respect of which the interest is paid is effectively connected with such permanent establishment. In such case the provisions of Article 7 shall apply.

5. Interest shall be deemed to arise in a Contracting State when the payer is a resident of that State. Where, however, the person paying the interest, whether he is a resident of a Contracting State or not, has in a Contracting State a permanent establishment in connection with which the indebtedness on which the interest is paid was incurred, and such interest is borne by such permanent establishment, then such interest shall be deemed to arise in the State in which the permanent establishment is situated.

6. Where, by reason of a special relationship between the payer and the beneficial owner or between both of them and some other person, the amount of the interest, having regard to the debt-claim for which it is paid, exceeds the amount which would have been agreed upon by the payer and the beneficial owner in the absence of such relationship, the provisions of this Article shall apply only to the last-mentioned amount. In such case, the excess part of the payments shall remain taxable according to the laws of each Contracting State, due regard being had to the other provisions of this Convention.

Article 12
Royalties

1. Royalties arising in a Contracting State and beneficially owned by a resident of the other Contracting State shall be taxable only in that other State.

2. The term 'royalties' as used in this Article means payments of any kind received as a consideration for the use of, or the right to use, any copyright of literary, artistic or scientific work including cinematograph films, any patent, trade mark, design or model, plan, secret formula or process, or for information concerning industrial, commercial or scientific experience.

3. The provisions of paragraph 1 shall not apply if the beneficial owner of the royalties, being a resident of a Contracting State, carries on business in the other Contracting State in which the royalties arise through a permanent establishment situated therein and the right or property in respect of which the royalties are paid is effectively connected with such permanent establishment. In such case the provisions of Article 7 shall apply.

4. Where, by reason of a special relationship between the payer and the beneficial owner or between both of them and some other person, the amount of the royalties, having regard to the use, right or information for which they are paid, exceeds the amount which would have been agreed upon by the payer and the beneficial owner in the absence of such relationship, the provisions of this Article shall apply only to the last-mentioned amount. In such case, the excess part of the payments shall remain taxable according to the laws of each Contracting State, due regard being had to the other provisions of this Convention.

Article 13
Capital gains

1. Gains derived by a resident of a Contracting State from the alienation of immovable property referred to in Article 6 and situated in the other Contracting State may be taxed in that other State.

2. Gains from the alienation of movable property forming part of the business property of a permanent establishment which an enterprise of a Contracting State has in the other Contracting State, including such gains from the alienation of such a permanent establishment (alone or with the whole enterprise), may be taxed in that other State.

3. Gains from the alienation of ships or aircraft operated in international traffic, boats engaged in inland waterways transport or movable property pertaining to the operation of such ships, aircraft or boats, shall be taxable only in the Contracting State in which the place of effective management of the enterprise is situated.

4. Gains derived by a resident of a Contracting State from the alienation of shares deriving more than 50 per cent of their value directly or indirectly from immovable property situated in the other Contracting State may be taxed in that other State.

5. Gains from the alienation of any property, other than that referred to in paragraphs 1, 2, 3 and 4, shall be taxable only in the Contracting State of which the alienator is a resident.

Appendix 1

[Article 14 – Independent personal services]

[Deleted]

Article 15
Income from employment

1. Subject to the provisions of Articles 16, 18 and 19, salaries, wages and other similar remuneration derived by a resident of a Contracting State in respect of an employment shall be taxable only in that State unless the employment is exercised in the other Contracting State. If the employment is so exercised, such remuneration as is derived therefrom may be taxed in that other State.

2. Notwithstanding the provisions of paragraph 1, remuneration derived by a resident of a Contracting State in respect of an employment exercised in the other Contracting State shall be taxable only in the first-mentioned State if:

   a) the recipient is present in the other State for a period or periods not exceeding in the aggregate 183 days in any twelve month period commencing or ending in the fiscal year concerned, and

   b) the remuneration is paid by, or on behalf of, an employer who is not a resident of the other State, and

   c) the remuneration is not borne by a permanent establishment which the employer has in the other State.

3. Notwithstanding the preceding provisions of this Article, remuneration derived in respect of an employment exercised aboard a ship or aircraft operated in international traffic, or aboard a boat engaged in inland waterways transport, may be taxed in the Contracting State in which the place of effective management of the enterprise is situated.

Article 16
Directors' fees

Directors' fees and other similar payments derived by a resident of a Contracting State in his capacity as a member of the board of directors of a company which is a resident of the other Contracting State may be taxed in that other State.

Article 17
Artistes and sportsmen

1. Notwithstanding the provisions of Articles 7 and 15, income derived by a resident of a Contracting State as an entertainer, such as a theatre, motion picture, radio or television artiste, or a musician, or as a sportsman, from his personal activities as such exercised in the other Contracting State, may be taxed in that other State.

2. Where income in respect of personal activities exercised by an entertainer or a sportsman in his capacity as such accrues not to the entertainer or sportsman himself but to another person, that income may, notwithstanding the provisions of Articles 7 and 15, be taxed in the Contracting State in which the activities of the entertainer or sportsman are exercised.

Article 18
Pensions

Subject to the provisions of paragraph 2 of Article 19, pensions and other similar remuneration paid to a resident of a Contracting State in consideration of past employment shall be taxable only in that State.

Article 19
Government service

1.

a) Salaries, wages and other similar remuneration, other than a pension, paid by a Contracting State or a political subdivision or a local authority thereof to an individual in respect of services rendered to that State or subdivision or authority shall be taxable only in that State.

b) However, such salaries, wages and other similar remuneration shall be taxable only in the other Contracting State if the services are rendered in that State and the individual is a resident of that State who:

(*i*) is a national of that State; or

(*ii*) did not become a resident of that State solely for the purpose of rendering the services.

2.

a) Any pension paid by, or out of funds created by, a Contracting State or a political subdivision or a local authority thereof to an individual in respect of services rendered to that State or subdivision or authority shall be taxable only in that State.

b) However, such pension shall be taxable only in the other Contracting State if the individual is a resident of, and a national of, that State.

3. The provisions of Articles 15, 16, 17, and 18 shall apply to salaries, wages and other similar remuneration, and to pensions, in respect of services rendered in connection with a business carried on by a Contracting State or a political subdivision or a local authority thereof.

Article 20
Students

Payments which a student or business apprentice who is or was immediately before visiting a Contracting State a resident of the other Contracting State and who is present in the first-mentioned State solely for the purpose of his education or training receives for the purpose of his maintenance, education or training shall not be taxed in that State, provided that such payments arise from sources outside that State.

Article 21
Other income

1. Items of income of a resident of a Contracting State, wherever arising, not dealt with in the foregoing Articles of this Convention shall be taxable only in that State.

2. The provisions of paragraph 1 shall not apply to income, other than income from immovable property as defined in paragraph 2 of Article 6, if the recipient of such income, being a resident of a Contracting State, carries on business in the other Contracting State through a permanent establishment situated therein and the right or property in respect of which the income is paid is effectively connected with such permanent establishment. In such case the provisions of Article 7 shall apply.

Chapter IV
Taxation of capital

Article 22
Capital

1. Capital represented by immovable property referred to in Article 6, owned by a resident of a Contracting State and situated in the other Contracting State, may be taxed in that other State.

2. Capital represented by movable property forming part of the business property of a permanent establishment which an enterprise of a Contracting State has in the other Contracting State may be taxed in that other State.

3. Capital represented by ships and aircraft operated in international traffic and by boats engaged in inland waterways transport, and by movable property pertaining to the operation of such ships, aircraft and boats, shall be taxable only in the Contracting State in which the place of effective management of the enterprise is situated.

4. All other elements of capital of a resident of a Contracting State shall be taxable only in that State.

Chapter V
Methods for elimination of double taxation

Article 23A
Exemption method

1. Where a resident of a Contracting State derives income or owns capital which, in accordance with the provisions of this Convention, may be taxed in the other Contracting State, the first-mentioned State shall, subject to the provisions of paragraphs 2 and 3, exempt such income or capital from tax.

2. Where a resident of a Contracting State derives items of income which, in accordance with the provisions of Articles 10 and 11, may be taxed in the other Contracting State, the first-mentioned State shall allow as a deduction from the tax on the income of that resident an amount equal to the tax paid in that other State. Such deduction shall not, however, exceed that part of the tax, as computed before the deduction is given, which is attributable to such items of income derived from that other State.

3. Where in accordance with any provision of the Convention income derived or capital owned by a resident of a Contracting State is exempt from tax in that State, such State may nevertheless, in calculating the amount of tax on the remaining income or capital of such resident, take into account the exempted income or capital.

4. The provisions of paragraph 1 shall not apply to income derived or capital owned by a resident of a Contracting State where the other Contracting State applies the provisions of the Convention to exempt such income or capital from tax or applies the provisions of paragraph 2 of Article 10 or 11 to such income.

Article 23B
Credit method

1. Where a resident of a Contracting State derives income or owns capital which, in accordance with the provisions of this Convention, may be taxed in the other Contracting State, the first-mentioned State shall allow:

   a) as a deduction from the tax on the income of that resident, an amount equal to the income tax paid in that other State;

   b) as a deduction from the tax on the capital of that resident, an amount equal to the capital tax paid in that other State. Such deduction in either case shall not, however, exceed that part of the income tax or capital tax, as computed before the deduction is given, which is attributable, as the case may be, to the income or the capital which may be taxed in that other State.

2. Where in accordance with any provision of the Convention income derived or capital owned by a resident of a Contracting State is exempt from tax in

that State, such State may nevertheless, in calculating the amount of tax on the remaining income or capital of such resident, take into account the exempted income or capital.

Chapter VI
Special provisions

Article 24
Non-discrimination

1. Nationals of a Contracting State shall not be subjected in the other Contracting State to any taxation or any requirement connected therewith, which is other or more burdensome than the taxation and connected requirements to which nationals of that other State in the same circumstances, in particular with respect to residence, are or may be subjected. This provision shall, notwithstanding the provisions of Article 1, also apply to persons who are not residents of one or both of the Contracting States.

2. Stateless persons who are residents of a Contracting State shall not be subjected in either Contracting State to any taxation or any requirement connected therewith, which is other or more burdensome than the taxation and connected requirements to which nationals of the State concerned in the same circumstances, in particular with respect to residence, are or may be subjected.

3. The taxation on a permanent establishment which an enterprise of a Contracting State has in the other Contracting State shall not be less favourably levied in that other State than the taxation levied on enterprises of that other State carrying on the same activities. This provision shall not be construed as obliging a Contracting State to grant to residents of the other Contracting State any personal allowances, reliefs and reductions for taxation purposes on account of civil status or family responsibilities which it grants to its own residents.

4. Except where the provisions of paragraph 1 of Article 9, paragraph 6 of Article 11, or paragraph 4 of Article 12, apply, interest, royalties and other disbursements paid by an enterprise of a Contracting State to a resident of the other Contracting State shall, for the purpose of determining the taxable profits of such enterprise, be deductible under the same conditions as if they had been paid to a resident of the first-mentioned State. Similarly, any debts of an enterprise of a Contracting State to a resident of the other Contracting State shall, for the purpose of determining the taxable capital of such enterprise, be deductible under the same conditions as if they had been contracted to a resident of the first-mentioned State.

5. Enterprises of a Contracting State, the capital of which is wholly or partly owned or controlled, directly or indirectly, by one or more residents of the other Contracting State, shall not be subjected in the first-mentioned State to any taxation or any requirement connected therewith which is other or more burdensome than the taxation and connected requirements to which other similar enterprises of the first-mentioned State are or may be subjected.

6. The provisions of this Article shall, notwithstanding the provisions of Article 2, apply to taxes of every kind and description.

Article 25
Mutual agreement procedure

1. Where a person considers that the actions of one or both of the Contracting States result or will result for him in taxation not in accordance with the provisions of this Convention, he may, irrespective of the remedies provided by the domestic law of those States, present his case to the competent authority of the Contracting State of which he is a resident or, if his case comes under paragraph 1 of Article 24, to that of the Contracting State of which he is a national. The case must be presented within three years from the first notification of thc action rcsulting in taxation not in accordance with the provisions of the Convention.

2. The competent authority shall endeavour, if the objection appears to it to be justified and if it is not itself able to arrive at a satisfactory solution, to resolve the case by mutual agreement with the competent authority of the other Contracting State, with a view to the avoidance of taxation which is not in accordance with the Convention. Any agreement reached shall be implemented notwithstanding any time limits in the domestic law of the Contracting States.

3. The competent authorities of the Contracting States shall endeavour to resolve by mutual agreement any difficulties or doubts arising as to the interpretation or application of the Convention. They may also consult together for the elimination of double taxation in cases not provided for in the Convention.

4. The competent authorities of the Contracting States may communicate with each other directly, including through a joint commission consisting of themselves or their representatives, for the purpose of reaching an agreement in the sense of the preceding paragraphs.

Article 26
Exchange of information

1. The competent authorities of the Contracting States shall exchange such information as is necessary for carrying out the provisions of this Convention or of the domestic laws concerning taxes of every kind and description imposed on behalf of the Contracting States, or of their political subdivisions or local authorities, insofar as the taxation thereunder is not contrary to the Convention. The exchange of information is not restricted by Articles 1 and 2. Any information received by a Contracting State shall be treated as secret in the same manner as information obtained under the domestic laws of that State and shall be disclosed only to persons or authorities (including courts and administrative bodies) concerned with the assessment or collection of, the enforcement or prosecution in respect of, or the determination of appeals in relation to the taxes referred to in the

first sentence. Such persons or authorities shall use the information only for such purposes. They may disclose the information in public court proceedings or in judicial decisions.

2. In no case shall the provisions of paragraph 1 be construed so as to impose on a Contracting State the obligation:

   a) to carry out administrative measures at variance with the laws and administrative practice of that or of the other Contracting State;

   b) to supply information which is not obtainable under the laws or in the normal course of the administration of that or of the other Contracting State;

   c) to supply information which would disclose any trade, business, industrial, commercial or professional secret or trade process, or information, the disclosure of which would be contrary to public policy (ordre public).

Article 27
Assistance in the collection of taxes[1]

1. The Contracting States shall lend assistance to each other in the collection of revenue claims. This assistance is not restricted by Articles 1 and 2. The competent authorities of the Contracting States may by mutual agreement settle the mode of application of this Article.

2. The term 'revenue claim' as used in this Article means an amount owed in respect of taxes of every kind and description imposed on behalf of the Contracting States, or of their political subdivisions or local authorities, insofar as the taxation thereunder is not contrary to this Convention or any other instrument to which the Contracting States are parties, as well as interest, administrative penalties and costs of collection or conservancy related to such amount.

3. When a revenue claim of a Contracting State is enforceable under the laws of that State and is owed by a person who, at that time, cannot, under the laws of that State, prevent its collection, that revenue claim shall, at the request of the competent authority of that State, be accepted for purposes of collection by the competent authority of the other Contracting State. That revenue claim shall be collected by that other State in accordance with the provisions of its laws applicable to the enforcement and collection of its own taxes as if the revenue claim were a revenue claim of that other State.

4. When a revenue claim of a Contracting State is a claim in respect of which that State may, under its law, take measures of conservancy with a view to ensure its collection, that revenue claim shall, at the request of the competent authority of that State, be accepted for purposes of taking measures of conservancy by the competent authority of the other Contracting State. That other State shall take measures of conservancy in respect of that revenue claim in accordance with the provisions of its laws as if the revenue claim were a revenue claim of that other State even if, at the time when such

measures are applied, the revenue claim is not enforceable in the firstmentioned State or is owed by a person who has a right to prevent its collection.

5. Notwithstanding the provisions of paragraphs 3 and 4, a revenue claim accepted by a Contracting State for purposes of paragraph 3 or 4 shall not, in that State, be subject to the time limits or accorded any priority applicable to a revenue claim under the laws of that State by reason of its nature as such. In addition, a revenue claim accepted by a Contracting State for the purposes of paragraph 3 or 4 shall not, in that State, have any priority applicable to that revenue claim under the laws of the other Contracting State.

6. Proceedings with respect to the existence, validity or the amount of a revenue claim of a Contracting State shall not be brought before the courts or administrative bodies of the other Contracting State.

7. Where, at any time after a request has been made by a Contracting State under paragraph 3 or 4 and before the other Contracting State has collected and remitted the relevant revenue claim to the first-mentioned State, the relevant revenue claim ceases to be

   a) in the case of a request under paragraph 3, a revenue claim of the first-mentioned State that is enforceable under the laws of that State and is owed by a person who, at that time, cannot, under the laws of that State, prevent its collection, or

   b) in the case of a request under paragraph 4, a revenue claim of the first-mentioned State in respect of which that State may, under its laws, take measures of conservancy with a view to ensure its collection the competent authority of the first-mentioned State shall promptly notify the competent authority of the other State of that fact and, at the option of the other State, the firstmentioned State shall either suspend or withdraw its request.

8. In no case shall the provisions of this Article be construed so as to impose on a Contracting State the obligation:

   a) to carry out administrative measures at variance with the laws and administrative practice of that or of the other Contracting State;

   b) to carry out measures which would be contrary to public policy (ordre public);

   c) to provide assistance if the other Contracting State has not pursued all reasonable measures of collection or conservancy, as the case may be, available under its laws or administrative practice;

   d) to provide assistance in those cases where the administrative burden for that State is clearly disproportionate to the benefit to be derived by the other Contracting State.

1. In some countries, national law, policy or administrative considerations may not allow or justify the type of assistance envisaged under this Article or may require that this type of assistance be restricted, e.g. to countries that have

similar tax systems or tax administrations or as to the taxes covered. For that reason, the Article should only be included in the Convention where each State concludes that, based on the factors described in paragraph 1 of the Commentary on the Article, they can agree to provide assistance in the collection of taxes levied by the other State.

Article 28
Members of diplomatic missions and consular posts

Nothing in this Convention shall affect the fiscal privileges of members of diplomatic missions or consular posts under the general rules of international law or under the provisions of special agreements.

Article 29
Territorial extension[1]

1. This Convention may be extended, either in its entirety or with any necessary modifications [to any part of the territory of (State A) or of (State B) which is specifically excluded from the application of the Convention or], to any State or territory for whose international relations (State A) or (State B) is responsible, which imposes taxes substantially similar in character to those to which the Convention applies. Any such extension shall take effect from such date and subject to such modifications and conditions, including conditions as to termination, as may be specified and agreed between the Contracting States in notes to be exchanged through diplomatic channels or in any other manner in accordance with their constitutional procedures.
2. Unless otherwise agreed by both Contracting States, the termination of the Convention by one of them under Article 30 shall also terminate, in the manner provided for in that Article, the application of the Convention [to any part of the territory of (State A) or of (State B) or] to any State or territory to which it has been extended under this Article.

1. The words between brackets are of relevance when, by special provision, a part of the territory of a Contracting State is excluded from the application of the Convention.

Chapter VII
Final provisions

Article 30
Entry into force

1. This Convention shall be ratified and the instruments of ratification shall be exchanged at . . . as soon as possible.
2. The Convention shall enter into force upon the exchange of instruments of ratification and its provisions shall have effect:

a) (in State A): . . . .

b) (in State B): . . . .

Article 31
Termination

This Convention shall remain in force until terminated by a Contracting State. Either Contracting State may terminate the Convention, through diplomatic channels, by giving notice of termination at least six months before the end of any calendar year after the year . . . In such event, the Convention shall cease to have effect:

a) (in State A): . . . .

b) (in State B): . . . .

Terminal clause[1]

1. The terminal clause concerning the signing shall be drafted in accordance with the constitutional procedure of both Contracting States.

Appendix 2

UK withholding taxes on outward interest and royalties

This appendix tabulates the basic UK tax treaty rates applicable to outward payments of interest and royalties that are sourced in the UK.

Notes are appended only in relation to those countries discussed in the book as the most frequent investors into the UK. These are indicated by shading.

Therefore, the tax rates indicated for the remaining countries should be assumed as subject to the conditions contained in the specific treaty.

Country	Dividends [1] %	Interest [2] %	Royalties [3] %
No treaty		20	22
Antigua		20	0
Argentina		12	
Australia		10	10[4]
Austria		0	0[4], [5]
Azerbaijan		10	5
Bangladesh		10	10
Barbados		15	0
Belarus		15	0
Belgium		15	0
Belize		20	0
Bolivia		15	15
Botswana		15	15
Brunei		20	0
Bulgaria		20	0
Canada		10	10[4], [6]
China		10	10
Croatia		10	10
Cyprus		10	0
Czech Republic		0	0
Denmark		0	0
Egypt		15	15
Estonia		10	10
Falkland Islands		0	0
Fiji		10	15

Country	Dividends [1] %	Interest [2] %	Royalties [3] %
Finland		0	0[4]
France		0	0[4]
Gambia		15	12
Germany		0	0[4]
Ghana		12½	12½
Greece		0	0
Grenada		20	0
Guernsey			
Guyana		15	10
Hungary		0	0
Iceland		0	0
India		15	15
Indonesia		10	15
Ireland		0	0[4]
Isle of Man			
Israel		15	0
Italy		10	8[4]
Ivory Coast		15	10
Jamaica		12½	10
Japan		10	10[4]
Jersey			
Jordan		10	10
Kazakhstan		10	10
Kenya		15	15
Kiribati			0
Korea		10	10
Kuwait		0	10
Latvia		10	10
Lesotho		10	10
Lithuania		10	10
Luxembourg		0	5[4]
Macedonia		10	10
Malawi		0	0
Malaysia		10	8
Malta		10	10
Mauritius		20	15
Mexico		15	10
Mongolia		10	5

Country	Dividends [1] %	Interest [2] %	Royalties [3] %
Montserrat		20	0
Morocco		10	10
Myanmar		20	0
Namibia		20	0
Netherlands		0	0[4]
New Zealand		10	10
Nigeria		12½	12½
Norway		0	0
Oman		0	0
Pakistan		15	12½
Papua New Guinea		10	10
Philippines		15	25
Poland		0	10
Portugal		10	5[4]
Romania		10	10
Russian Federation		0	0
St Kitts & Nevis		0	0
Sierra Leone		20	0
Singapore		10	10[4]
Slovak Republic		0	0
Slovenia		10	10
Soloman Islands		20	0
South Africa		10	0
Spain		12	10[4]
Sri Lanka		10	10
Sudan		15	10
Swaziland		20	0
Sweden		0	0[4]
Switzerland		0	0[4]
Thailand		20	15
Trinidad and Tobago		10	10
Tunisia		12	15
Turkey		15	10
Tuvalu		20	0
Uganda		15	15
Ukraine		0	0
USSR		0	0
United States		0[7]	0[7]

Country	Dividends [1] %	Interest [2] %	Royalties [3] %
Uzbekistan		5	5
Venezuela		5	7
Vietnam		10	10
Yugoslavia		10	10
Zambia		10	10
Zimbabwe		10	10

Notes re main conditions

(1) Basically non-taxable to non-residents (see paragraph **28.3** et seq).

(2) See **Chapter 19.** Note also that interest or royalties paid to EU affiliates is due to be free of withholding tax from 1 January 2004 (see paragraph **19.15**).

(3) See **Chapter 6**.

(4) Includes equipment rents (see **Chapter 31**).

(5) 10% if paid to an Austrian company controlling 50% or more of UK company's voting powers.

(6) 0% for copyright royalties except for films and videotapes.

(7) Extensive limitation of benefits provisions (see paragraph **27.24**).

Appendix 3

Controlled foreign companies ('CFCs'): an overview

Introduction

The purpose of this overview is to attempt to briefly summarise the broad principles of the CFC legislation applying in those of the selected jurisdictions where it is in force. It is beyond the scope of this work to describe each country's system in detail.

The overview is highly relevant in relation to tax planning for inward UK investment. Its purpose is to identify for each of the 21 countries the limitations on, but in particular the scope for, properly accumulating income and gains in a third country jurisdiction, and so reducing potential taxes in both the UK, and the home country of the foreign investor.

The overview is then referred to in the text whenever relevant to the cycle of transactions discussed in the various Chapters.

The CFC countries

Of the 21 selected countries the following (well over half) have specific CFC legislation: Australia, Canada, Denmark, Finland, France, Germany, Italy, Japan, Portugal, Spain, Sweden and USA.

In addition the following countries have legislation which inhibits accumulation of income and gains in low-tax subsidiaries:

Belgium

Although the Belgian tax legislation contains no CFC rules as such, article 344(2) of the Consolidated Income Tax Code has the effect that any transfer of shares, debentures, loans, intellectual property or cash, resulting in the accrual of income to a foreign company, permits the Belgian tax authorities to ignore the transfer.

However these rules are inapplicable in cases where the transferor receives continuing income subject to tax in Belgium. So, for example, funds might be lent to a foreign subsidiary at normal interest rates, thus allowing the foreign subsidiary to invest the cash proceeds of the loan into assets generating a higher income yield. For example, acquiring or developing intellectual property producing royalty income.

There is also an exception from the rules if it can be demonstrated that the transfer of assets was for bona fide commercial reasons.

Ireland

There are no CFC rules applicable to Irish resident companies.

When an Irish resident individual directly or indirectly transfers assets to a foreign entity, he or she can be taxed on the consequential income accruing to the foreign entity unless it can be demonstrated that the transfer was for bona fide commercial reasons, and not to avoid Irish tax. For example, incorporating a UK trading company to conduct a UK business.

The individual shareholders of a closely-owned Irish company could be taxed under this rule if, for example, their Irish company set up an offshore finance company unless the above bona fide test could be met.

Under a separate rule, Irish resident individuals and close companies may be taxed on certain gains accruing to foreign companies in which they have a direct or indirect interest. However Ireland's right to tax these gains may be curtailed under a double tax treaty between Ireland and the country of residence of the foreign company (see article 13.5 of the OECD Model Convention, **Appendix 1**).

Ireland also has general anti-avoidance legislation which could be applied by the Irish Revenue to recharacterise certain artificial transactions which involve a tax advantage to the taxpayer. Genuine business transactions should not be affected.

The Netherlands

Although there are no CFC rules as such, article 28b of the Corporate Income Tax Act 1969 may inhibit the utilisation of foreign companies carrying out passive investment activities.

In principle, a Dutch company with a 25% or more direct or indirect shareholding in a foreign company whose activities are exclusively or almost exclusively (90% ore more) passive, is taxed annually on the increase in value of its direct or indirect shareholding in the foreign company. However the following exceptions apply:

(a) It is possible that the foreign company may carry out trading activities to the extent that the investment activities are not its exclusive or almost exclusive function.

(b) Investments in EU subsidiaries to which the participation exemption applies (generally active subsidiaries) are outside the scope of article 28b.

(c) If the passive investment activity has a function within the corporate group it will not be considered passive. For example, a foreign subsidiary providing finance or licensing rights to the corporate group for the purpose of active functions would not be considered passive.

With regard to individuals, s 4.14 of the Income Tax Act will tax Dutch resident individuals owning 5% or more of the shares in a foreign passive investment company. However the taxable amount is limited to 4% of the value of the investment, taxed at a rate of 25%.

The CFC rules

CFC legislation has the effect of attributing the profits (and usually, gains) of companies located in low-tax jurisdictions to residents of high-tax jurisdictions who directly or indirectly control such companies.

In most jurisdictions the CFC rules apply to foreign low-tax companies, whether controlled by companies, or by individuals resident in the home country jurisdiction. Some jurisdictions have separate sets of rules for companies and individuals.

Invariably, the rules only apply where the foreign company is controlled by residents of the home country. France is an exception to this, requiring only a 10% holding. In any event, in the situations envisaged in this book it will be generally inevitable that the UK business or investment will be directly or indirectly controlled by residents of the foreign jurisdiction. One possible exception to this might be joint ventures in which the joint venturers may be from different jurisdictions with no single person having a controlling interest (see **Chapter 16** and paragraph **16.20**).

'Passive' income and gains

The rules are cast to tax passive income and gains accumulated in the controlled foreign company; basically, dividends, interest, royalties and capital gains. However a number (but not all) of the selected jurisdictions also treat trading profits as passive income when the purchase or sale end of the trading transaction is from or to a related party. Quite a few jurisdictions, for example France and Japan, treat all trading transactions as passive unless there is a real business presence in the foreign jurisdiction sufficient to support the trading activities.

An interesting contrast is Canada. Its 'FAPI' legislation in fact treats passive income as active, and so outside its ambit, when it arises from active income of a foreign affiliate. Typically:

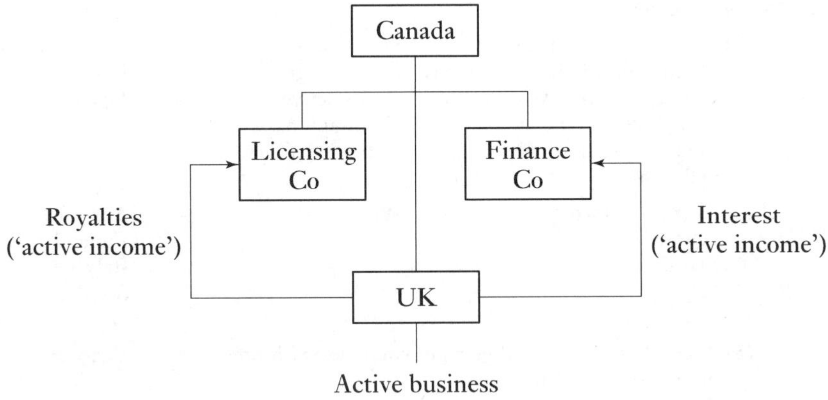

The royalties and interest receivable by the offshore licensing and finance companies are regarded as active income.

Low-tax jurisdictions, Black Lists and White Lists

In general there is a requirement for the rate of tax payable by the CFC to be below a certain percentage if its income is to be taxed under the CFC rules.

In order to simplify the system and to bring certainty to it, a number of countries publish a 'White List' or a 'Black List', tabling those jurisdictions that are or are not considered to impose a rate of tax sufficiently low for CFCs resident there to have their passive income and gains taxed on shareholders resident in the home jurisdiction. Clearly, well-known tax havens such as the Bahamas and Cayman Islands are vulnerable; however, so are countries offering special tax concessions in some of the home jurisdictions, such as Luxembourg and the Netherlands. Countries publishing lists include Australia, Finland, Italy and Sweden.

Some interesting exceptions

The following examples illustrate some of the situations in which income and gains may accrue to related companies in low-tax jurisdictions outside the ambit of CFC rules in the home country jurisdiction.

Type of income	*Examples*
(1) Passive income classified active. See above.	Canada
(2) 'Same country exception'. Payments (such as interest and royalties) out of the active income of, say, a UK subsidiary to another company incorporated in the UK.	USA

Type of income	*Examples*
(3) Inter-company dividends. Often a local holding company in the foreign country will receive dividends from its active subsidiaries in the same country. Although passive in nature, such dividends are often treated as active and so outside CFC taxation.	Denmark USA Japan
(4) Accrual of income and gains in 'White List' countries. See above.	Australia Finland Italy Sweden
(5) Accrual of income and gains in countries with rate of tax not regarded as low. See above.	Various
(6) Trading profits, especially where affiliates not involved. See above.	Various
(7) Passive income not significant. In some jurisdictions the CFC rules do not apply to passive income of a CFC if it is not significant in relation to the CFC's trading profits.	Australia Netherlands
(8) Gains on sale of shares in subsidiaries. Such gains are basically passive. However a number of countries exempt the gain from CFC taxation particularly where: the foreign holding company's gain would be exempt from tax if directly realised in the home country; the subsidiary carries on an active business; or the rate of tax in the holding company's jurisdiction is not regarded as low even though no tax is payable on the gain.	Australia (proposed) Canada Finland Germany Portugal Spain
(9) Joint venture companies. Absence of local country control because of a joint venture with investors in other jurisdictions (see **Chapter 17**).	All (except France)
(10) Tax treaties. The Schneider decision in France [Conseil d'Etat 28 June 2002, Société Schneider Electric, no 232 276] held that France's CFC rules were overridden by the permanent establishment article of the then article 7(1) of the France/Swiss tax treaty (since amended). The French company's Swiss subsidiary had no permanent establishment in France so its profits could not be taxed in France. Similar claims may be available under other tax treaties.	Various

Type of income	*Examples*
This contrasts with the UK decision in *Bricom Holdings Ltd v IRC* [1997] STC 1179 where it was held that the UK/Netherlands tax treaty did not prevent the application of UK CFC rules. The apportionment of the income to UK shareholders is of an amount equal to the CFC's income, not the income itself [ICTA 1988, s 747(3)]. Nevertheless, the UK and Australia have taken pre-emptive action in relation to any such claims that may be made under the non-discrimination article of the new treaty of 21 August 2003 as yet unratified (see paragraph **19.10**).	
(11) EU discrimination. For shareholders in EU jurisdictions it is arguable that CFC rules are discriminatory insofar as they may inhibit freedom of establishment in an EU subsidiary in contravention of articles 43 and 48 of the EC treaty; for example, a Belgian co-ordination centre or an Irish trading company. In relation to UK CFC rules, a Group Litigation Order against the Revenue was made in the High Court on 30 July 2003. It is understood that the European Commission may be reviewing the validity of CFC legislation in EU jurisdictions.	Various

Appendix 4

Inland Revenue Statement of Practice SP 1/90 Company residence

1 Residence has always been a material factor, for companies as well as individuals, in determining tax liability. But statute law has never laid down comprehensive rules for determining where a company is resident and until 1988 the question was left solely to the courts to decide. FA 1988, s 66 introduced the rule that a company incorporated in the UK is resident here for the purposes of the Taxes Acts. Case law still applies in determining the residence of companies excepted from the incorporation rule or which are not incorporated in the UK.

A The incorporation rule

2 The incorporation rule applies to companies incorporated in the UK subject to the exceptions in FA 1988, Sch 7 for some companies incorporated before 15 March 1988. Paragraphs 3 to 8 below explain how the Revenue interpret various terms used in the legislation.

Carrying on business

3 The exceptions from the incorporation test in FA 1988, Sch 7 depend in part on the company carrying on business at a specified time or during a relevant period. The question whether a company carries on business is one of fact to be decided according to the particular circumstances of the company. Detailed guidance is not practicable but the Revenue take the view that 'business' has a wider meaning than 'trade'; it can include transactions, such as the purchase of stock, carried out for the purposes of a trade about to be commenced and the holding of investments including shares in a subsidiary company. Such a holding could consist of a single investment from which no income was derived.

4 A company such as a shelf company whose transactions have been limited to those formalities necessary to keep the company on the register of companies will not be regarded as carrying on business.

5 For the purposes of the case law test (see B below) the residence of a company is determined by the place where its real business is carried on. A company which can demonstrate that in these terms it is or was resident outside the UK will have carried on business for the purposes of FA 1988, Sch 7.

'Taxable in a territory outside the UK'

6 A further condition for some companies for exception from the incorporation test is provided by FA 1988, Sch 7 paras 1(1)(c), 5(1). The company has to be

taxable in a territory outside the UK. 'Taxable' means that the company is liable to tax on income by reason of domicile, residence or place of management. This is similar to the approach adopted in the residence provisions of many double taxation agreements. Territories which impose tax on companies by reference to incorporation or registration or similar criteria are covered by the term 'domicile'. Territories which impose tax by reference to criteria such as 'effective management', 'central administration', 'head office' or 'principal place of business' are covered by the term 'place of management'.

7 A company has to be liable to tax on income so that a company which is, for example, liable only to a flat rate fee or lump sum duty does not fulfil the test. On the other hand a company is regarded as liable to tax in a particular territory if it is within the charge there even though it may pay no tax because, for example, it makes losses or claims double taxation relief.

'Treasury consent'

8 Before 15 March 1988 it was unlawful for a company to cease to be resident in the UK without the consent of the Treasury. Companies which have ceased to be resident in pursuance of a Treasury consent, as defined in FA 1988, Sch 7 para 5(1), are excepted from the incorporation rule subject to certain conditions. A few companies ceased to be resident without Treasury consent but were informed subsequently by letter that the Treasury would take no action against them under the relevant legislation. Such letter is not a retrospective grant of consent and the companies concerned cannot benefit from the exceptions which depend on Treasury consent.

B The case law test

9 This test of company residence is that enunciated by Lord Loreburn in *De Beers Consolidated Mines v Howe* ([1906] AC 455; 5 TC 198, HL) at the beginning of this century—

> 'A company resides, for the purposes of income tax, where its real business is carried on . . . I regard that as the true rule; and the real business is carried on where the central management and control actually abides.'

10 The 'central management and control' test, as set out in *De Beers*, has been endorsed by a series of subsequent decisions. In particular, it was described by Lord Radcliffe in the 1959 case of *Bullock v Unit Construction Company* ([1960] AC 351; 38 TC 712, HL) (1959) 38 TC 712 at 738 as being—

> 'as precise and unequivocal as a positive statutory injunction . . . I do not know of any other test which has either been substituted for that of central management and control, or has been defined with sufficient precision to be regarded as an acceptable alternative to it. To me . . . it seems impossible to read Lord Loreburn's words without seeing that he regarded the formula he was propounding as constituting *the* test of residence.'

Nothing which has happened since has in any way altered this basic principle for a company the residence of which is not governed by the incorporation rule; under current UK case law such a company is regarded as resident for tax purposes where central management and control is to be found.

Place of 'central management and control'

11 In determining whether or not an individual company outside the scope of the incorporation test is resident in the UK, it thus becomes necessary to locate its place of 'central management and control'. The case law concept of central management and control is, in broad terms, directed at the highest level of control of the business of a company. It is to be distinguished from the place where the main operations of a business are to be found, though those two places may often coincide. Moreover, the exercise of control does not necessarily demand any minimum standard of active involvement: it may, in appropriate circumstances, be exercised tacitly through passive oversight.

12 Successive decided cases have emphasised that the place of central management and control is wholly a question of fact. For example, Lord Radcliffe in *Unit Construction* said that 'the question where control and management abide must be treated as one of fact or "actuality" ' [(1959) 38 TC 712 at 741]. It follows that factors which together are decisive in one instance may individually carry little weight in another. Nevertheless the decided cases do give some pointers. In particular a series of decisions has attached importance to the place where the company's board of directors meet. There are very many cases in which the board meets in the same country as that in which the business operations take place, and central management and control is clearly located in that one place. In other cases central management and control may be exercised by directors in one country though the actual business operations may, perhaps under the immediate management of local directors, take place elsewhere.

13 But the location of board meetings, although important in the normal case, is not necessarily conclusive. Lord Radcliffe in *Unit Construction* pointed out [(1959) 38 TC 712 at 738] that the site of the meetings of the directors' board had *not* been chosen as '*the* test' of company residence. In some cases, for example, central management and control is exercised by a single individual. This may happen when a chairman or managing director exercises powers formally conferred by the company's Articles and the other board members are little more than cyphers, or by reason of a dominant shareholding or for some other reason. In those cases the residence of the company is where the controlling individual exercises his powers.

14 In general the place of directors' meetings is significant only insofar as those meetings constitute the medium through which central management and control is exercised. If, for example, the directors of a company were engaged together actively in the UK in the complete running of a business which was wholly in the UK, the company would not be regarded as resident outside the UK merely because the directors held formal meetings outside the UK. While it is possible to identify extreme situations in which central management and control plainly is, or is not, exercised by directors in formal meetings, the conclusion in any case is wholly one of fact depending on the relative weight to be given to various factors. Any attempt to lay down rigid guidelines would only be misleading.

15 Generally, however, where doubts arise about a particular company's residence status, the Revenue adopt the following approach:

(i) they first try to ascertain whether the directors of the company in fact exercise central management and control;

(ii) if so, they seek to determine where the directors exercise this central management and control (which is not necessarily where they meet);

(iii) in cases where the directors apparently do *not* exercise central management and control of the company, the Revenue then look to establish where and by whom it is exercised.

Parent/subsidiary relationship

16 It is particularly difficult to apply the 'central management and control' test in the situation where a subsidiary company and its parent operate in different territories. In this situation, the parent will normally influence, to a greater or lesser extent, the actions of the subsidiary. Where that influence is exerted by the parent exercising the powers which a sole or majority shareholder has in general meetings of the subsidiary, for example to appoint and dismiss members of the board of the subsidiary and to initiate or approve alterations to its financial structure, the Revenue would not seek to argue that central management and control of the subsidiary is located where the parent company is resident. However, in cases where the parent usurps the functions of the board of the subsidiary (such as *Unit Construction* itself) or where that board merely rubber stamps the parent company's decisions without giving them any independent consideration of its own, the Revenue draw the conclusion that the subsidiary has the same residence for tax purposes as its parent.

17 The Revenue recognise that there may be many cases where a company is a member of a group having its ultimate holding company in another country which will not fall readily into either of the categories referred to above. In considering whether the board of such a subsidiary company exercises central management and control of the subsidiary's business, they have regard to the degree of autonomy which those directors have in conducting the company's business. Matters (among others) that may be taken into account are the extent to which the directors of the subsidiary take decisions on their own authority as to investment, production, marketing and procurement without reference to the parent.

Conclusion

18 In outlining factors relevant to the application of the case law test, this statement assumes that they exist for genuine commercial reasons. Where, however, as may happen, it appears that a major objective underlying the existence of certain factors is the obtaining of tax benefits from residence or non-residence, the Revenue examine the facts particularly closely in order to see whether there has been an attempt to create the appearance of central management and control in a particular place without the reality.

19 The case law test examined in this statement is not always easy to apply. The courts have recognised that there may be difficulties where it is not possible to identify any one country as the seat of central management and control. The principles to apply in those circumstances have not been fully developed in case law. In addition, the last relevant case was decided almost 30 years ago, and there have been many developments in communications since then, which in particular may enable a company to be controlled from a place far distant from where the day-to-day management is carried on. As the Statement makes clear, while the general principle has been laid down by the courts, its application must depend on the precise facts.

C Double taxation agreements

20 In general our double taxation agreements do not affect the UK residence of a company as established for UK tax purposes. But where the partner country adopts a different definition of residence, it may happen that a UK resident company is treated, under the partner country's domestic law, as also resident there. In these cases, the agreement normally specifies what the tax consequences of this 'double' residence shall be.

21 Under the double taxation agreement with the United States, for example, the UK residence of a company for UK tax purposes is unaffected. But where that company is also a US corporation, it is excluded from some of the reliefs conferred by the agreement. On the other hand, under a double taxation agreement which follows the 1977 OECD Model Taxation Convention (now superseded by the 1992 text of the Convention), a company classed as resident by both the UK and the partner country is, for the purposes of the agreement, treated as resident where its 'place of effective management' is situated.

22 The commentary in article 4 paragraph 3 of the OECD Model records the UK view that, in agreements (such as those with some Commonwealth countries) which treat a company as resident in a state in which 'its business is managed and controlled', this expression means 'the effective management of the enterprise'. More detailed consideration of the question in the light of the approach of Continental legal systems and of Community law to the question of company residence has led the Revenue to revise this view. It is now considered that effective management may, in some cases, be found at a place different from the place of central management and control. This could happen, for example, where a company is run by executives based abroad, but the final directing power rests with non-executive directors who meet in the UK. In such circumstances the company's place of effective management might well be abroad but, depending on the precise powers of the non-executive directors, it might be centrally managed and controlled (and therefore resident) in the UK.

23 The incorporation rule in FA 1988, s 66(1) determines a residence which supersedes a different place 'given by any rule of law'. This incorporation rule determines residence under UK domestic law and is subject to the provisions of any applicable double taxation agreement. It does not override the provisions of a double taxation agreement which may make a UK incorporated company a resident of an overseas territory *for the purposes of the agreement* (see paras 20, 21 above).

Appendix 5

The BDO European Holding Companies Table (April 2003)

Factor	*Austria*	*Belgium*	*Denmark*	*France*	*Germany*	*Ireland*	*Luxembourg**	*Netherlands*	*Spain*	*Switzerland*	*UK*
Treatment of dividends (1)	Exempt (7)	95% Exempt (10)	Exempt (20)	95% Exempt	Exempt (30)	Taxable (61)	Exempt (7)	Exempt (47)	Exempt (51)	Exempt	Taxable (61)
Minimum holding for dividends	25%	10% or €1.2m (10)	20%	5%	None	0%–25% (36)	10% or cost acquisition of €1.2m	5% (48)	5% (52)	20% or CHF2m (56)	10%
Treatment of capital gains (2)	Exempt	Exempt (11)	Exempt (20)	Taxable (25)	Exempt	Taxable (37)	Exempt (40)	Exempt (47)	Exempt (51)	Exempt (57)	Exempt (62)
Minimum holding for gains	25%	None (12)	None	N/A	None	N/A	10% or cost of acquisition of €6m	5% (48)	5% (52)	20% (57)	10%
Minimum ownership period	2 yrs (div) (8) 2 yrs (gains) (8)	None (13)	1 yr (div) 3 yrs (gains)	2 yrs (div) 2 yrs (gains) (26)	None	N/A	1 yr (div) 1 yr (gains) (41)	None	1 yr (div) 1 yr (gains)	1 yr (gain) (57)	1yr (gains) (62)
Must subsidiary be active (3)	Yes	No	Yes (21)	No	No	N/A	No (42)	Yes	Yes	No	Yes (63)
Must subsidiary be liable to tax (4)	Yes	Yes (14)	Yes (22)	No	No	N/A	Yes (40)	Yes	Yes	No	No
CT rate	34%	33.99% (15)	30%	35.33% (27)	27.96% (31)	12.5% (38)	22.88%	34.5% (49)	35% (53)	18–32% (58)	30% (64)
Normal WHT on dividends paid (5) **	25%	25%	Nil (23)	25%	20%	Nil (39)	20% (43)	25%	15% (54)	35%	Nil

Factor	*Austria*	*Belgium*	*Denmark*	*France*	*Germany*	*Ireland*	*Luxembourg**	*Netherlands*	*Spain*	*Switzerland*	*UK*
WHT on liquidation**	No (9)	Yes (16)	Nil (23)	25%	20% (32)	No	No	25%	15% (55)	35%	No
Interest deduction (6)	No	Yes	Yes (24)	Yes	Yes (33)	Yes	Yes (44)	No (50)	Yes	Yes	Yes (65)
Debt/ equity restrictions	No	7:1 (17)	4:1	3:2 (28)	3:1 (34)	No	85:15 (45)	85:15 (45)	3:1	Yes (59)	1:1 (66)
CFC rules	No	No (18)	Yes	Yes	Yes	No	No	No (18)	Yes	No	Yes
Binding pre-transaction rulings	Sometimes	Yes	Yes	Sometimes	Sometimes	No	Yes	Yes	Yes	Yes	No
Other taxes	1% CD	0.5% CD (19)	None	€230 CD, TT (29) €3,049 STT MAX	TT (35)	1% CD 1% STT	1% CD NWT 0.5% (46)	0.55% CD	1% CD	1% CD 0.15%-0.3% (60)	0.5% STT
Treaty network	Good	Good	Good	Good	Good	Good	Good	Excellent	Good	Good	Excellent

Abbreviations

CD Capital duty

CT Corporation tax

TT Trade tax

NWT Net worth tax

STT Share transfer tax

WHT Withholding tax

CFC Controlled foreign company

Other considerations not mentioned that may be of relevance are, eg whether the particular country offers a favourable income tax regime for expatriates, the treatment of start-up losses and the treatment of foreign exchange gains and losses.

The table can only give a brief indication of the tax rules. Whilst every care and attention has been taken to ensure the accuracy of the contents of this table, the information is intended for general guidance only. There is no substitute for detailed advice from local professionals. Please contact BDO Stoy Hayward's International Tax Team if you would like any specific advice on any matter.

All details are correct at time of going to press and subject to change.

** For European Union countries, the Parent Subsidiary Directive applies.

It stipulates a minimum holding period in order for distributions of profit to be paid free of withholding tax. This minimum holding period may be reduced by domestic legislation. In the case of France, Germany and Spain, domestic anti-avoidance provisions may deny the benefit of the Parent Subsidiary Directive where the recipient is not a qualifying parent company located in an EU Member State.

Notes

(1) Conditions other those shown may apply (eg activities of holding company may be restricted). Certain anti-avoidance rules may apply in Belgium.

(2) Austria, Germany and Spain tax gains on disposals of local companies. Denmark taxes gains on disposal of a company if it is held for less than three years.

(3) Whether the exemption requires the subsidiary to have, broadly, an active trade or business.

(4) General rule. Each case must should be reviewed in detail.

(5) In the absence of a tax treaty and, for EU members, outside the application of the EU Parent Subsidiary Directive.

(6) Whether interest on a loan applied to acquire the subsidiary is tax-deductible.

(7) No tax exemption if tax on foreign subsidiary's profits is less than 15%.

(8) There is no minimum ownership period and no minimum holding for dividends from local companies.

(9) In the absence of a tax treaty, the foreign shareholder must file a tax return if the gain on liquidation exceeds €3,630.

(10) The parent company must own at least 10% of its subsidiary's share capital. The distributing company must be subject to a similar tax as Belgian corporate income tax. The participations must be held during an uninterrupted period of at least one year. A minimum 15% taxation condition must also be met, however, this condition does not apply to companies resident in an EU country. Dividends from certain types of companies such as financing, treasury, investment and companies resident in a jurisdiction, which does not have similar tax base, are taxed at the normal corporate income tax rates.

(11) The minimum taxation conditions apply.

(12) All other conditions for dividend exemption must be satisfied.

(13) The one year minimum holding condition applies for dividend received deduction.

(14) 15% minimum taxation condition applies.

(15) Including 3% additional crisis contribution.

(16) 10% withholding tax may apply to proceeds from a 'liquidation boni'.

(17) Where paid to persons exempt from tax or taxed at a low rate. 1:1 in respect of loans from individual directors, shareholders and non-resident corporate directors.

(18) There is no CFC legislation, but specific anti-avoidance rules may have broadly the same effect.

(19) 0% for the so-called 'fusion a l'anglaise'.

(20) If not situated in a low tax country.

(21) Only if the subsidiary is conducting an active business and not financial activity.

(22) Taxable if foreign subsidiary's business is financial and if total foreign tax liability is less than 75% of what would have been paid in Denmark.

(23) The standard rate of WHT is 28%. Dividends to an EU parent company or a parent company resident in a treaty country may be paid without the deduction of WHT.

(24) Denied in certain circumstances.

(25) Long term gains qualify for a reduced rate 19.57% or 20.67% in 2002. Higher rate includes a social surcharge due if tax is in excess of €763,000.

(26) Minimum holding period for the reduced rate on gains.

(27) The effective tax rate 35.33%, includes French Surtax 3% and the Social Surtax 3.3%. Social Surtax applies on the amount of French tax payable in excess of €763,000 and the tax payable on long term gains is also taken into account in determining this amount.

(28) Only applies if loan provided from parent company.

(29) Local business tax but not based on profits.

(30) Dividends received from domestic or foreign companies are exempt from German tax. Of the foreign dividends received, 5% are treated as a non-deductible business expense, however, directly attributable expenses to foreign dividends are tax deductible. The directly attributable expenses to dividends from domestic sources are not tax deductible.

(31) The corporation tax rate for the year 2003 is 26.5% (2002: 25%; 2004: 25%); however, a solidarity surcharge of 5.5% also applies making it an effective rate of 27.96%.

(32) Distributions in excess of shareholders contributions.

(33) Interest on borrowings to acquire domestic subsidiaries is not tax deductible, however, in the case of an Organschaft, a deduction for the interest is available to the German parent company as the dividends from its subsidiary included within an Organschaft are taxable income for the German parent. Interest on a loan to acquire a foreign subsidiary is fully deductible subject to 5% of the foreign dividends deemed to be a non-business expense.

(34) Applies to holding companies only. Debt: Equity restrictions do not apply if the loan would have been available on the same conditions from a bank.

(35) Trade tax on income and capital (average effective rates). The rate of trade tax depends on the municipality where the company is located. A rate of 19% may apply.

(36) Holding requirement for underlying tax credit depends on particular treaty provision. Under domestic law, a 25% holding is required for unilateral tax credit.

(37) The tax rate on gains is 20%.

(38) The standard rate of tax on trading income is 12.5%. A 10% rate applies for certain manufacturing/IFSC/Shannon companies. Investment income is taxed at a higher rate of 25%.

(39) No WHT on dividends paid to companies which are controlled by persons who are resident in an EU Member State or in a tax treaty country, or companies not resident in the State which are themselves resident in an EU Member State or in a tax treaty country, or companies the principal class of whose shares or the shares of its 75% parent are substantially and regularly traded on a Stock Exchange in a tax treaty country or an EU Member State.

(40) For non-EU subsidiaries, the exemption only applies if tax rate on the subsidiary's profits is 15% or more.

(41) 12 months at the date at which the capital gain is realised.

(42) While the company need not have an active trade or business, it must be fully taxable.

(43) Dividends distributed to a branch of a company resident in a treaty jurisdiction are exempt.

(44) Only to the extent that payments exceed exempt income.

(45) No statutory rule. Applied generally in practice.

(46) Net asset tax on net assets less liabilities. Value of holdings in qualifying subsidiaries is exempt.

(47) The foreign company must be subject to tax in the country of residence. Portfolio investments held in non-EU companies via an EU intermediary company does not qualify; however, portfolio investments held in an EU company will qualify provided certain conditions are met.

(48) A lower percentage may qualify under very strict conditions.

(49) First €22,689 of profit taxable at 29%.

(50) Interest payable on a loan obtained to finance the purchase of a Dutch subsidiary is deductible. A court case is pending with the EU Court of Justice with the possibility that the non-deductibility of interest costs might be discriminatory. If this were to follow, the Netherlands domestic legislation could be amended.

(51) The subsidiary must have a commercial activity and subject to tax similar to Spanish corporation tax.

(52) Generally, 5% applies, however, if the acquisition costs is more than €6m, the minimum holding percentage is deemed to be satisfied.

(53) Small companies with a group turnover of below €5m are taxed at a reduced rate of 30% on the first €90,152.

(54) WHT @15% on dividends if the shareholders of an ETVE holding company are resident in a fiscal paradise.

(55) The company is obliged to retain 35% as being the Spanish capital gains tax liability if the shareholders are resident in a fiscal paradise.

(56) Federal tax: minimum 20% or CHF 2m. Cantonal/communal taxes – no minimum holding is required.

(57) Federal tax: exemption for acquisitions after 31 December 1996 or for disposals after 31 December 2006 in respect of acquisitions pre 1 January 1997. Minimum ownership period is one year. Cantonal/communal taxes: always exempt for holding companies and usually no minimum holding period.

(58) Total tax rate, including federal, cantonal and communal taxes, varies between cantons.

(59) In a circular of 6 June 1997 the federal tax administration issued detailed safe haven rules. The level of connected party debt which can be supported without recharacterisation, as 'hidden equity' will depend upon the value and nature of the asset held in the balance sheet.

(60) This is payable on certain transactions related to securities for certain holding companies.

(61) With foreign tax credit.

(62) If held for a continuous period of at least 12 months in the last two years preceding the disposal.

(63) The company must be a trading company or a holding company of a trading group or the holding company of a trading sub-group.

(64) The starting rate for profits up to £10,000 is 0% and small companies with profits up to £250,000 pay corporation tax at 19%, marginal relief applies both for profits falling between £10,000 and £50,000 and also between £250,000 and £1,500,000. The effective corporation tax rates for profits falling within marginal relief bands are 23.25% and 32.75% respectively.

(65) Interest deductible on an accruals basis unless to a connected overseas company, when it must be paid within 12 months of the end of accounting period to obtain a deduction. If not paid within 12 months, then relief available when the interest is actually paid.

(66) No statutory rule. Inland Revenue assertion is generally 1:1 but may vary according to circumstances.

(67) Following the ECJ *Lankhorst – Hohorst* GmbH decision in relation to German debt:equity restrictions, it is arguable that these are also inapplicable in the other EU jurisdictions when interest is paid to an EU affiliate.

Appendix 6

Research and development expenditure

A UK permanent establishment or company incurring revenue (as opposed to capital) expenditure on research and development may be entitled to significant tax reliefs.

For tax purposes, research and development is defined by ICTA 1988, s 837A by reference to generally accepted accounting practice. Resource must therefore be had to SSAP 13 (*Accounting for Research and Development*) which limits research and development to spending in the fields of science and technology and classifies it into one of the following three categories:

(a) pure or basis research;

(b) applied research; and

(c) development.

Pure or basic research is 'experimental or theoretical work undertaken primarily to acquire new scientific or technical knowledge for its own sake rather than directed towards any specific aim or application'. Applied research, on the other hand, is 'original or critical investigation undertaken in order to gain new scientific or technical knowledge and directed towards a specific practical aim or objective'. Development is the 'use of scientific or technical knowledge in order to produce new or substantially improved materials, devices, products or services, to install new processes or systems prior to the commencement of commercial production or commercial applications, or to improving substantially those already produced or installed'.

What chiefly distinguishes research and development (R&D) activity from non-research activity, according to SSAP 13, is the presence in R&D of an appreciable amount of innovation, as may be deduced from the above definitions. If the activity departs from routine and breaks new ground, it will normally constitute, or include, R&D.

As a basic rule, all persons (including natural persons) carrying on a trade who incur expenditure on research and development are entitled to deduct that expenditure in computing their taxable profits, even if they would not be entitled to do so under the general 'wholly and exclusively' rule [ICTA 1988, s 82A]. The same entitlement extends to payments made to approved research associations to carry out scientific research to the taxpayer's trade [ICTA 1988, s 82B].

However, additional relief may be available from the two special relief schemes. A company that is a small or medium-sized enterprise (SME) may claim a deduction of 150% of its qualifying expenditure on R&D, whereas a large company may claim a deduction of 125%.

Qualifying expenditure in any period for an SME must be no less than £25,000 (for accounting periods beginning on or after a day yet to be named it will be reduced to £10,000), and must satisfy the following criteria:

(a) it is attributable to R&D directly undertaken by the company or undertaken on its behalf;

(b) it must be subsidised;

(c) it is incurred on staffing costs, consumable stores, externally provided workers or on qualifying subcontracted R&D;

(d) it is not incurred on work contracted out to the company by another person;

(e) it is related to the trade carried on by the company or to a trade it intends to carry on;

(f) any intellectual property created by the R&D vests or will be vested in the company (alone or jointly with other persons).

Payments to externally provided workers qualify if they are payments to a third party for providing workers directly and actively engaged in carrying out R&D work for the company. If the external provider is a connected person, the whole of the payment to the external provider qualifies (or, if it is less, the provider's expenditure on those workers). However, it is a condition that the provider has brought all of the payment into account in computing its profits. Where they are not connected, only 65% qualifies, but the company and the provider may elect for connected persons' treatment.

Similarly, only 6% of expenditure on subcontracted R&D is qualifying expenditure unless the company and the subcontractor are connected or elect to be treated as connected. The same conditions apply as for external providers.

If the company makes a loss in an accounting period in which it has qualifying R&D expenditure, it may, instead of claiming the 150% deduction, claim an R&D tax credit instead. The amount of the credit is the smaller of:

(a) 16% of the company's 'surrenderable loss'; and

(b) its total PAYE and Class 1 NIC liability for payment periods (these will be PAYE months) ending in the accounting period.

The Inland Revenue published a consultation paper on 9 July 2003 aimed at widening the scope of R&D tax relief.

Index

Introduction. The index covers Chapters 1 to 35. Index entries are to paragraph numbers and Appendix numbers eg App 3.